THE MYTH *of the* GOOD WAR

THE MYTH *of the* GOOD WAR

AMERICA IN THE SECOND WORLD WAR, REVISED EDITION

JACQUES R. PAUWELS

JAMES LORIMER & COMPANY LTD., PUBLISHERS
TORONTO

Notice to educators

This book is available for purchase in both print and ebook form. Copies can be purchased from our website at www.lorimer.ca. Copies of individual chapters or portions of the full text in print or digital form are also available for sale at reasonable prices. Contact us for details at rights@lorimer.ca.

The publisher and the author of this work expect that portions of this work will be useful for education, and expect reasonable compensation for this use. This can be readily achieved by arranging to purchase these portions from the publisher. Contrary to the view of university administrators and their legal advisors, it is unlikely that use of a chapter or 10% of this work for educational purposes with no payment to the publisher or author would be found to be fair dealing under the Canadian Copyright Act.

James Lorimer & Company Ltd., Publishers acknowledges the support of the Ontario Arts Council. We acknowledge the financial support of the Government of Canada through the Canada Book Fund for our publishing activities. We acknowledge the support of the Canada Council for the Arts which last year invested $24.3 million in writing and publishing throughout Canada. We acknowledge the Government of Ontario through the Ontario Media Development Corporation's Ontario Book Initiative.

   Canada Council for the Arts   Conseil des Arts du Canada

Cover photo: National Archives and Records Administration (NARA) in Washington, DC.

Library and Archives Canada Cataloguing in Publication

Pauwels, Jacques R., author
        The myth of the good war : America in the Second World
War / Jacques R. Pauwels. -- Revised edition.

A revised edition of the 2002 English translation with updated foreword.
Includes bibliographical references and index.
Issued in print and electronic formats.
ISBN 978-1-4594-0872-2 (pbk.).--ISBN 978-1-4594-0873-9 (epub)

        1. World War, 1939-1945--United States. I. Title.

D769.P38 2015   940.53'73   C2014-908287-8
                                                   C2014-908288-6

James Lorimer & Company Ltd., Distributed in the United   Distributed in the United
Publishers   States by: Kingdom by:
317 Adelaide Street West, Suite Casemate   Casemate UK
1002   2114 Darby Road, 2nd Floor   17 Cheap Street
Toronto, ON, Canada   Havertown, PA 19083   Newbury, RG14 5DD
M5V 1P9
www.lorimer.ca

Printed and bound in Canada.

CONTENTS

FOREWORD TO THE NEW ENGLISH EDITION

This book was originally written in Dutch, more specifically the variety of Dutch spoken in Belgium and known as Flemish, and it was first published in Belgium in 2000. The English edition was published two years later, in 2002. Since these early years of the twenty-first century, we have come to look at the world through different glasses on account of the tragic events of September 11, 2001, as well as the so-called "war on terrorism" thus engendered. "Nine-eleven" was proclaimed to be another Pearl Harbor, and stateside the "war on terrorism" was — and continues to be — presented by the authorities and the mainstream media as another "good war," like the Second World War.

However, countless people inside and outside the United States have come to question the official rationales for the "war on terrorism" and are convinced that it is really — though not necessarily exclusively — about resources such as oil, obviously a commodity of great interest to oil trusts associated with former president George W. Bush, and about profits for the "military-industrial complex," exemplified by corporations such as Halliburton, closely associated with former vice-president Dick Cheney. In this context it has become less difficult to accept the notion, put forward in this book, that even in World War II, America's quintessential "good war," the role of the United States was determined far more by the interests of the country's big corporations and banks than by the idealistic motives conjured up at the time by the authorities and echoed ever since in the media, in schools and universities, in history books, and, of course, in Hollywood productions. World War II, allegedly America's "best war ever" (Michael C. C. Adams), is no longer the "untouchable" historiographical sacred cow it still was a dozen years ago.

Since 2002, also, numerous new books and articles have been produced on relevant topics such as the economic history of Nazi Germany and the American economic penetration of Europe in general and Germany in particular. As an example, we can cite Adam Tooze's *The Wages of Destruction: The Making and Breaking of the Nazi Economy* (2006). Most important for our purposes, naturally, were the new publications dealing with the collaboration of US corporations with Germany's Nazi regime before and during the war. Henry Ashby Turner's study of Opel, the German subsidiary of General Motors, entitled *General Motors and the Nazis: The Struggle for Control of Opel, Europe's Biggest Carmaker* (2005), is a good example, and so is Edwin Black's *Nazi Nexus: America's Corporate Connections to Hitler's Holocaust* (2009).

Much more is now known than a decade ago about the collaboration of major corporations and banks — not only American but also German, French, Swiss, et cetera — with fascist movements and regimes in general and with Nazism in particular. (I have examined these connections in a book published in 2013 in French, *Big Business avec Hitler*; an English edition will hopefully be available soon.) New facts and insights have thus come to light that confirmed the interpretation presented in the first edition of *The Myth of the Good War* and made it possible to strengthen and illustrate many of the arguments put forth in the original edition of this book. They have, of course, been integrated into this new edition.

Some new information, on the other hand, made it necessary, or at least desirable, to rewrite parts of the book. For example, this new edition contains a more elaborate discussion, as well as a plausible explanation, of the tragic raid on Dieppe in August 1942, in which, not coincidentally, mostly Canadian troops were led to the slaughter. And a longer and more detailed chapter is now devoted to another "enigma" of the Second World War, namely the infamous bombing of Dresden. That chapter was rewritten in response to the publication and success, especially (and not surprisingly) in Britain and Germany, of a rather sensational book purporting to "rehabilitate" this horrible but seemingly senseless raid, namely Frederick Taylor's *Dresden: Tuesday, February 13, 1945,* published in 2004. It was also considered appropriate to include an entirely new chapter on the true turning point of World War II, not the landings in Normandy, not even the titanic Battle of Stalingrad, but the Battle of Moscow, fought in the fall of 1941. This relatively unheralded battle, and especially the start of the Red Army's counteroffensive on December 5, 1941, marked the end of Germany's hitherto extremely successful blitzkrieg or "lightning-war" strategy. And so it doomed Nazi Germany to lose the war, as not only Hitler and his generals but also some well-informed foreign observers (such as the Vatican and the Swiss secret services) already realized at the time.

It is remarkable that this "turning of the tide" took place a few days before the US entered the war against Nazi Germany, which happened on December 11, 1941. And it is also noteworthy that the tide turned years before the landings in Normandy of June 1944, all too often, and totally wrongly, lionized as the beginning of the end for Nazi Germany. It is fair to argue, and it will be argued here, that the Americans and their British and Canadian allies landed in Normandy to ensure that the Red Army did not single-handedly defeat Nazi Germany, liberate Europe, and reap the fruits of this achievement.

Remarkable also is the fact that America did not walk into the war against Nazi Germany with a cool head and open eyes, but was involuntarily and unexpectedly "pulled into" that war, as a popular and celebrated American historian, Stephen Ambrose, has put it, namely when, a few days after the Japanese attack on Pearl Harbor, Hitler gratuitously declared war on the US. An effort has been made in this new edition to clarify the circumstances of the Japanese attack on Pearl Harbor and the convoluted way in which this event caused America to stumble into the war against Germany. This book still focuses on the war against Germany, the war in the "European theatre," but in this new edition much more attention is paid to America's war against Japan. In contrast to the war against Germany, the conflict against Japan was very much wanted by the US establishment, which expected great dividends from it. It is for that reason that it was in many ways provoked by the Roosevelt administration, as Robert B. Stinnett has persuasively argued in his book *Day of Deceit: The Truth about FDR and Pearl Harbor* (2000).

Finally, this new edition has also benefitted from the fact that, during the last decade or so, the author has had an opportunity to become acquainted with the very insightful work of a number of Italian scholars, including historians and philosophers: the late Filippo Gaja, author of *Il Secolo Corto: La Filosofia del Bombardamento, La Storia da Riscrivere* (1994); Luciano Canfora, *La Democrazia: Storia di un'Ideologia* (2008); and, above all, Domenico Losurdo, of whose impressive opus the most relevant for our purposes happened to be *Il Linguaggio dell'Impero: Lessico dell'Ideologia Americana* (2007). I say *"molto grazie!"* to my good Italian friend Silvio Calzavarini, who also translated *The Myth of the Good War* into the language of Dante, for bringing these scholars to my attention.

Foreword
OBJECTIVES AND METHODOLOGY

This book is not the fruit of arduous research undertaken in Washington's monumental National Archives or in other imposing collections of documents; in order to create it, little or no use was made of what historians call "primary sources." Moreover, the pages that follow do not offer any dramatic revelations or hitherto unknown facts. Nevertheless, this concise study will hopefully bring something valuable, namely a new and possibly surprising interpretation of historical facts that are already familiar to many of us.

Studies that do rely mainly on primary sources are virtually always monographs, in other words detailed analyses of a historical subject, and they tend to illuminate only small pieces of the great puzzles of complex historical events such as the Second World War. The scholarly books and essays written by historical experts are examples of this type of analysis, which are not normally written for the general public, for whom they are often impenetrable, but for learned colleagues. Of these opuses, it is sometimes respectfully said that they serve to advance the frontier of historical knowledge. Such monographs can indeed be extremely useful, but they rarely if ever offer a comprehensive overview or a more or less convincing interpretation of a major historical problem in all its complexity; they do not show the puzzle itself, but only its parts.

Consequently, we require not only analyses but also another type of historical study, syntheses. These are far less interested in the details than in the totality of a historical drama. Unlike analyses, syntheses do offer an overview and an interpretation; they are mainly based on secondary rather than primary sources, on existing analyses, and also on what social scientists call a "paradigm," that is, a general theory that inspires the interpretation.

The study that follows is not an analysis, but aims to be a synthesis. It is an attempt to offer a relatively short sketch as well as a consistent interpretation of the role played by the United States in the Second World War. This intriguing and important theme has already been the subject of numerous syntheses within the last twenty years in America itself. The present study, however, differs in many important ways from the orthodox overviews of the history of the Second World War in general, and of the role played by the United States in that conflict. For one thing, it is argued here that the role of the United States, or more accurately, the wartime role of America's political and economic leadership, was not guided primarily by idealistic motives, as is generally assumed. The overwhelming majority of conventional syntheses dealing with the role of the United States in the Second World War are typical examples of so-called "feel-good history." This term refers to the heartwarming historical literature that tends to confirm what the average American first learns at school, and subsequently hears over and over again from the nation's media: that in the Second World War, the idealistic United States took upon itself the leadership of the crusade for democracy and against dictatorship, and proceeded to win this crusade virtually single-handedly. The present study does not fit into this category. It does not belong to what a British historian, Nikolai Tolstoy, has called the "drum-and-trumpet" school of military historiography. Instead, it asks difficult questions and points to what an American political scientist, Michael Parenti, refers to as "dirty truths," instead of limiting itself to the agreeable and convenient realities.[1] This type of interpretation will disturb some readers; others, it is hoped, will approve of it, and find it liberating. The purpose of this study is to challenge readers and stimulate reflection.

Moreover, in contrast to the orthodox accounts that tend to treat the war as a problem of international relations and, in numerous cases, as an almost purely military event, this study offers a kind of political economy. An attempt is made here to explain the extremely important role played by the United States in the Second World War in light of its leaders' economic, social, and political aspirations, difficulties, and opportunities. Consequently, much attention is paid to the interconnections between, for example, America's internal social and economic problems and Washington's international diplomacy and military strategy.

There are further differences between this book and conventional studies on the United States' role in the great Armageddon of the twentieth century. Not only the war itself receives our attention, but also the important pre-war and even post-war developments. In other words, this book deals with chronological interconnections. It emphasizes the continuity between the 1920s, the 1930s, the war years themselves, and the post-war era, including relatively recent developments such as the reunification of Germany. It seeks to answer questions such as: Why did so many influential Americans favour fascism before the war? Why did it take so long before America brought itself to support the democracies against Nazi Germany? And why did it require a Japanese attack on an American possession, Hawaii, for the United States to be inadvertently drawn into the war against Nazi Germany, instead of purposely entering it?[2] Indeed, it was Nazi Germany that declared war on the United States, and not vice versa. As for the post-war era, why did US policymakers not eradicate all forms of fascism in Germany and elsewhere after 1945? Why did they choose to oppose the anti-fascists instead?

In addition, this study will also focus on the enormous influence of the war on American society, the American role in the post-war world in general, and American relations with Germany and the Soviet Union in particular. It will be shown, for example, that in some ways the war aims of the US leaders were fully realized only at the end of the Cold War. The division of Germany into two antagonistic states, and their eventual reunification, will be analyzed in this context. Readers will undoubtedly be struck by the continuity and consistency of Washington's pre-war, wartime, and post-war policy at home and abroad. It is a policy that has been guided not primarily by the ideals of freedom, justice, and democracy, but by the interests of American industry, of America's "big business" (and finance), in other words, of America's power elite.

On which analyses and on which paradigm is this study based? No synthesis can take into account all the analyses that have ever been published on such a complex theme. Every synthesis is inevitably based on a restricted selection of available analyses, and so is this one. In order to produce this account, moreover, selective use was made not only of purely historical analyses, but also of studies in economics and political science, and of inter- and multidisciplinary essays published not only in North America and Great Britain but also in Germany, France, Italy, and other countries.

This unorthodox synthesis was inspired primarily by a series of original and controversial historical studies produced as early as the 1960s, but in some cases also in more recent years; studies that have not been used, so far, for the purpose of constructing a like-minded overview, no matter how concise, of the United States' role in the Second World War. In this hetero- geneous family of studies we find, first of all, the works of so-called revision- ist historians, who achieved notoriety in America at the time of the Vietnam War. Revisionists such as William Appleman Williams and Gabriel Kolko attracted attention for their critical perspective on American foreign policy before, during, and after the Second World War, during the early years of the Cold War, and during the Vietnam War. Another well-known revisionist is Gar Alperovitz, whose thorough studies of America's "atomic diplomacy" of 1945 caused some commotion in the United States in 1995, on the occasion of the fiftieth anniversary of the obliteration of Hiroshima.[3]

The term revisionist causes some confusion, because it is also used to refer to all those who seek to "revise" the history of the Second World War and of Nazi Germany in the sense that they deny the historical reality of the Holocaust. America's revisionist historians, however, for whom the term "radical historians" might be more appropriate, have absolutely nothing in common with those who seek to negate the Holocaust and to rehabilitate Hitler. The historians who have inspired this study are revisionists in the sense that they have engaged in a critical examination of America's histor- ical role, and of its role in Second World War in particular. Such revision- ists may also be found outside the United States. In Germany, for example, some very interesting critical studies of the little-known role played by America in the occupation and post-war division of that country were pub- lished in the 1990s.

The intimate but highly profitable connections that big American corporations such as Coca-Cola, IBM, Ford, General Motors, and ITT maintained with their own subsidiaries and/or German partner firms in Hitler's Germany before the Second World War, and that continued to play an important role during and after the war, have not received much attention from mainstream historians. This scholarly reticence has undoubtedly much to do with the fact that the influential corporations involved in business deals with the Nazis prefer to keep the lid on that Pandora's box. Nevertheless, some compelling studies about this sensitive subject have actually been published, including Charles Higham's *Trading with the Enemy*; Ed Cray's *Chrome Colossus*; and *Working for the Enemy*, written by the German-American team of Reinhold Billstein, Karola Fings, Anita Kugler, and Nicholas Levis; and Edwin Black's *IBM and the Holocaust*. Their findings will also be taken into account here. While many — but not nearly enough — facts of US corporate involvement in Nazi Germany are already well known, this study will explore the reasons for this involvement and its ramifications on Washington's foreign policy.

This synthesis was inspired by the aforementioned studies, and shares not only their critical view of the policies pursued by America's leaders in times of peace as well as in times of war, but also certain aspects of their methodology. In order to find an explanation for complex and sometimes controversial historical events, for example, a particularly effective method consists in asking a question that is often asked by detectives during their investigative work, namely, who profited? *Cui bono?*

Not only historians, but also critical American political scientists have had a great deal of influence on this synthesis. Two examples are C. Wright Mills, the author of a classical study of America's political, social, economic, and military elites, and Michael Parenti, a well-known maverick political scientist from California, who has exploded many myths of American politics and history in books such as *Democracy for the Few*. Noam Chomsky also deserves to be mentioned here; in his interdisciplinary work, he has drawn attention to America's historical contribution to the development of the contemporary world economy, a development in which the Second World War constituted an extremely important stage. Chomsky asks us, for example, to empathize with the people of the Third World, for whom that world conflict must have loomed as a bloody settlement of accounts between brigands who fought over territorial loot, such as Hong Kong and

Pearl Harbor, which those brigands — the colonial powers — had snatched from third parties.[5] The ideas of Chomsky, Williams, Kolko, and above all Parenti, collectively constitute the paradigm, the general theory, on which this synthesis is based: that the development of the capitalist economy of the United States requires that the American social, economic, and therefore also political elites consistently pursue their class interests at home and abroad — with the help of democrats or dictators, with peaceful means or with violence, and without much regard for the values of democracy, liberty, and justice of which America claims to be the great champion.

This study is not perfectly objective, and that is unavoidable. Its theme is not a physical phenomenon such as the movement of a planet around the sun, in other words, the kind of phenomenon of which a totally objective study was long believed to be possible — until Heisenberg demonstrated the illusory nature of that belief. Our study focuses on a historical drama from which it is not easy to distance oneself, a drama that cannot possibly be approached with perfectly cool objectivity. Historical interpretations that are totally objective simply do not exist. However, with respect to objectivity, this study does claim some modest merits. First, much of what pretends to be objectivity is in reality nothing more, as Parenti writes, than the orthodoxy's "established familiarity and unanimity of bias," the "dominant view which parades as the objective one"; of this spurious kind of objectivity this book is guaranteed to be entirely free.[6] Furthermore, the reader will undoubtedly be happy to notice the absence of the blatant subjectivity that was so typical of most mainstream historiography in the Cold War era, when certain things simply could not be said. However, it is now possible for an author to mention, for example, the undisputable historical fact that the Soviet Union made the biggest contribution to the Allied victory over Nazi Germany, without being branded as a puppet of Moscow. A much more objective look at the history of Second World War has become possible since the end of the Cold War, and this greater degree of objectivity is hopefully reflected in these pages.

But enough about objectivity. In the case of a synthesis, there are other qualities that are important. First, the interpretation ought to be as free as possible from contradictions; it must be consistent. Second, we are entitled to expect that a new interpretation explain to us issues that cannot be explained, or are difficult to explain, in light of other syntheses and interpretations. In other words, a crucial quality of any synthesis is its comparative — and, indeed, competitive — persuasive power. Every reader will have to decide for her- or himself how consistent and how persuasive this interpretation is in comparison to others.

Finally, it ought to be mentioned that this study is also to a great extent the result of many discussions with professors and students of North American universities, with friends and strangers in bars and planes, and with fellow visitors — sometimes war veterans — to battlefields and war cemeteries from Monte Cassino via Normandy to Pearl Harbor, to concentration camp memorials like the one at Buchenwald, and to other landmarks of the Second World War. It was also because of such discussions and this kind of dialogue that the image of the Second World War in general, and of the United States' role in particular, underwent a gradual change and started to differ increasingly from the traditional interpretation repeatedly offered — albeit with minor variations — in conventional syntheses. In this book, then, the Second World War is not presented in the conventional manner as the "good war," as the great American crusade against fascism and militarism, but as a conflict whereby business interests, money, and profits were at stake.

Chapter 1
INTRODUCTION: AMERICA AND THE MYTH OF THE "GREAT CRUSADE"

Everybody knows that the United States made a huge contribution to the Allied victory over German Nazism, European fascism in general, and, of course, Japanese militarism. Equally well known is the fact that a considerable part of Europe was liberated by the Americans themselves. The gratitude and goodwill that they have been able to enjoy in post-war Europe are therefore certainly not unmerited. But why did the United States really go to war? Many if not most Europeans never learned the answer to that question in elementary or secondary school; the history that was taught there preferred to concentrate on the glorious achievements of Caesar, Columbus, and other heroes from the distant and therefore safe past, rather than on the earth-shaking and traumatic events of our own twentieth century. In any event, European school children never learned much about the history of the admittedly important but distant United States, the land of cowboys and Indians, gangsters, and movie stars, and last but not least, a country that was often said — totally wrongly, but with conviction — not to have much history anyway.

What we know — or, more precisely, assume — about the role of the United States in the Second World War, we appear to have learned primarily from Hollywood; that is, from the American movie industry. The countless popular war movies produced by Tinseltown in the fifties and sixties, such as the D-Day epic *The Longest Day*, propagated in a far from subtle yet very effective way the idea that an idealist USA had gone to war in order to restore freedom and justice in Europe and just about everywhere in the world.[1] Already during the war itself, this was how the American authorities presented their cause to the American people and to the rest of the world. General Eisenhower, the commander-in-chief of the Western Allied armies in Europe, liked to describe his country's intervention in the Second World War as "the great crusade," and President Franklin D. Roosevelt spoke of a war in which America fought for values such as liberty, justice, and even — as he once put it in all sincerity — of "our religion."[2]

It is generally accepted that the war aims of the United States and of its transatlantic British partner were best summarized in the Atlantic Charter, a document issued jointly by President Franklin D. Roosevelt and Prime Minister Winston Churchill of Great Britain during their meeting on a battleship in the coastal waters of Newfoundland on August 14, 1941. At that moment Washington, though not yet formally at war, functioned as a de facto ally of Great Britain because of its active moral and material support of the British. In this "charter" the two partners declared that they opposed Nazi Germany for the sake of the self-determination of all nations and for the so-called "four freedoms," that is, freedom of speech, freedom of religion, freedom from want, and freedom from fear.

However, those beautiful (and very vague) words ought to be taken with a grain of salt. Washington and London clearly did not intend to allow the populations of their own colonial (or semi-colonial) possessions or protectorates, such as British India, or the American-dominated Philippines, to enjoy all these freedoms. In any event, the proclamation of the Atlantic Charter served to launch the idea that America, together with its British ally, fought for freedom and justice, and this idea was actively propagated in the months and years that followed the Allied summit off the coast of Newfoundland. An illustration created by the popular American artist Norman Rockwell served as an important tool in this myth-making process. Rockwell's sentimental evocation of the "four freedoms" made its first appearance in the popular magazine *The Saturday Evening Post,* and millions of copies were subsequently distributed in America and abroad in the form of posters, then still a very important propaganda medium. Innumerable individuals, certainly not exclusively Americans, thus came to believe that the United States had responded to a "divine mission to save the world," as the philosopher and historian Isaiah Berlin, then a British diplomat in Washington, put it in a contemporary report to London.[3] The official discourse thus spawned an official truth, or rather, an official mythology, according to which sterling idealistic motives had determined the role of the United States in the Second World War.

It was not only thanks to Rockwell's posters, Hollywood's war movies, the many American documentaries about the Second World War, and American periodicals such as *The Saturday Evening Post, Life,* and *Reader's Digest,* that this mythology was disseminated all over the world during and after the war. In countries that were actually liberated by the Americans, the dramatic words of Roosevelt and Eisenhower about freedom and justice found an eager echo in the official language used annually by dignitaries during commemorations in the shadow of American war memorials in Normandy, the Belgian Ardennes, and elsewhere. This kind of discourse also serves to corroborate the same comfortable official truth in the minds of the many grateful citizens and devoted school children who faithfully attend these ceremonies.

American (as well as British and Canadian) war veterans attending such occasions generally feel flattered by this official praise. However, informal and sometimes cynical remarks by war veterans indicate that they definitely did not go to war on idealistic impulses. Moreover, oral histories such as those of the American author Studs Terkel, as well as a number of excellent studies of the motivation and the conduct of American soldiers during the war, also make it clear that the ordinary American soldiers — the GIs — had taken up arms for all sorts of reasons, but definitely not out of a desire to destroy fascism and militarism and to restore democracy and justice in Europe, as the official mythology suggests.

On the eve of the Second World War, most Americans were simply not in the mood for a crusade against fascism in general and its German variety, Hitler's National Socialism (Nazism) in particular. They knew little or nothing about all these European "isms," and they themselves were not directly threatened by fascism. Neither were they bothered much by militarism of the German or Japanese variety; after all, in the United States itself militarism and violence have traditionally been glorified rather than condemned. The GIs would later complain, incidentally, that it was in their own army that they first became acquainted with fascist (or at least quasi-fascist) practices, in the form of the daily petty mistreatments and humiliations that became known as "chickenshit."[4] Most American soldiers also had little knowledge of, or interest in, the people and countries they liberated. The famous General Patton — a capable military leader, but also a megalo-maniac who terrorized his own men with monumental chickenshit — was certainly not the only American who displayed more sympathy for German citizens and military personnel than for the starved, sick, and filthy human wrecks they came upon in the concentration camps.[5]

To the previous generation of Americans, the First World War had been presented as the "war to end all wars," or, as President Wilson had stated, a "war for democracy." However, the outcome of the horrible carnage had given the lie to this beautiful phraseology, and the outlook of the disen-chanted America of the twenties and thirties was therefore decidedly anti-war.[6] The generation of Americans that was predestined to fight a second "Great War" was no longer susceptible to the idealistic Wilsonian phrases that now gushed forth from the mouths of Roosevelt and Eisenhower. This generation had really no idea why they were fighting; on an ideological level its representatives fought, as the American historian (and war veteran) Paul Fussell writes, "in a vacuum." "The troops in the field," writes the same author, "were neither high- nor particularly low-minded. They were not -minded at all." The American soldiers had not wanted this war, and they did not fight for the beautiful ideals of freedom, justice, and dem-ocracy; they fought to survive, to win the war in order to end it, in order to be able to leave the army, in order to be able to go home. When they heard an idealistic rationalization for the war, they usually responded with a pithy "Bullshit!" The GIs were driven by an absurd but compelling logic, as Fussell writes, "To get home you had to end the war. To end the war was the reason you fought it. The only reason."[7] The same motif pervades the movie *Saving Private Ryan*, in which one of the American soldiers makes a remark to the effect that they were fighting "for the right to go home."[8]

Neither did the majority of American civilians have a clear idea what this war was really all about. A Gallup poll of September 1942 revealed that 40 per cent of Americans had no idea at all why their country was involved in the war, and that less than one-quarter of Americans had ever heard of the

Atlantic Charter. Only 7 per cent were able to name one of the "four free-doms." For the American people the war was not a crusade for freedom and democracy but simply, as *Fortune* magazine wrote, "a painful necessity"— a deplorable but inescapable misfortune.[9]

It did not really matter what American soldiers or civilians thought, because their opinion did not play a role in the decision-making process that led to their country's entry into the Second World War. The United States is a democracy in the sense that American women and men are allowed from time to time to elect either Republican or Democratic candidates for the presidency and for the Congress; they actually do take advantage of this right if they value the sometimes very subtle differences between the two political parties, but this is clearly not the case for a very high percentage of Americans. In any event, the existence of an electoral ritual does not mean that ordinary US citizens have much influence in the corridors of power in the White House, the Capitol, the Pentagon, or anywhere else in Washington. The American government's decisions concerning domestic and foreign policy tend to be only a very pale reflection of the opinions and interests of ordinary Americans.

On the other hand, it would also be wrong to believe that the president monopolizes the decision-making process like an all-powerful dictator, even though he is widely believed to be the most powerful man on earth. In reality, American presidents enjoy far less power than is commonly assumed; they cannot even count on the automatic support of the members of their own party in the House of Representatives and the Senate, and they also have to take into account the opinions of Pentagon generals, influential members of Cabinet, high-ranking bureaucrats, the media, and all sorts of powerful lobbyists. In addition, it is no longer a secret that the FBI and the CIA often pursue official and unofficial American policy objectives at home and abroad, sometimes without the knowledge of the tenant in the White House. American policy during the war should therefore not be explained primarily as a function of President Roosevelt's personal motives and objectives, as is usually done by the many historians who still subscribe to the nineteenth-century notion that "great men" determine the course of history.[10] This kind of historiography does not sufficiently take into account the anonymous economic and social factors that make it possible for certain individuals — "great men" like Napoleon, Hitler, Churchill, or Roosevelt — to play a leading role in the drama of history at some time or another. History thus degenerates all too often into biography. This study, on the other hand, proceeds from the premise that history determines who the great men (and women) are, rather than that great men determine the course of history; it therefore seeks to understand the American role in the Second World War in light of forces within American society whose importance far surpass that of an admittedly important president, such as Roosevelt.

In America, important public-policy decisions are made neither by the president alone, nor by the American people in general. As Michael Parenti has written, the United States may be defined as a "democracy for the few," that is, a state which looks like a democracy in many ways, but in which only a small group of powerful and usually very wealthy individuals pull the strings. Whatever Washington does or does not do tends to reflect and promote the interests of the nation's political, social, economic, and military elites — an establishment described as the "power elite" in a book of the same name by C. Wright Mills, a well-known sociologist who taught at Columbia University in New York. The members of this power elite, Mills wrote, "are in command of the major hierarchies and organizations of modern society. They rule a veritable triangle of power." However, whereas Mills tended to treat all sections of the power elite — "the warlords," "the political directorate," "the corporate rich," et cetera — as roughly equal in power and importance, this study emphasizes the primordiality of economic interests and therefore of the economic elite. Seen from this perspective, the US power elite is motivated first and foremost by economic interests, by business interests, and its real nerve centres are the major industrial firms of America, such as Ford, General Motors (GM), ITT, and IBM – often collectively referred to as "big business." These big corporations enjoy enormous influence in Washington, and it is not an exaggeration to say that in many ways the American government functions primarily to serve their needs and promote their interests. With the US power elite committed first and foremost to the interests of American corporations, the United States is indeed a "corporate state," as Michael Parenti writes. This was already the case long before the Second World War, as in the twenties, when President

Calvin Coolidge stated flatly but truthfully that "the business of America is business."

What are the interests of America's industry, of America's businesses, of the nation's corporations? And how is the American state supposed to defend and promote them? Now as in the past, America's corporate leaders expect that the domestic and foreign policy of their country will seek to remove all restraints on business activities, to keep American workers as docile as possible and their wages as low as possible, to secure sources of raw materials as well as markets for their products, and to minimize the risks of domestic and foreign competition, so that American corporations (and individual entrepreneurs) may earn the highest possible profits. In other countries, big business expects a similar commitment from the political leadership, a similar dedication to the cause of making money; and much the same is expected from supranational bureaucratic organizations such as the European Community, which have taken over many if not all essential functions from the national governments, which happen to be more or less democratically elected and therefore not totally reliable from the corporate perspective. However, there is arguably no major country in the world where business has as much influence on government as the United States, and where the government has tried as hard to indulge the demand that "enterprise" be totally "free," that capitalism be truly "unfettered." Even so, spokesmen for American business never cease to lament that Washington is insufficiently sensitive to corporate expectations.

Within the ranks of the power elite, opinions naturally differ now, as they did in the thirties and forties, over how corporate objectives may best be achieved, about how the state may best serve the cause of making money, the cause of "capital accumulation." Like everywhere else on earth, in the US business is not monolithic, but is divided within itself, not only in countless enterprises big and small, but also, and more importantly, in factions with conflicting interests and therefore very different opinions about all sorts of issues of domestic and foreign policy. (Some authors have spoken in this respect of "elite pluralism.") In 1939, some factions of corporate America thus believed that they would benefit from continuing neutrality, while others expected advantages from an alliance with Great Britain. The traditional rivalry between the Republican and Democratic

Parties similarly reflects the important distinction between those who expect salvation from the consistent application of laissez-faire principles and those who believe in the wisdom of a more interventionist and socially oriented course in public policy.

Considering this fragmentation of American business and the pressures on the makers of public policy from other sources such as labour unions and the media, and the resulting concessions and compromises, neither the domestic nor the foreign policies of Washington ever receive the enthusiastic approval of all business factions, but are instead constantly subjected to all sorts of criticism. The American government can simply never satisfy business, no matter how hard it tries, but precisely because of this the general public is less likely to notice that Washington's policies, whether fashioned by the Republicans or the Democrats, consistently aim to serve the corporate interest. And so the American people are all the more easily impressed by the official mythology, which proclaims that their political system is a pluralist one, where all interest groups — business, the unions, farmers, and so on — enjoy roughly equal input into the public-policy process, so that power is widely dispersed rather than concentrated in the hands of an elite.[11]

This study purports to explain why and how, after war had broken out in Europe in 1939, the interests of America's power elite were at first best served by neutrality, but were eventually served even better by America's active participation in the war. Our attention will thereby focus on the crucial economic and social issues that confronted America in the thirties and forties, filled the nation's power elite with fears as well as hopes, determined the course of Washington's domestic and foreign policy, and eventually led to war with Japan and Germany. The most important military developments will be cited and explained within this framework, but will not be dealt with in detail; aficionados of martial minutiae can find them — and a profusion of illustrations as well — in the countless publications that are almost exclusively concerned with the military aspects of the Second World War and approach them from the American point of view.

Those who have learned the history of the Second World War with the help of the didactic material made available by Hollywood and *Reader's Digest* will perhaps perceive this study to be anti-American, but in reality it is not. First of all, this synthesis is based primarily — but by no means exclusively — on American sources; the inspiration, the underlying paradigm, most of the data, and many specific insights were provided by American authors. Moreover, this book is by no means a diatribe against the United States as such, and certainly not against the brave and generous American people, that is, the male and female civilians and soldiers who made the sacrifices required to win a Herculean struggle against a particularly evil enemy. On the contrary, sympathy for those unsung heroes is actually an important leitmotif here. This study does offer a highly critical view of the role of the US power elite and of the policy pursued by the American government before, during, and even after the Second World War. This, too, is far from anti-American, because Americans themselves never tire of criticizing the conduct of their government and the role of the political, social, and economic elites of the country who have so much influence on that conduct. It is similarly obvious that it is not "anti-German" to condemn the conduct of the Nazis who ruled that country from 1933 to 1945, and that it is not "anti-Spanish" to criticize Franco, et cetera. What is also critically reviewed here is the mythology concerning the United States' role in the war, a mythology that, more than fifty years after the end of that world-shaking conflict, continues to be peddled as the official truth, not only in America itself, but also in Europe and virtually everywhere else on the globe. This official truth may well flatter the jingoistic egos of certain Americans, but it does not really render a service to the United States, and it is therefore not pro-American. The reason for this is that America is better served by a critical and realistic look at its own recent history than by myths and illusions. This is also true for Germany and Japan, countries that are frequently chided — particularly by American officials, scholars, and journalists — for their reluctance to engage in critical historical introspection with regard to the Second World War. This war was most definitely not a simple, black-and-white confrontation between good and evil, but a complex historical drama, from which no actor emerged with clean hands — although it is evident that in comparison to the unprecedented crimes of the Nazis, the misdeeds of their antagonists amounted to minor infractions. Consequently, it behooves not only the vanquished, but also the victors, including the Americans, to critically confront their wartime history.

Condemning a critical examination of the American role in the Second World War automatically as anti-American, then, is as wrong as sweepingly condoning the uncritical, "feel-good" view as pro-American. Finally, in the present era of globalization, the origins of which will be traced back in this book to the Second World War, we are all deeply affected by the policies of the world's only superpower; conversely, the stance we adopt may somehow help to shape those policies. We therefore have not only a right but also a duty to carefully and critically scrutinize the role played by Washington on the stage of recent world history.

Chapter 2
THE AMERICAN POWER ELITE AND FASCISM

Rightly or wrongly, the United States has long been considered — and has considered itself — the cradle of liberty and democracy. It is understandable, therefore, that conventional historiography usually postulates that in the crisis culminating in the Second World War, America sympathized from the start with the side of freedom, democracy, and justice, as opposed to the side of fascist dictatorship, though for some reason it did not enter the war until a rather late stage. While innumerable people on both sides of the Atlantic Ocean embrace this view simply because it conjures up such good feelings, closer examination reveals that the historical reality fails utterly to conform to it.

First of all, while American governments have always proclaimed their love of democracy in theory, they have often displayed a preference for dictatorship in practice. In Latin America alone, long before the Second World War, numerous dictators such as Trujillo (in the Dominican Republic) and Somoza (in Nicaragua) were able to embark on lengthy careers thanks to the active support they received from Uncle Sam. Moreover, even after the Second World War and the traumatic experiences with fascists such as Hitler and Mussolini, at a time when America became the leader of an international community that proudly styled itself the "free world," Washington tolerated the presence within this community of brutal civilian as well as military dictatorships, for example in Spain, Portugal, Greece, Turkey, Iran,

Taiwan, Indonesia, the Philippines, Argentina, and Chile. In fact, many of these dictatorships would not have been able to survive as long as they did without the active support of the American government and its counterinsurgency experts.[1]

Let us turn to the case of the German and Italian fascist dictatorships of the thirties, which are much more relevant to our purpose. Sad to say, these dictatorships enjoyed a lot more sympathy and admiration in America than is commonly assumed, not only during the thirties but until the very moment of Hitler's declaration of war on the United States at the end of 1941. It is hardly a secret that many Americans of German or Italian descent adored the Führer and Il Duce. Far less well known, however, is the fact that fascism particularly fascinated Catholic and, more importantly, upper-crust Americans.

The millions of American Catholics — many of them of Irish, Polish, and Italian origin — were undoubtedly influenced by the example of Rome. Already in the twenties, the Vatican had enthusiastically endorsed Mussolini's regime. Il Duce's rise to power did not result from the highly trumpeted "march on Rome," which was actually a charade, but from the active support of the pope as well as the Italian king, the army, the large landowners, and other pillars of the Italian power elite. Via the establishment of a fascist dictatorship, this elite purported to suppress a revolutionary movement that threatened to transform Italy and put an end to the power and privileges of the country's elite. The Vatican's favourable view of fascism was also dramatically revealed by the concordat it concluded with Nazi Germany as early as July 20, 1933, barely one half-year after Hitler had come to power. It was an initiative of Cardinal Eugenio Pacelli, the former papal nuncio in Germany who was later to become Pope Pius XII. This concordat constituted Hitler's first major diplomatic triumph, and it legitimated his regime in the eyes of Catholic Germans; it was correctly perceived by American Catholics as a kind of *nihil obstat* with regard to National Socialism and fascism in general. Furthermore, many influential American prelates followed the Vatican's example and openly proclaimed their sympathy for Mussolini and Hitler; this was the case with George Mundelein, the archbishop of Chicago, and with Francis Spellman, auxiliary bishop of Boston from 1932 on and later the high-profile archbishop of New York. If Catholic Americans tended to have a favourable view of fascist dictators, then, it was unquestionably because the Catholic Church elite liked and supported fascism. Much more important from our point of view, however, is the fact that numerous members of the social, economic, and political elite of the US also revealed themselves to be admirers of Mussolini and Hitler.[2]

Like their German counterparts, wealthy and conservative Americans had originally been suspicious of Hitler, a plebeian upstart whose ideology was called National *Socialism*, whose party identified itself as a *Workers'* party, and who spoke ominously of bringing about "revolutionary" change. However, again like their German colleagues, they realized soon enough that Hitler's Teutonic type of fascism, like every other variety of fascism, was not revolutionary but conservative and even reactionary in nature, and therefore potentially extremely useful for their purposes. Moreover, after massive financial and political support from the German establishment had made it possible for Hitler to come to power,[3] the American and international elites found to their great satisfaction that Hitler did indeed conduct himself extremely conservatively in social and economic respects. The Nazis' so-called revolution did nothing to threaten the social and economic privileges of the German elites, and for the loss of their political power these elites were more than compensated by the ruthless elimination of the labour unions and of all left-wing political parties. The "Bohemian corporal," as President von Hindenburg of Germany had condescendingly called Hitler before his usefulness was revealed to the German establishment, appeared to have nothing against the principle of private property, the cornerstone of the capitalist system. It was not a coincidence that a huge sign above the main gate of the concentration camp of Buchenwald, where inmates were supposedly re-educated in the essentials of National Socialist doctrine, proclaimed the slogan *Jedem das Seine*, "to each his own."

Such a slogan would have impressed the owners, shareholders, and managers of America's innumerable firms big and small. The majority of American businesses were going through very hard times in the thirties, that is, during the grave economic crisis that has gone down in history as the Great Depression. These bad times were often blamed on the supposedly greedy labour unions, on blacks who were said to steal jobs from white folks, or on the "covetous" Jews. The Americans who saw things that way recognized a soulmate in Hitler, who similarly blamed scapegoats for Germany's misfortune, and so they admired him as a clear-eyed man, a politician who dared to speak the truth, and a leader who did not hesitate to resort to the tough measures required by the situation. American businessmen were particularly impressed by two achievements of Hitler's. First, after coming to power in early 1933, he had immediately eliminated the socialist and communist parties and dissolved the labour unions. Second, during the following years he had led Germany out of the desert of the Great Depression by means of unorthodox but seemingly very effective methods such as the construction of highways and other public works, and above all, large-scale rearmament.

The German dictator and his fascist ideas were particularly liked and admired by the owners, managers, and shareholders of those American enterprises that had already made considerable investments in Germany or had entered into joint ventures or strategic partnerships with German firms in the 1920s. Their German subsidiaries and/or partner firms, such as Coca-Cola's bottling plant in Essen, General Motors' Opel automobile factory in Rüsselsheim near Mainz, Ford's Ford-Werke in Cologne, IBM's facility in Berlin, or Standard Oil's infamous German partner, IG Farben, flourished under a Hitler regime that had swept away the unions, whose rearmament program caused a flood of orders, and with whom all sorts of highly profitable deals could be concluded thanks to the services of corrupt Nazi bigwigs such as Hermann Göring, unscrupulous bankers such as the notorious Hjalmar Schacht, and financial institutions in Germany itself or in Switzerland.[4]

Coca-Cola's German subsidiary, for example, increased its sales from 243,000 cases in 1934 to 4.5 million cases by 1939. This success had a lot to do with the fact that, as the Hitler-admiring and -imitating national manager Max Keith explained, the caffeinated soft drink revealed itself to be a functional alternative to beer as a refreshment for Germany's workers, who were being driven "to work harder [and] faster." In Hitler's Third Reich, where labour unions and working-class political parties had been banned, the workers "were little more than serfs forbidden not only to strike, but to change jobs," and their wages "were deliberately set quite low." This, writes

Mark Pendergrast, combined with the higher sales volume, considerably enhanced the profitability of Coca-Cola, as it did for all corporations active in Germany.[5]

Ford's German subsidiary, the Ford-Werke, which had posted heavy losses in the early thirties, saw its annual profits rise spectacularly under the auspices of the Hitler regime, from a pitiful 63,000 RM (reichsmarks) in 1935 to a respectable 1,287,800 RM in 1939. This success was made possible not only by lucrative government contracts within the framework of Germany's rearmament drive, but also by Hitler's elimination of labour unions and working class parties, which made it possible to cut labour costs from 15 per cent of business volume in 1933 to only 11 per cent in 1938. As for Ford-Werke's total assets, they mushroomed between 1933 and 1939 from 25.8 to 60.4 million RM. (The official exchange rate at the time was 2.5 RM for one dollar, and the value of the dollar in the late thirties was approximately seven times higher than at present.)

GM's Opel factory fared even better under the Third Reich. Opel's share of the German automobile market grew from 35 per cent in 1933 to more than 50 per cent in 1935, and the German subsidiary of General Motors, which had posted losses in the early thirties, became extremely profitable thanks to the economic boom caused by Hitler's rearmament program. Earnings of 35 million RM — almost 14 million dollars — were recorded in 1938. A year later, the total value of Opel was estimated at 86.7 million dollars, more than double the amount GM had invested in the firm a decade earlier, namely 33.3 million dollars.[6] "The German branch of the American business which a few years earlier was only a lame duck, proved in the long run to be the goose that laid the golden egg," wrote Henry Ashby Turner, the famous American historian who was asked by General Motors to write the history of its German branch during the Third Reich and published a book on this subject.[7] In 1939, on the eve of the war, the chairman of General Motors, Alfred P. Sloan, publicly justified doing business in Hitler's Germany by pointing to the highly profitable nature of GM's operations under the Third Reich. In that same year, GM and Ford together controlled 70 per cent of the German car market and were poised to supply the German army with all sorts of equipment required by the coming war.[8]

Yet another American corporation that enjoyed a bonanza in Hitler's

Third Reich was IBM. Its German subsidiary, Dehomag, provided the Nazis with the punch-card technology — forerunner of the computer — required to automate production in the country, doing everything from making the trains run on time to identifying Jews for the purpose of confiscation and, eventually, extermination. Edwin Black has documented this sorry corporate saga in great detail in his book *IBM and the Holocaust*. All that mattered to IBM, however, was that in Germany it made money, lots of money. Already in 1933, the year Hitler came to power, Dehomag made a profit of $1 million, and during the early Hitler years the German branch plant was to pay IBM in the United States some $4.5 million in dividends. By late 1938, still in full Depression, "the net worth of the company [Dehomag] had essentially doubled from its RM 7.7 million total investment in 1934 to more than RM 14 million," writes Black, and "annual earnings were about RM 2.3 million, a 16 per cent return on net assets." In 1939 Dehomag's profits were to increase spectacularly again to just about 4 million RM.[9] If IBM founder and chairman Thomas Watson, like so many other American tycoons with assets in Germany, admired and loved Hitler, it was not because of the Führer's allegedly irresistible charm or charisma, but quite simply because one could do business with Hitler, and because doing business with Hitler was immensely profitable.

Many US corporations had first invested in Germany when that country was still a parliamentary democracy known as the Weimar Republic. However, the stock of American investments in Germany increased considerably after Hitler came to power in 1933 and transformed the democratic Weimar Republic into a fascist dictatorship known as the Third Reich. One of the reasons for this mushrooming of US investment stocks was that profits made by foreign firms could no longer be repatriated, at least in theory. In reality, this embargo could be circumvented by stratagems such as billing the German subsidiary for "royalties" and all sorts of "fees," as we will see later. In any event, the restriction meant that profits were largely reinvested within Germany, for example in the modernization of existing facilities, in the construction or purchase of new factories, and in the purchase of Reich bonds and the acquisition of real estate. IBM, for example, reinvested its considerable earnings in a new factory in Berlin-Lichterfelde, in an expansion of its facilities at Sindelfingen near Stuttgart, in numerous branch offices throughout the Reich, and in the purchase of rental properties in Berlin and other real estate and tangible assets.[10] American corporate involvement in Germany thus continued to expand under Hitler, and by the time of Pearl Harbor the total size of US investments in Hitler's Third Reich would be estimated at 475 million dollars.[11]

An elite of about twenty large and powerful American corporations benefitted from a German connection during the thirties. This elite included Ford, GM, Standard Oil of New Jersey (as Charles Higham puts it, the chief jewel in the crown of the Rockefeller empire, now known as Exxon),[12] Du Pont, Union Carbide, Westinghouse, General Electric, Goodrich, Singer, Eastman Kodak, Coca-Cola, IBM, and — last but certainly not least — ITT. In addition, US corporations had also invested hundreds of millions of dollars in fascist Italy. Finally, a considerable number of American law firms, investment companies, and banks were also actively and profitably involved in America's investment offensive in the fascist countries, among them the banks J. P. Morgan and Dillon, Read and Company, as well as the renowned Wall Street law firm Sullivan & Cromwell. The "stars" of Sullivan & Cromwell were two brothers, John Foster and Allen Dulles, about whom we will hear more later on. Another player in the lucrative "game" of US investment in Germany (and vice versa) was a relatively small and obscure bank known as the Union Bank of New York. It was closely connected to the financial and industrial empire of Thyssen, the German steel baron, who is known to have provided a large part of the financial support without which Hitler would never have been able to come to power. This bank was managed by Prescott Bush, father of President George Bush senior and grandfather of President George W. Bush. It is alleged that Prescott Bush was also an ardent supporter of Hitler, to whom he sent money via Thyssen, and that he was rewarded for this with business deals with Nazi Germany. He made a lot of money in the process and used a part of that lucre to launch his son George into the Texas oil industry.[13]

The gigantic Du Pont trust, financial parent of General Motors, had invested heavily in the German armament industry. It also smuggled weapons and ammunition into Germany via the Netherlands, and possibly profited more than any other American firm from Hitler's aggressive policies and his rearmament program. In this context, it is hardly surprising that

Du Pont's chairman adored Hitler. However, like Ford and Rockefeller, he had already provided generous financial support for the Nazi movement long before Hitler came to power in 1933. Another American corporation that enjoyed intimate relations with the Nazi regime was ITT, whose founder and president, Sosthenes Behn, made no secret of his sympathy for Hitler. (ITT would retain its predilection for fascist dictators long after Behn's disappearance from the scene; its connection with the Pinochet regime in Chile is well known.) The big boss of the oil giant Texaco, Torkild Rieber, was another powerful American entrepreneur who admired Hitler, and he was also a personal friend of Göring; under his guidance Texaco not only profited from all sorts of business deals with Nazi Germany, but also helped Franco's fascists to win the Spanish Civil War with deliveries of oil that contravened US neutrality laws.[14] A member of the German secret service reported about Rieber that he was "absolutely pro-German" and "a sincere admirer of the Führer."[15]

There were of course limits to the American businessmen's fondness for Hitler and his Nazi regime. For example, as traditional champions of free enterprise they were opposed in principle to the fact that the Nazis regimented the activities of firms in Germany, including US subsidiaries — e.g. by restricting the repatriation of profits — and that German-owned enterprises were frequently favoured over US- and other foreign-owned competitors. But these were minor nuisances. Hitler's supreme merit in the eyes of virtually all leaders of corporate America was that thanks to the rearmament boom, their German assets were accumulating riches of which they could only dream in Depression-ridden America, and that under the Third Reich they were not bothered by labour unions, as they certainly were at home. A strike in an American subsidiary in Germany immediately triggered an armed response by the Gestapo, resulting in arrests and dismissals, as was the case in the Opel factory in Rüsselsheim in June 1936.[16] (As the Thuringian teacher and anti-fascist resistance member Otto Jenssen wrote after the war, Germany's corporate leaders were happy "that fear for the concentration camp made the German workers as meek as lap-dogs."[17]) We can therefore understand that the chairman of General Motors, William Knudsen, described Nazi Germany after a visit there in 1933 as "the miracle of the twentieth century," and that many other representatives of the

American power elite had high words of praise for Hitler and his Nazi state. Quite a few of them even dreamed openly or secretly of the coming of a similar fascist saviour on their side of the Atlantic Ocean.[18] Du Pont and many other corporations even provided generous financial support to America's own fascist organizations, such as the infamous "Black Legion."[19]

The racial hatred propagated by Hitler did not offend American sensibilities in the twenties and thirties as much as it would now. After the abolition of slavery at the time of the Civil War, blacks had continued to be considered and treated by many as inferior human beings, and racism was by no means universally stigmatized but remained socially acceptable. Lynchings were a common occurrence in the southern states in the twenties and thirties, even for alleged petty offenses, and proposals for moderate anti-lynching laws were repeatedly turned down by Congress. A strict segregation between whites and blacks was enforced not only south of the Mason-Dixon Line but also in Washington, DC, and would even survive the Second World War. During the war, blacks had to be seated in the back of streetcars and theatres in southern states, sometimes behind German prisoners of war. The American army was itself rife with racism. "White" and "black" blood plasma were strictly segregated in its hospitals, and quite a few generals — including Eisenhower, Marshall, and Patton — were just as convinced as the Nazis of the superiority of the white race. After the war, black veterans married to white war brides or, for that matter, white veterans returning with Asian brides, were not allowed to settle in the many states where statutes continued to feature miscegenation laws forbidding interracial marriages. As for the strongly racist eugenic theories that in Nazi Germany would lead to all sorts of inhuman experiments in "racial hygiene," including sterilization and euthanasia, they found an eager echo in the United States of the thirties, where immigration laws, for example, officially discriminated against persons of "non-Nordic" origin.[20] It is an "irony of history," writes the well-known American historian Stephen Ambrose, that "we fought our greatest war against the world's worst racist with a segregated army while maintaining, either by law or custom, a system of racial separation at home."[21]

During the 1930s, then, all too many Americans did not object to the racism of the Nazis, as was revealed by "polls showing the affinity of

American with German notions of racial hierarchy."[2] Neither was the anti-Semitism of Hitler and his fascist cronies a big issue in America. Anti-Semitism was rather fashionable in the twenties and thirties not only in Germany, but in many other countries, including the United States. Many Americans were anti-Semitic themselves and were therefore tolerant of, if not sympathetic to, Nazi anti-Semitic actions.[23] American industrialists and bankers, and the country's elite in general, did not constitute an exception to this general rule. In the exclusive clubs and fine hotels they patronized, for example, Jews were usually not admitted. America's most notorious anti-Semite was the industrialist Henry Ford, an influential man who admired Hitler, supported him financially, and inspired him with his anti-Semitic book, *The International Jew*, which had been published in the early twenties. The admiration was mutual; the Führer kept a portrait of Ford in his office, acknowledged him as a source of anti-Semitic inspiration, and in 1938 honoured him with the highest medal that Nazi Germany could bestow on a foreigner. Ford also funded the pro-Nazi propaganda campaign waged vigorously throughout the United States by the famous aviator Charles Lindbergh, a friend of Göring. Another fiery and influential American anti-Semite was Charles E. Coughlin, a Catholic priest from Michigan, who in daily radio broadcasts incited his millions of listeners against a Judaism that he equated with Bolshevism, precisely as Hitler did. As for America's businessmen, a large number of them, possibly a majority, thoroughly despised President Roosevelt's policy known as the New Deal, which they condemned as "socialist" interference in the country's economy. The anti-Semites concluded that it was part of a Jewish plot, and they denigrated the New Deal as the "Jew Deal." They similarly considered the president to be a crypto-communist and therefore an agent of the Jews, as a crypto-Jew, and they frequently referred to him as "Rosenfeld."[24] American bankers visiting Germany in June 1934 complained to the ambassador of their country in Berlin that the Roosevelt administration was "full of Jews."[25]

It is clear that, generally speaking, American businessmen and bankers did not despise Nazism or fascism in general for its anti-Semitism; on the contrary, they sympathized with the fascists, and with Hitler in particular, because of their anti-Semitism. Led, directly or indirectly, by such men,

America was not prepared to embark on a European crusade on account of Hitler's anti-Semitism. Even though an inscription on the base of the Statue of Liberty invites to the haven of America all the earth's "tired, poor, huddled masses yearning to breathe free," and even though the US government saw fit from time to time to express its displeasure with certain aspects of Hitler's anti-Semitic policies, precious few Jewish refugees from Germany were granted papers to immigrate to the United States.[26] In the spring of 1939, a ship full of refugees from Germany — the *St. Louis* — was refused permission to disembark its passengers in America or, for that matter, in Cuba, then still a de facto US protectorate. The ship was forced to return to Germany, but received permission *in extremis* to set course for Antwerp, and its Jewish passengers received asylum in Belgium, the Netherlands, France, and Great Britain.[27] During the war, also, Washington worried little, if at all, about the fate of the Jews in Germany and in occupied Europe, even though it became increasingly evident that a systematic genocide was being perpetrated. In 1945, at the time of the American conquest of Germany and directly after the German capitulation, numerous survivors of the Holocaust were kept in concentration camps by the American authorities, to be systematically neglected and even mistreated there. This deplorable situation only came to an end after President Truman was forced to admit in September 1946 that "we apparently treat the Jews the same way as the Nazis did, with the sole exception that we do not kill them," and gave General Eisenhower an order to intervene.[28] It was only years after the end of the war that Jews started to enjoy a measure of respect in the United States, namely, after the new state of Israel — which, with its kibutzim, originally loomed as an unwelcome kind of socialist experiment — revealed itself as a very useful ally of America in the hornet's nest of the Middle East.[29]

It also deserves mention that Hitler did not suddenly forfeit the considerable fund of sympathy he had commanded in high circles in the United States when he unleashed the dogs of war with his attack on Poland on September 1, 1939, or when in May 1940 his military machine overran the Netherlands, Belgium, Luxembourg, and France. When on June 26, 1940, a German commercial delegate organized a dinner at the Waldorf-Astoria Hotel in New York in order to celebrate the victories of the Wehrmacht in Western Europe, the evening was attended by leading industrialists such as James D. Mooney, a top executive of General Motors. As a result of GM's services to Nazi Germany, Mooney had already been honoured by Hitler with the same medal Henry Ford had received from the Führer. (Yet another American mogul who had made himself deserving of the Third Reich and therefore received a medal from Hitler during a 1937 visit to Germany, was IBM's Thomas Watson.) Five days later the German victories were again celebrated in New York, this time by means of a party hosted by the previously mentioned pro-fascist Texaco boss, Rieber. Among the leaders of corporate America who attended this function were the same James D. Mooney and Henry Ford's son, Edsel. In that same summer — the zenith of Hitler's career — Rieber also provided generous moral and material support to a German emissary who visited the United States in order to make propaganda for the cause of the Third Reich.[30]

It was not without reason that America's automobile manufacturers and oil tycoons shared in the German triumph. Without the trucks, tanks, planes, and other equipment supplied by the German subsidiaries of Ford and GM, and without the large quantities of strategic raw materials, notably rubber as well as diesel oil, lubricating oil, and other types of fuel shipped by Texaco and Standard Oil via Spanish ports, the German air and land forces would not have found it so easy to defeat their adversaries in 1939 and 1940. Albert Speer, Hitler's architect and wartime armament minister, would later state that without certain kinds of synthetic fuel made available by US firms, Hitler "would never have considered invading Poland." The American historian Bradford Snell agrees; alluding to the controversial role played by Swiss banks during the war, he comments that "the Nazis could have attacked Poland and Russia without the Swiss banks, but not without General Motors." Hitler's military successes were based on a new form of warfare, the blitzkrieg, consisting of extremely swift and highly synchronized attacks by air and by land. But without the aforementioned American support and without state-of-the-art communications and information technology provided by ITT and IBM, the Führer could only have dreamed of blitzkriege and blitzsiege ("lightning wars" followed by "lightning victories").[31]

Hitler was by no means admired by all Americans. As was the case in other countries, including Germany itself, opinions about Hitler and about fascism in general were divided. In the United States too, countless people despised the German dictator, some US citizens liked Hitler in certain respects but disliked him in others, and then as now many Americans took little or no interest in the affairs of other countries and in international relations and had therefore no particular opinion about the Führer and his fellow fascists. Furthermore, opinions about Hitler fluctuated with the ups and downs of his career. After his attack on Poland, for example, his prestige ebbed considerably stateside, where in cities such as Chicago many people are proud of their Polish origins. What is important, however, is that before and even after the outbreak of war in Europe Hitler and his National Socialism, and fascism in general, enjoyed a disproportionate amount of sympathy within the ranks of the American power elite.

Chapter 3
AMERICA AND THE RED PERIL

The American power elite liked European fascism in general, and Hitler's Nazism in particular, because fascist regimes defended and promoted the interests of big business (and big finance); in other words, because they proved to be "good for business." Another equally important reason was that fascism, the contemporary embodiment of right-wing extremism, was far less distasteful to the American establishment than its left-wing extremist alternative, communism, or "Bolshevism," to use a term fashionable at the time. In the eyes of the corporate leaders of the United States, communism posed a far greater danger than fascism. Moreover, fascism seemed to provide an effective solution to the so-called Red Peril. The socio-economic elites of Europe saw things the same way; they too flirted with fascism in the hope of exorcizing the evil spirit of Bolshevism. Attitudes toward fascism, in the United States as in Europe, can only be fully understood in light of attitudes toward communism.

When the news of the Russian Revolution reached the other side of the Atlantic Ocean in 1917, even before the Great War had run its murderous course, it polarized American public opinion. Quite naturally, the political and economic elites, those who had built up the American capitalist system and profited from it, wholeheartedly repudiated a movement that purported to overthrow capitalism not only in Russia but all over the world.[1] Among lower- and even middle-class Americans, on the other hand, there was considerable enthusiasm for a revolutionary movement that aimed to replace the capitalist system with a new and egalitarian socio-economic alternative. The Bolshevik cause found considerable sympathy and support in the relatively radical American labour movement, particularly in the revolutionary union IWW (International Workers of the World), and among America's socialists and anarchists, who were still numerous at the time. But pacifist citizens, intellectuals, and other respectable representatives of the middle class also reacted positively to the news of the "Red" revolution in Russia. A well-known example is the journalist John Reed, who sought to influence American public opinion in favour of Lenin and his comrades with his reports from Russia and with a best-selling book, *Ten Days That Shook the World*.[2]

Reds such as Reed and the members of the IWW were a thorn in the side of the American government and of the American establishment, who despised Bolshevism and feared that it might inspire a similar revolutionary movement, or at least demands for radical change, in the United States itself. (A similar fear also haunted the power elites of the European countries.) All proponents and sympathizers of Bolshevism were therefore mercilessly persecuted. The IWW was destroyed, and with the help of the media the government orchestrated a campaign aimed at persuading the American people of the dangers of "godless Bolshevism." The flames of the Red Scare were fanned primarily by the newspapers of press baron William Randolph Hearst, who would provide the inspiration for Orson Welles's famous movie, *Citizen Kane*.[3] A. Mitchell Palmer, the attorney general of the supposedly idealistic and democratic President Woodrow Wilson, in many respects a racist and an anti-democrat, arranged to have thousands of Reds and other real or imaginary radicals prosecuted and/or summarily deported during the so-called "Palmer raids" of 1919–20.[4] In addition, American troops joined the contingents of British, French, and other foreign forces that were sent to Russia by their governments in 1918–20 in order to assist the czarist "Whites" in the merciless fight against the Bolsheviks.[5]

A particularly eager assistant of Palmer, J. Edgar Hoover, was totally obsessed with the Red Peril. Later, during his long career as director of the FBI, he would reveal himself to be much more active in the hunt for real or imaginary Reds than in the struggle against gangsters like Al Capone.[6] A student of the history of the FBI, William W. Turner, has described Hoover as "the God-the-Father of the anti-communist theology" and as a man who looked for communists "under every bed."[7] One half-century after the original Red Scare, Hoover would continue to hunt for Reds at home and even abroad; in the 1970s the FBI kept a voluminous file on Prime Minister Pierre Trudeau of Canada, suspected by Hoover to be a "closet communist."[8]

With domestic repression and armed intervention in Russia, then, the American government did battle against the Red Peril, while in Europe the Great War was coming to an end. However, in Russia the Bolsheviks triumphed and established a new state, the Union of Socialist Soviet Republics (USSR). Within the United States itself, the Reds were down but not out; they survived the Red Scare and retrenched in a new Communist Party. Communism retained a considerable measure of sympathy and influence among the American working class and provided some of the most dynamic activists within the trade union movement.[9] And so the American establishment continued to be haunted by the spectre of Bolshevism. The fear of a red revolution even flared up again when the infamous Wall Street Crash of 1929 heralded the onset of the worldwide economic crisis known as the Great Depression. This economic plague brought unprecedented unemployment and untold misery. It also appeared to verify Marx's theory about the development and inevitable demise of the capitalist system, an analysis that had inspired the Bolshevik revolutionaries. In any event, the Great Depression dramatically revealed the shortcomings of American and international capitalism, the more so since the homeland of Bolshevism, which under Stalin was industrializing rapidly, experienced neither an economic crisis nor massive unemployment. On the contrary, in the 1930s the Soviet Union underwent a veritable industrial revolution. An American historian, John H. Backer, has even compared this rapid development of the Soviet economy with the economic boom of West Germany after the Second World War, the widely celebrated "economic miracle."[10] Initially, huge sacrifices had been required of the population of the Soviet Union, but according to Robert W. Thurston, author of a recent American study of Russia in the 1930s, their standard of living improved "slowly but steadily" and "some tangible progress [was made] toward general well-being" after 1933, at a time when for many Americans the situation was becoming increasingly desperate. Not surprisingly, American workers, unemployed, intellectuals, and artists developed a keener interest in socialism and in the communist model of a new, alternative society that was being constructed with so much energy and singularity of purpose, and ostensibly success-fully, in the USSR.[11] A young American writer, Malcolm Cowley, gave voice to these feelings:

> All through the 1930s the Soviet Union was a second father-
> land for millions of people in other countries, including
> our own. It was the land where men and women were sac-
> rificing themselves to create a new civilization, not for Russia
> alone but for the world. It was not so much a nation, in the
> eyes of Western radicals, as it was an ideal, a faith and an
> international hope of salvation.[12]

It is not without reason that in the United States the thirties are some-times referred to as the Red Thirties. In some ways it was a romanticized Soviet Union that served as a model in the United States and elsewhere for all sorts of anti-capitalist plans, because unquestionably the extremely rapid industrialization of the USSR and the concomitant construction of social-ism were accompanied by harsh regimentation and demanded a very high price in human and ecological terms. On the other hand, the mere exist-ence of the Soviet Union, the considerable social and economic progress being made there, and, to a larger extent, the possible future success of that Bolshevik experiment, were perceived as a real threat by the social, econom-ic, and political elite of America. After all, the Soviets offered America's own workers, unemployed, and intellectuals a source of inspiration as well as a practical model of a non-capitalist society, no matter how imperfect. "The Soviet Union [was] not regarded as a military power of the first rank prior to World War II, [and therefore not a military threat]"wrote an American expert in the field, James R. Millar, in the 1980s, and he added:

> Insofar as [the USSR] was regarded as a threat, it was an
> ideological threat. The fear was that [American] workers, and

> *especially the unemployed among them, would see in Bolshevik*
> *Russia a preferred alternative to capitalism.*[13]

In the thirties, America's power elite was far more worried about Bolshevism than about fascism and Nazism. In spite of their revolutionary language, these movements of the extreme right did not seek to overthrow the capitalist system but were easily "reconcil[able] with the American totem-poles of liberty and individualism."[14] In the eyes of most representatives of the American elites, Bolshevism was dangerous, while fascism — including Hitler's Nazism — was not. Furthermore, fascism in general, but German fascism in particular, offered a solution to the problem of the Red Peril. Mussolini and Hitler were outspoken anti-Bolsheviks, who in their own countries had proceeded to politically and often physically eliminate the communists (as well as the socialists and the leaders of the labour unions) from the moment they came to power. They had demonstrated how to get rid of the communist threat, and the labour movement in general, and were consequently admired by the power elites not only of the United States, but also of Great Britain, France, and all other countries where these elites felt threatened by the Red Peril or pressured by labour. Precisely these considerations had prompted the traditional power elites of Italy and Germany to become the "enablers" of Mussolini and Hitler.[15]

In addition, Hitler broadcast to the world that he intended sooner or later to settle the account of the communist homeland, not in order to provide Germany with the *Lebensraum* ("living space") it presumably needed, but to rid the globe once and for all of the state that served as the source of inspiration for Reds everywhere. Anti-Bolshevism — with Bolshevism defined as a Jewish conspiracy — was the leitmotif of *Mein Kampf,* and it is fair to say that Hitler considered the destruction of the Soviet Union as his great mission in life, a task entrusted to him by Providence itself.[16] "Hitler's fundamental political conviction, his self-imposed duty from the moment he had embarked on his political career," emphasizes the German historian Bernd Martin, "was the eradication of Bolshevism."[17]

In the 1930s the Führer concentrated on the restoration of the formidable military might Germany had lost as a result of its defeat in the

Great War. Thus he loomed increasingly like a mighty Siegfried who not only wanted, but was also able, to crush the head of the dragon of international communism, the Soviet Union. Everywhere in the industrialized world there were statesmen, corporate leaders, press barons, and other influential personalities who encouraged him openly or discreetly to realize his great anti-Soviet ambition.[18] In the United States, Nazi Germany was praised as an insurance or a bulwark against communism; for example, by *Time* magazine, whose publisher, Henry Luce, considered "Nazism as ... an antidote against Bolshevism."[19] And Hitler was encouraged to use the might of Germany to destroy the Soviet Union by people such as Herbert Hoover, Roosevelt's predecessor in the White House. (According to Charles Higham, Hoover had lost "extensive Russian oil holdings during the communist revolution," and his attitude toward the Soviet Union was that somehow "it must be crushed.")[20]

Hitler was keenly aware that he was the "great white hope" of anti-communism, and he skillfully took advantage of this goodwill to violate the Treaty of Versailles with impunity. Thus, having first remilitarized Germany in violation of international agreements, he also managed to annex Austria and Czechoslovakia, neighbours whose territory as well as human and material resources happened to be useful, if not indispensable, for the realization of his great eastern ambition. In view of the invaluable service they expected of him, the British, French, and American leaders would not begrudge him this loot — so Hitler speculated, and he was right.

It was primarily in Europe itself that the social and political elites expected great anti-Soviet achievements of Hitler. In Great Britain, for example, the eastern ambitions of the Führer enjoyed at an early stage the approval of respectable and influential politicians, such as Lloyd George; Lord Halifax; Lord Astor and his circle of friends, the so-called "Cliveden Set"; Montagu Norman of the Bank of England; and even of members of the royal family. The Duke of Windsor, who was briefly king in 1936 under the name of Edward VIII, and his American wife, Wallis Simpson, even travelled to Berchtesgaden to have tea with Hitler in his Bavarian mountain retreat and encouraged him in his ambition to attack Russia.[21] Much later, in 1966, the Duke acknowledged this:

> *[Hitler] made me realize that Red Russia [sic] was the only*
> *enemy, and that Great Britain and all of Europe had an*
> *interest in encouraging Germany to march against the east*
> *and to crush communism once and for all . . . I thought that*
> *we ourselves would be able to watch as the Nazis and the Reds*
> *would fight each other.*[22]

It was clear that from this coming titanic struggle the Duke of Windsor —
like virtually all other Western leaders — hoped to see Nazism emerge in
triumph.

And so it came to the infamous "appeasement" policy, the theme of a
brilliant study by two Canadian historians, Clement Leibowitz and Alvin
Finkel, published in 1997. The quintessence of this policy was as follows: Great Britain and France ignored Stalin's proposals for international
cooperation against Hitler, and sought by means of all kinds of diplomatic
contortions and spectacular concessions to stimulate Hitler's anti-Soviet
ambitions and to facilitate their realization. This policy reached its nadir
in the Munich Pact of 1938, whereby Czechoslovakia was sacrificed to the
Führer as a kind of springboard for military aggression in the direction of
Moscow. But Hitler ultimately demanded a higher price than the British
and the French were prepared to pay, and this led in the summer of 1939 to
a crisis over Poland. Stalin, who understood the true objectives of appeasement, took advantage of the opportunity and made a deal of his own with
the German dictator in order to gain not only precious time but also a *gla-*
cis — a strategically important space — in Eastern Europe, without which
the USSR would almost certainly not have survived the Nazi onslaught in
1941. Hitler himself was prepared to deal with his arch-enemy because he
felt cheated by London and Paris, who refused him Poland. And so the
appeasement policy of Great Britain and France collapsed in dismal failure,
first, because the USSR did not disappear from the face of the earth, and second, because after a short blitzkrieg in Poland, Nazi Germany would attack
those who had hoped to manipulate him in order to rid the earth of communism. The so-called ironies of history can be extremely cruel indeed.[23]

When the fiasco of appeasement is mentioned in American history texts,
the finger is usually pointed at London and Paris. And indeed, British and

French statesmen such as Chamberlain and Daladier were the main architects of that abominable policy. Of American foreign policy in the thirties,
on the other hand, it cannot be said that it sought to appease Hitler to
the same extent, and this was for a number of reasons. For example, the
idea of a German crusade against the motherland of communism was all
the more attractive in Great Britain and France because those countries
believed that they would derive a double benefit from it. Not only would
the Soviet Union be wiped off the face of the earth by Hitler's host, but a
new Teutonic venture in Eastern Europe would also conveniently remove
the threat of German revanchism to Western Europe. On the other side of
the Atlantic Ocean, however, fear of German revanchism was not much of a
factor in comparison to the desire to see the Soviet Union destroyed. Since
much more was at stake for London and Paris, Washington could leave the
dishonourable job of appeasement to its Western European colleagues. And
so US leaders found it easy, after the debacle of that policy, to wash their
hands of it. Furthermore, there was no consistent American appeasement
policy because certain factions within America's leading circles had started
to develop an interest in developing good relations with the USSR.

During the thirties, the Bolshevik motherland not only did not fall victim
to the economic crisis, but its economy developed very rapidly, and this
created a demand for all sorts of goods that America's Depression-ridden
industry, or at least some of its sectors and corporations, were very eager to
supply. Thus, while some American firms chose to bank on their German
connections, other corporations perceived a promising alternative strategy
in exporting to the Soviet Union. The result was some disagreement within the American power elite in terms of policy preferences: while most of
its representatives continued to argue in favour of a Germanophile, pro-
fascist, and anti-Soviet policy along the lines of appeasement, some now
propagated a normalization of relations with the USSR and a less indulgent
stance vis-à-vis Nazi Germany.[24]

President Roosevelt briefly flirted with the second policy option. Shortly
after his election, in November 1933, the United States actually entered into
normal diplomatic relations with the Soviet Union, whose existence had
hitherto not been recognized by Washington. However, the power elite's
pro-fascist and Germanophile element was very strongly entrenched in the

State Department, which was dominated by anti-Bolshevik diplomats and bureaucrats, including many with close connections to corporations with investments in Nazi Germany. These officials worked very hard to promote a pro-German and anti-Soviet course along the lines of appeasement.[25] In addition, appeasement enjoyed some public support. Many Americans had little respect for the Treaty of Versailles, which had never been officially recognized by their country, and so they harboured a good measure of understanding, even sympathy for some of Hitler's territorial demands.[26] Thus we can understand how, in spite of reported personal misgivings, President Roosevelt allowed his administration to follow suit when the British and French appeasers went to work. Hitler's aggressions were ignored or rationalized, and usually eventually recognized, by Washington. The annexation of Austria, for example, was legitimated by American diplomats and politicians as a natural and therefore unavoidable development of no importance whatsoever to their own country. The appeasement policy practised by London and Paris was henceforth discreetly supported by Washington, and the British-French concessions to Hitler received Roosevelt's seal of approval.[27] America's policy, writes the American historian Gabriel Kolko, "tacitly, and later explicitly, fell behind British and French appeasement policy." After the conclusion of the Munich Pact, whereby Czechoslovakia was sacrificed to Hitler, President Roosevelt even saw fit to loudly praise arch-appeaser Chamberlain.[28]

The appeasement policy collapsed in the late summer of 1939 on account of the Polish crisis. Appeasement was now officially defunct, but its ghost continued to haunt the corridors of power on both sides of the Atlantic. Appeasers like Chamberlain remained in power in London and Paris, and clandestinely they continued to pursue the goals of that discredited policy. Public opinion had forced them to declare war on Nazi Germany, but it was indeed a "phoney war," a "strange little war" (drôle de guerre) as the French said or, as the Germans put it, a Sitzkrieg (a "sitting war"), during which the British and the French merely sat on their hands and watched as Poland was crushed. London and Paris clearly kept hoping that Hitler would eventually turn against the Soviet Union after all, and arrangements were made to assist him in this mission. The French and British governments and army high commands busily hatched all sorts of plans of attack during the winter of 1939–40, not against Germany, but against the USSR, for example in the form of an operation from the Middle East against the oil fields of Baku.[29] In the United States also, many leading personalities kept hoping that Hitler would soon come to an agreement with Great Britain and France, and would then be free to devote his undivided attention to the Soviet Union. After Germany's victory in Poland, for example, the American ambassador in Berlin, Hugh R. Wilson, expressed the hope that the British and French would see fit to resolve their inconvenient conflict with Germany, so that the Führer would finally have an opportunity to crush the Bolshevik experiment of the Soviets for the benefit of the entire "Western Civilization." A few months later, on March 4, 1940, the aforementioned James D. Mooney, a vice-president of General Motors, visited Hitler in Berlin as an unofficial emissary of President Roosevelt. He made a plea for peace in Western Europe, but suggested "that Americans had understanding for Germany's standpoint with respect to the question of living space" — in other words, that they had nothing against his territorial claims in the East. The idea that Germany needed a free hand in Eastern Europe was also promoted by Wilson's colleague in London, Joseph P. Kennedy, father of the later president, JFK. As for the American mainstream media, they tried very hard to convince the American people that international communism, headquartered in Moscow, represented a far greater danger to their country than the German or Italian versions of fascism. In Catholic as well as Protestant periodicals, "communist subversion" was identified as "the great threat to the country" and, conversely, Hitler was praised as the great "savior from Bolshevism." Those who insisted that fascism was the greater danger were stigmatized as dupes of Moscow; anti-fascism would become popular later, during the war, but America's pre-war anti-fascists — best exemplified by the courageous members of the Lincoln Brigade who fought against Franco's forces in the Spanish Civil War — made the mistake, in the eyes of the US establishment, of being "premature anti-fascists."[30]

And so it happened that in spite of fascist aggression in Europe, the United States witnessed the orchestration of a new anti-communist (and anti-Soviet) Red Scare. During this second so-called "little Red Scare," President Roosevelt found it expedient to declare himself to be a "militant anti-communist." The USSR admittedly provided grist for the mill of this new Red Scare by waging a border war against the Finnish neighbour, who had rejected a Soviet offer to exchange territory. As a result of the border adjustments wrested from the Finns in this "winter war," the Soviets would be able to strengthen the defensive system around the city of Leningrad with its vitally important industries, including tank factories. When war came in 1941, this would turn out to be a decisive factor, as the city was able, but just barely, to withstand a ferocious siege that was to last eight hundred days. However, the Bolshevik homeland paid dearly for the inglorious little war against Finland in terms of lost international goodwill and prestige.[31]

Chapter 4
THE WAR IN EUROPE AND AMERICA'S ECONOMIC INTERESTS

In 1939-1940 opinions about the war were divided, within the population at large and also within the American power elite. However, the US power elite remained anti-communist rather than anti-fascist, and a core group of influential pro-fascist Americans kept hoping that sooner or later Hitler would fulfill their fondest fantasies by turning against the Soviet Union. They were therefore prepared also to sacrifice Western Europe on the altar of anti-communism and anti-Sovietism, just as London and Paris had already sacrificed Eastern Europe. Outspoken Hitler-sympathizers like Henry Ford and Charles Lindbergh set the tone in the "America First" movement, which opposed any form of intervention in the European conflict; and in Congress a so-called isolationist majority resisted any attempts to involve the United States in the war in Europe. Taking a stand against the isolationists were the interventionists, who argued in favour of an American intervention on the side of Great Britain, Hitler's only remaining enemy. The interventionists were motivated by factors such as important business relations but also cultural, ethnic, intellectual, and purely sentimental ties with Great Britain, genuine concern about the fate of democracy in Europe, and fear that sooner or later the United States itself might become the victim of Nazi aggression.

The American government was likewise divided. The idea of intervention on the side of Great Britain seemed to be supported by President

Roosevelt, but remained out of the question because of the strength of the isolationists in Congress. And so it was expected in Washington — with approval or with resignation — that the "new order" established in Europe by the Nazis would not evaporate soon. With regard to foreign relations, this meant, for example, that the American government saw no reason to withdraw its ambassador from Berlin, and that normal diplomatic relations were maintained with the French collaborator regime of Marshal Pétain in Vichy. Vichy would eventually break off diplomatic relations with the United States in November 1941, following the American-British landings in French North Africa, which will be discussed later.[1]

However, the war in Europe opened up particularly interesting opportunities for American industry, mired for nearly a decade in a deep economic crisis. The causes of the Great Depression, which ravaged not only America but all industrialized countries in the thirties, with the notable exception of the Soviet Union, can be found in the rapid development of the capitalist industrial system. Productivity had increased to such an extent that the supply of goods had started to exceed the demand for them. As a result of chronic overproduction, prices as well as profits decreased, inventories of unsold products were building up, and factories laid off workers or simply closed their doors, thereby increasing unemployment. The resulting decrease of purchasing power caused aggregate demand to drop even further, which worsened the crucial problem of overproduction. The infamous Wall Street Crash in the fall of 1929 did not cause the Great Depression, as is often alleged or implied, but merely reflected these fatal structural trends: stock market shares plunged in value when it became obvious that there were no longer any prospects of sustained industrial growth and, therefore, of further increases in profits and returns on investments.

In 1932 America elected the Democratic candidate, Franklin D. Roosevelt, to the presidency. He had intimated that under his leadership the state would do something to fight the economic crisis, while his Republican rival, Herbert Hoover, preferred to remain faithful to the orthodox liberal laissez-faire principles of Adam Smith, which call for the state to refrain as much as possible from intervening in economic life. Roosevelt's new administration did indeed tackle the crisis with new policy instruments, including gigantic state-sponsored projects such as the construction of dams in the Tennessee Valley. Essentially, the idea was to stimulate demand by creating employment. However, the huge expenditures associated with this policy — which was denigrated by the champions of laissez-faire as a nefarious socialist experiment — threatened to cause the national debt to skyrocket. Roosevelt's unorthodox and inflationary kind of economic policy initiatives, which differed only little from the policy of road construction and rearmament used by Hitler to fight the economic crisis in Germany, contributed to inspire a new economic theory, linked with the name of the British economist John Maynard Keynes. In this sense, at least, Roosevelt's new approach to the economic crisis was Keynesian, although it would be wrong to label Roosevelt himself as a Keynesian and although his (far from consistent) policies were far from faultless from a Keynesian perspective. In any event, with this newfangled economic policy, which became known as the New Deal, Roosevelt did not succeed in leading America out of the desert of the Great Depression.

The conflict in Europe, on the other hand, opened up extremely interesting prospects for the American economy. It was to be expected that, as in the First World War, the belligerent nations would need all sorts of armaments and equipment, at least if the war would again prove to be a protracted one. If American industry could supply these goods, this might provide a solution for the economic crisis and the unemployment problem. But which warring nations were potential customers of Uncle Sam? Which countries might become markets for American export products? In the early stages of the First World War, the neutral United States had done business with the Entente, and above all with Great Britain. Between 1914 and 1916, the total value of American exports to Great Britain and France had increased dramatically, from 824 million to 3.3 billion dollars, while the volume of exports to Germany and Austria-Hungary had declined to merely 1 million dollars. These statistics reflected not American sympathy for the Entente but the simple fact that the British naval blockade made it impossible to supply the Germans with the goods for which their war industry was starved.[2]

At the start of the Second World War, the so-called Cash and Carry laws of the United States required that belligerent countries could only purchase goods in America in return for payment in cash; these countries had to make their own arrangements to have the goods carried to their destination. As the Royal Navy still ruled the Atlantic, this meant that the Germans were unable to shop for war supplies in the United States. After the campaign in Western Europe, much as in the First World War, only Great Britain remained as a potential market for American industry.[3] Payment in cash was required because a lesson had been learned in the Great War. Originally, the British had been allowed to buy on credit. In 1917, when the British and French threatened to lose the war, the United States was forced to intervene militarily in order to prevent the collapse of their customer and debtor.[4] It is understandable, therefore, that when the Second World War got underway the neutral Americans proved to be more cautious and insisted on cash payment. However, when the hard-pressed British started to suffer from a shortage of cash, America's leaders could not face the prospect of discontinuing their country's profitable transatlantic business with Great Britain. In spite of its high tariffs, Great Britain had absorbed more than 40 per cent of America's exports before the war and the US did not want to lose such an important partner, especially since its wartime business might help pull its economy out of the slump of the Great Depression. In any event, in spite of its depleted cash reserves, Great Britain remained creditworthy in some respects, because it was an empire boasting huge geopolitical capital in the form of overseas possessions. In exchange for a collection of antiquated destroyers for the Royal Navy, the United States thus took over a number of naval and air force bases in September 1940 in British territories in the Caribbean and on Newfoundland, a British Dominion that was to join Canada only after the war, in 1949. President Roosevelt eventually managed to persuade Congress to grant the British easy terms of payment in the form of a system that was ambiguously called Lend-Lease. This term created the impression that it was a purely business-like and mutual arrangement between the two countries. Lend-Lease, officially introduced in March 1941, provided London with virtually unlimited credits, to be used to purchase American weapons, ammunition, and similar urgently required supplies. The total value of American exports to Great Britain would thus increase spectacularly, from 505 million dollars in 1939 to 1 billion in 1940, 1.6 billion in 1941, 2.5 billion in 1942, 4.5 billion in 1943, and no less than 5.2 billion in 1944. As far as American business was concerned, Lend-Lease proved to be a dream come true, because it opened up a huge market for the export products of the United States.[5]

The Lend-Lease deliveries were also associated with an important British concession known as "the consideration." London committed itself to a post-war dismantlement of the protectionist system of "imperial preference" tariffs, which had not prevented but certainly limited American exports to Great Britain and its dependencies. "Lend-Lease," write two American historians, Justus D. Doenecke and John E. Wilz,

> *was not nearly as generous as it was long believed . . . the deliveries did not amount to a selfless gift, because payment was postponed, but required in the end . . . the ultimate bill did not necessarily have to be settled with money or with deliveries in reverse. [It was expected that] the British imperial preference tariffs would be abolished, so that American products would in future more easily reach the many markets which had hitherto been dominated by England [sic].[6]*

Thanks to Lend-Lease, the export products of American industry would in future no longer run into a relatively closed economy in Great Britain, but instead enjoy the benefit of a so-called open door. This opened up prospects for a solution to the crisis of the Great Depression in the United States, namely, free access to the British market, and eventually to all world markets, for American products. The burgeoning of international trade, then, was expected to eliminate the key problem of the demand deficit.[7]

The Lend-Lease system was a classical Keynesian remedy for the economic crisis of the thirties: the state "primed the pump" of the economy by means of large-scale Lend-Lease orders, and financed this scheme primarily by borrowing the required capital. The national debt would increase considerably as a result of Lend-Lease and of America's now rapidly increasing military expenditures — from approximately 3 billion dollars in 1939 to almost 5 billion in 1941, 20 billion in 1942, and 45 billion in 1945. But it was expected that eventually high profits would generate sufficient taxation revenue to enable Washington to liquidate its debts. All this was pure theory, Keynesian theory. In reality, the scheme came down to this: the

American state used its general revenues to pay the hefty bills presented by the large corporations that virtually monopolized Lend-Lease business and war production in general. These bills were mostly paid by means of direct and indirect taxes, which during the war — primarily as a result of the regressive *Revenue Act* of October 1942, introducing the euphemistically named "Victory Tax" — would be paid increasingly by ordinary US citizens rather than by the wealthy Americans and the big corporations. Enormous private profits were thus financed by the American public.[8] "The burden of financing the war," observes the American historian Sean Dennis Cashman,"[was] sloughed . . . firmly upon the shoulders of the poorer members of society."[9]

Great Britain also benefitted from Lend-Lease, at least in the short run, because imports of American weapons and other equipment made it possible to continue the war against Hitler after the fall of France and, a few years later, to emerge victoriously from the ordeal. In the long run, however, Great Britain would pay the price of its status as a political and economic world power. Lend-Lease proved to be the foot in the door that allowed the United States to penetrate Great Britain and its entire empire economically and eventually to dominate it. Lend-Lease irrevocably led to a very intimate but also extremely asymmetrical military, political, and economic American-British partnership wherein Great Britain was predestined to play the role of junior partner, the role of America's faithful sidekick in Europe. It would come to that well before the end of the Second World War, and it is still that today.[10] (Some contemporary Allied leaders, for example Camille Gutt, the very capable finance minister of the Belgian government-in-exile in London, understood only too well that Lend-Lease help would permit the United States after the war "to dictate to other countries the commercial and economic conditions" of their bilateral relations and would thus result in a high degree of economic dependency on America, and that it was therefore wise to use Lend-Lease credits only sparingly. In comparison to the British, however, the Belgians enjoyed the advantage that they were able to pay for American supplies with important minerals from their Congolese colony, such as copper, cobalt, and above all uranium, which would be used by the Americans to build their nuclear bomb.)[11]

The war that had broken out in Europe provided American big business with an unprecedented window of opportunity. Many owners and managers of American corporations who threw themselves at the chance to profit from the lucrative trade with Great Britain undoubtedly had more sympathy for Hitler than for Churchill, more sympathy for fascism than for democracy. However, the totally businesslike American-British trade relationship, which began with Cash and Carry and metamorphosed into Lend-Lease, started to affect the sentiments of even the most hard-nosed American entrepreneurs. As American industry oriented itself increasingly toward profitable trade with Great Britain, that country gradually earned more and more sympathy in the United States. Conversely, the cause of Nazi Germany found less and less understanding in America, even among the businessmen who had wished Hitler well only a little earlier, but who were now making a pretty penny from the booming trade with Great Britain.

There were other, purely economic reasons why Nazi Germany enjoyed less and less sympathy within the ranks of the American power elite. The political and industrial leaders of the United States were unanimous in their conviction "that foreign trade was essential to American prosperity," as the historians Peter N. Carroll and David W. Noble write in a vignette of Roosevelt and his advisors, so they wanted open doors for their export products.[12] However, it gradually became clear that as part of their preparations for war the Nazis strove to achieve autarky, thereby reducing imports and turning Germany into one of those "closed economies" loathed by American businessmen. Exports from the United States to Germany declined in the thirties, first slowly and then more rapidly as the implementation of the Nazi autarky schemes gained momentum. Between 1933 and 1938, Germany's share of America's export volume sunk from 8.4 to 3.4 per cent; by 1938, the value of all US exports to Germany amounted to only 406 million dollars, compared to two billion dollars ten years earlier. To American corporations with branch plants in Germany itself, this development may not have presented a considerable problem, but American corporate leaders who were not so privileged — and politicians convinced that US prosperity depended on foreign trade — were extremely perturbed by this trend.[13] (In spite of its search for autarky, one commodity Germany had to continue importing was oil, of which US firms clandestinely supplied huge amounts via neutral countries, as we have already seen.)

Even more irritating to many America's industrialists and politicians, including personalities with favourable views of Hitler, must have been the success of Berlin's aggressive international trade policy in Latin America. Ever since the proclamation of the Monroe Doctrine at the start of the nineteenth century, the Americans had considered Central and South America as their very own commercial bailiwick. However, during the 1930s the German share of the import volume of countries such as Brazil, Chile, and Mexico was growing rapidly at the expense — and to the displeasure — of the hitherto unthreatened American competition.[14] The American historian Patrick J. Hearden writes:

> The Nazi trade offensive in South America continued to score big gains at the expense of the United States. Germany's share of total Latin American imports increased from 9.5 per cent in 1929 to 16.2 per cent in 1938, while the figures for the United States declined from 38.5 to 33.9 per cent. The State Department was disturbed. "The competition is getting keener all the time," [an official] noted in May 1938. "More and more dissatisfaction is being expressed by American exporters."[15]

Commercially, then, Nazi Germany was becoming the "most irksome competitor" of the United States in that part of the world, as the German ambassador to Mexico put it in 1938 in a report to Berlin.[16]

From an American perspective, the problem of Germany's "closed economy" was exacerbated in 1938, 1939, and 1940. This was due to the appeasement policy first, and then to the victories of the Wehrmacht, factors which permitted the Nazis to establish their economic hegemony over most of Eastern Europe as well as France and the Low Countries. Henceforth it was no longer Germany alone but its entire Grossraumwirtschaft ("greater economic zone") on the Continent which closed its doors to US export products. The American corporations with subsidiaries in Germany actually managed to secretly profit from this development, as we will see later, but to the industrial and political leaders of America in general it amounted to another slap in the face by Nazi leaders for whom many of them had earlier displayed so much admiration.

It was against this backdrop that in late 1940 and early 1941 the enticing business opportunities of trade with Great Britain — and the potential of Lend-Lease in terms of creating open doors — revealed themselves. No wonder that with regard to the war in Europe the sympathy of corporate America shifted perceptibly from Germany to Great Britain, and that in the media soon nothing positive was said anymore about Hitler, so that American public opinion in general also increasingly espoused the cause of Great Britain.

In business, the bankruptcy of an important customer can be extremely costly to a supplier. Consequently, the United States could not afford to see Great Britain lose the war. On the other hand, the interests of American industry did not require the British to win the war, something that seemed totally out of the question after the fall of France. Most advantageous to corporate America was a scenario whereby the war in Europe dragged on as long as possible, so that the big corporations might continue to supply the British partner indefinitely. According to his biographer, David Lanier Lewis, Henry Ford thus "expressed the hope that neither the Allies nor the Axis would win [the war]," and at one point he actually suggested that the United States should supply both Britain and the Axis powers with "the tools to keep on fighting until they both collapse."[17] Ford practised what he preached, and arranged for his factories at home and abroad to supply the Germans as well as the British with all sorts of war equipment. Another tycoon with lucrative investments in Germany, IBM's Thomas Watson, was equally nonchalant about the prospect of a permanent Nazi dominion in continental Europe. "Like many [other US businessmen]," writes Edwin Black, "Watson expected that America would stay out of the war"; Germany would remain master of Europe, and IBM — already firmly ensconced in the Third Reich via Dehomag — would benefit by "[ruling] the data domain." Watson was not at all perturbed that Nazi-occupied Europe seemed predestined to become a nightmarish power block such as the one conjured up in Orwell's *Nineteen Eighty-Four*; on the contrary, he looked forward to providing Big Brother with the technological tools for total control — and to profiting accordingly.[18] In view of all this, it is understandable that while American leaders increasingly sympathized with Great Britain, they had no plans for their country to become an active belligerent. At the time of the fall of France and the evacuation from Dunkirk the situation momentarily looked critical for the British. However, after the summer of 1940 and the epic Battle of Britain, brilliantly won by the Royal Air Force, it was clear that tough little Albion would not knuckle under, at least not as long as the United States would continue to supply it with the wherewithal to fight on. The war in Europe, then, was expected to last a very long time. If in the meantime the Nazis remained the masters of the European continent and were free to establish their "new order" there, that did not bother Washington very much. America had no desire to become actively involved in the conflict in Europe, and on the occasion of the presidential elections in the fall of 1940 Roosevelt assured the American people that during his next term in office "[our] boys are not going to be sent into any foreign wars."[19] When in the fall of 1941 a series of incidents between German submarines and US Navy destroyers escorting freighters bound for Britain led to a further deterioration of relations with Nazi Germany, even this crisis — known as the "undeclared naval war" — did not lead to active American involvement in the war in Europe.[20] America's power elite was simply not interested in a crusade against Nazi Germany, and Nazi Germany, which had attacked the Soviet Union in June of 1941, was not interested in declaring war on America. Eventually, in December 1941, the United States would become an active belligerent. However, as Stephen Ambrose has pointed out, America was not to "enter" the Second World War in the sense that "[to] enter" is an active verb, implying some positive deed; the United States was "pulled in [to]" the war, he rightly emphasizes, and this happened "despite, rather than because of, the actions of the American president" and, it might be added, the wishes of the power elite he represented.[21]

Chapter 5
FALL 1941: THE TIDE OF WAR TURNS IN FRONT OF MOSCOW

War against the Soviet Union was what Hitler had wanted from the beginning. He had already made this very clear on the pages of *Mein Kampf*, written in the mid-1920s. Furthermore, as a German historian has recently convincingly demonstrated,[1] it was a war against the Soviet Union, and not against Poland, France, or Britain, that Hitler had wanted and planned to unleash in 1939. On August 11 of that year, Hitler explained to Carl J. Burckhardt, an official of the League of Nations, that "everything he undertook was directed against Russia," and that "if the West [i.e., the French and the British] is too stupid and too blind to comprehend this, he would be forced to reach an understanding with the Russians, turn and defeat the West, and then turn back with all his strength to strike a blow against the Soviet Union."[2] This is in fact what happened. The West did turn out to be "too stupid and blind," as Hitler saw it, to give him "a free hand" in the east, so he did make a deal with Moscow — the infamous "Hitler-Stalin Pact" — and then unleashed war against Poland, France, and Britain. But his ultimate objective remained the same: to attack and destroy the Soviet Union as soon as possible.

Hitler and the German generals were convinced they had learned an important lesson from World War I. Devoid of the raw materials, such as oil and rubber, needed to win a modern war, Germany could not win their planned new edition of the "Great War." In order to win such a war, Germany would have to win it fast, very fast. This is how the blitzkrieg concept was born, that is, the idea of warfare (*Krieg*) fast as lightning (*Blitz*). Blitzkrieg meant motorized war, so in preparation for such a war Germany, during the thirties, cranked out massive numbers of tanks and planes as well as trucks to transport troops. In addition, gargantuan amounts of oil and rubber were imported and stockpiled. As we have seen, much of this oil was purchased from US corporations, some of which also kindly made available the "recipe" for producing synthetic fuel from coal. In 1939 and 1940, this equipment permitted the Wehrmacht and Luftwaffe to overwhelm the Polish, Dutch, Belgian, and French defences with thousands of planes and tanks in a matter of weeks; blitzkriege, "lightning-fast wars," were invariably followed by blitzsiege, "lightning-fast victories."

The victories against Poland, France, et cetera were spectacular enough, but they did not provide Germany with much loot in the form of vitally important oil and rubber. Instead, "lightning warfare" actually depleted the stockpiles built up before the war. Fortunately for Hitler, in 1940 and 1941 Germany was able to continue importing oil from the still neutral United States, mostly via other neutral (and friendly) countries such as Franco's Spain. Moreover, under the terms of the Hitler-Stalin Pact the Soviet Union herself also supplied Germany rather generously with oil. However, it was most troubling for Hitler that, in return, Germany had to supply the Soviet Union with high-quality industrial products and state-of-the-art military technology, which was used by the Soviets to modernize their army and improve their weaponry.[3] Another headache for Hitler was the fact that the terms of his deal with the Soviets had permitted the latter to occupy eastern Poland, thus shifting their border, and their defences, a few hundred kilometres to the west, making the planned march to Moscow much longer for the German military. (As the Wehrmacht did actually make it to the outskirts of Moscow in late 1941, it can be argued that they would probably have taken the city, and perhaps won the war, had they been able to launch their attack from positions further east.)

In 1939, Hitler had reluctantly shelved his plan for war against the Soviet Union. But he resurrected it very soon after the defeat of France, in the summer of 1940. A formal order to prepare plans for such an attack, to be code-named Operation Barbarossa (*Unternehmen Barbarossa*) was given a few months later, on December 18, 1940.[4] By 1940 nothing had changed as far as Hitler was concerned: "The real enemy was the one in the east."[5] Hitler simply did not want to wait much longer before realizing the great ambition of his life, that is, destroying the country he had defined as his arch-enemy in *Mein Kampf*. Moreover, he knew that the Soviets were frantically preparing their defences for a German attack which, as they knew only too well, would come sooner or later. (The notion that, on account of their 1939 non-aggression pact, Nazi Germany and the Soviet Union were friendly "allies" is hopelessly erroneous.) Since the Soviet Union was getting stronger by the day, time was obviously not on Hitler's side. How much longer could he wait before the window of opportunity would close?

Furthermore, waging a blitzkrieg against the Soviet Union promised to provide Germany with the virtually limitless resources of that huge country, including Ukrainian wheat to provide Germany's population, experiencing wartime shortages, with plenty of food; minerals such as coal, from which synthetic oil and rubber could be produced; and — last, but certainly not least — the rich oil fields of Baku and Grozny, where the gas-guzzling Panzers and Stukas would be able to fill their tanks to the brim at any time. Steeled with these assets, it would then be a simple matter for Hitler to settle accounts with Britain, starting, for example, with the capture of Gibraltar. Germany would finally be a genuine world power, invulnerable within a European "fortress" stretching from the Atlantic to the Urals, possessed of limitless resources, and therefore capable of winning even long, drawn-out wars against any antagonist — including the US — in one of the future "wars of the continents" conjured up in Hitler's feverish imagination.

Hitler and his generals were confident that the blitzkrieg they prepared to unleash against the Soviet Union would be as successful as their earlier lightning wars against Poland and France had been. They considered the Soviet Union as a "giant with feet of clay," whose army, presumably decapitated by Stalin's purges of the late 1930s, was "not more than a joke," as Hitler himself put it on one occasion.[6] In order to fight and, of course, win the decisive battles, they allowed for a campaign of four to six weeks, possibly to be followed by some mopping-up operations, during which the remnants of the Soviet host would "be chased across the country like a bunch of beaten Cossacks."[7] In any event, Hitler felt supremely confident, and on the eve of the attack, he "fancied himself to be on the verge of the greatest triumph of his life."[8]

In Washington and London, the military experts likewise believed that the Soviet Union would not be able to put up significant resistance to the Nazi juggernaut, whose military exploits of 1939–40 had earned it a reputation of invincibility. The British secret services were convinced that the Soviet Union would be "liquidated within eight to ten weeks," and the chief of the Imperial General Staff averred that the Wehrmacht would slice through the Red Army "like a warm knife through butter," and that the Red Army would be rounded up "like cattle." According to expert opinion in Washington, Hitler would "crush Russia [sic] like an egg."[9]

The German attack started on June 22, 1941, in the early hours of the morning. Three million German soldiers and almost 700,000 allies of Nazi Germany crossed the border. Their equipment consisted of 600,000 motor vehicles, 3,648 tanks, more than 2,700 planes, and just over 7,000 pieces of artillery.[10] At first, everything went according to plan. Huge holes were punched in the Soviet defences, impressive territorial gains were made rapidly, and hundreds of thousands of Red Army soldiers were killed, wounded, or taken prisoner in a number of spectacular "encirclement battles." The road to Moscow seemed to lay open. However, all too soon it became evident that the blitzkrieg in the east would not be the cakewalk that had been expected. Facing the most powerful military machine on earth, the Red Army predictably took a major beating but, as propaganda minister Joseph Goebbels confided to his diary as early as July 2, also put up a tough resistance and hit back very hard on numerous occasions. General Franz Halder, in many ways the "godfather" of Operation Barbarossa's plan of attack, acknowledged that Soviet resistance was much stronger than anything the Germans had faced in Western Europe. Wehrmacht reports cited "hard," "tough," even "wild" resistance, causing heavy losses in men and equipment on the German side. More often than expected, Soviet forces managed to launch counterattacks that slowed down the German advance. Some Soviet units went into hiding in the vast Pripet Marshes and elsewhere, organized deadly partisan warfare, and threatened the long and vulnerable German lines of communication.[11] It also turned out that the Red Army was much better equipped than expected. German generals were "amazed," writes a German historian, by the quality of Soviet weapons such as the Katyusha rocket launcher (a.k.a. "Stalin Organ") and the T-34 tank. Hitler was furious that his secret services had not been aware of the existence of some of this weaponry.[12]

The greatest cause of concern, as far as the Germans were concerned, was the fact that the bulk of the Red Army managed to withdraw in relatively good order and eluded destruction in a huge encirclement battle, in the kind of repeat of Cannae or Sedan that Hitler and his generals had dreamed of. The Soviets appeared to have carefully observed and analyzed the German blitzkrieg successes of 1939 and 1940 and to have learned useful lessons. They must have noticed that in May 1940 the French had massed the bulk of their forces right at the border as well as in Belgium, thus making it possible for the German war machine to encircle them. (British troops were also caught in this encirclement but managed to escape via Dunkirk.) The Soviets did leave some troops at the border, of course, and these troops predictably suffered the Soviet Union's major losses during the opening stages of Barbarossa. But — contrary to what is claimed by historians such as Richard Overy[13] — the bulk of the Red Army was held back in the rear, avoiding entrapment. It was this "defence in depth" — facilitated by the acquisition of a "glacis," a territorial "breathing space," in Poland in 1939 — that frustrated the German ambition to destroy the Red Army in its entirety. As Marshal Zhukov was to write in his memoirs, "the Soviet Union would have been smashed if we had organized all our forces at the border."[14]

As early as the middle of July, as Hitler's war in the east started to lose its *Blitz*-qualities, countless Germans, military as well as civilians, of low as well as high rank, including Hitler himself, lost their belief in a quick victory. And by the end of August, at a time when Barbarossa should have been winding down, the Wehrmacht's high command (*Oberkommando der Wehrmacht*, or OKW) acknowledged that it might no longer be possible to win the war in 1941.[15] A major problem was the fact that, when Barbarossa started on June 22, the available supplies of fuel, tires, spare parts, et cetera, were good enough for only about two months. This had been deemed sufficient because it was expected that within two months the Soviet Union would be on its knees and its unlimited resources — industrial products as well as raw materials — would therefore be available to the Germans.[16] However, by late August the German spearheads were nowhere near those distant regions of the Soviet Union where oil, that most precious of all martial commodities, was to be had. If the tanks managed to keep on rolling, though increasingly slowly, into the seemingly endless Russian and Ukrainian expanses, it was to a large extent by means of fuel and rubber imported, via Spain and occupied France, from the US.

The flames of optimism flared up again in September, when German troops captured Kiev, and, further north, made progress in the direction of Moscow. Hitler believed, or at least pretended to believe, that the end was now near for the Soviets. In a public speech in the Berlin *Sportpalast* on October 3, he declared that the eastern war was virtually over. And the Wehrmacht was ordered to deliver the *coup de grâce* by launching Operation Typhoon (*Unternehmen Taifun*), an offensive aimed at taking Moscow. However, the odds for success looked increasingly slim, as the Soviets were busily bringing in reserve units from the Far East. (They had been informed by their master spy in Tokyo, Richard Sorge, that the Japanese, whose army was stationed in northern China, were no longer considering attacking the Soviets' vulnerable borders in the Vladivostok area.) To make things worse, the Germans no longer enjoyed superiority in the air, particularly over Moscow. Also, sufficient supplies of ammunition and food could not be brought up from the rear to the front, since the long supply lines were severely hampered by partisan activity.[17] Finally, it was getting chilly in the Soviet Union, though no colder than usual at that time of the year. But the German high command, confident that their eastern blitzkrieg would be over by the end of the summer, had failed to supply the troops with the equipment necessary to fight in the rain, mud, snow, and freezing temperatures of a Russian fall and winter.

Taking Moscow loomed as an extremely important objective in the minds of Hitler and his generals. It was believed, though probably wrongly, that the fall of its capital would "decapitate" the Soviet Union and thus bring about its collapse. It also seemed important to avoid a repeat of the scenario of the summer of 1914, when the seemingly unstoppable German advance into France had been halted *in extremis* on the eastern outskirts of Paris, during the Battle of the Marne. This disaster — from the German perspective — had robbed Germany of nearly certain victory in the opening stages of the Great War and had forced it into a lengthy struggle that, lacking sufficient resources and blockaded by the British navy, it was doomed to lose. This time, in a new Great War fought against a new arch-enemy, the Soviet Union, there was to be no "miracle of the Marne," that is, no defeat just outside the capital, and Germany would therefore not have to once more fight, resourceless and blockaded, a long, drawn-out conflict it would be doomed to lose. Unlike Paris, Moscow would fall, history would not repeat itself, and Germany would end up being victorious.[18] Or so they hoped in Hitler's headquarters.

The Wehrmacht continued to advance, albeit very slowly, and by mid-November some units found themselves only thirty kilometres from the capital. But the troops were now totally exhausted and running out of supplies. Their commanders knew that it was simply impossible to take Moscow, tantalizingly close as the city may have been, and that even doing so would not bring them victory. On December 3, a number of units abandoned the offensive on their own initiative. Within days, however, the entire German army in front of Moscow was simply forced on the defensive. Indeed, on December 5, at three in the morning, in cold and snowy conditions, the Red Army suddenly launched a major, well-prepared counterattack. The Wehrmacht's lines were pierced in many places, and the Germans were thrown back between 100 and 280 kilometres with heavy losses of men and equipment. It was only with great difficulty that a catastrophic encirclement could be avoided. On December 8, Hitler ordered his army to abandon the offensive and to move into defensive positions. He blamed this setback on the supposedly unexpected early arrival of winter, refused to pull back further to the rear, as some of his generals suggested, and proposed to attack again in the spring.[19]

Thus ended Hitler's blitzkrieg against the Soviet Union, the war that, had it been victorious, would have realized the great ambition of his life, the destruction of the Soviet Union. More importantly, such a victory would also have provided Nazi Germany with sufficient oil and other resources to make it a virtually invulnerable world power. As such, Nazi Germany would very likely have been capable of finishing off stubborn Great Britain, even if the US would have rushed to help its Anglo-Saxon cousin, which, in early December of 1941, was not yet in the cards. A blitzsieg, that is, a rapid victory against the Soviet Union, then, was supposed to have made a German defeat impossible, and would in all likelihood have done so. (It is probably fair to say that if Nazi Germany had defeated the Soviet Union in 1941, Germany would today still be the hegemon of Europe, and possibly of the Middle East and North Africa as well.) However, defeat in the Battle of Moscow in December 1941 meant that Hitler's blitzkrieg did *not* produce the hoped-for blitzsieg. In the new "Battle of the Marne" just to the west of Moscow, Nazi Germany suffered the defeat that made victory impossible, not only victory against the Soviet Union itself, but also victory against Great Britain and victory in the war in general. It ought to be noted that the United States was not yet involved in the war against Germany.

Bearing in mind the lessons of World War I, Hitler and his generals had known from the start that, in order to win the new Great War they had unleashed, Germany had to win fast, lightning-fast. But on December 5, 1941, it became evident to everyone present in Hitler's headquarters that a blitzsieg against the Soviet Union would not be forthcoming, and that Germany was doomed to lose the war, if not sooner, then later. According to General Alfred Jodl, chief of the operations staff of the OKW, Hitler then realized that he could no longer win the war.[20] And so it can be argued, as a German historian, an expert on the war against the Soviet Union, has done, that the success of the Red Army in front of Moscow was unquestionably the "major break" (*Zäsur*) of the entire world war.[21]

In other words, the tide of World War II can be said to have turned on December 5, 1941. However, as real tides turn not suddenly but rather gradually and imperceptibly, the tide of the war turned not on a single day, but over a period of days, weeks, and even months, in the period of approximately three months that elapsed between the (late) summer of 1941 and early December of that same year. The tide of the war in the east turned gradually, but it did not do so imperceptibly. Already in August 1941, astute observers had started to doubt that a German victory, not only in the Soviet Union but in the war in general, still belonged to the realm of possibilities. The well-informed Vatican, for example, initially very enthusiastic about Hitler's "crusade" against the Soviet homeland of "godless" Bolshevism, started to express grave concerns about the situation in the east in late summer 1941; by mid-October, it came to the conclusion that Germany would lose the war.[22] Likewise in mid-October, the Swiss secret services reported that "the Germans can no longer win the war."[23] By late November, a defeatism of sorts had started to infect the higher ranks of the Wehrmacht and of the Nazi Party. Even as they were urging their troops forward toward Moscow, some generals opined that it would be preferable to make peace overtures and wind down the war without achieving the great victory that had seemed so certain at the start of Operation Barbarossa.[24]

When the Red Army launched its devastating counteroffensive on December 5, Hitler himself realized that he would lose the war. But he was not prepared to let the German public know that. The nasty tidings from the front near Moscow were presented to the public as a temporary setback, blamed on the supposedly unexpectedly early arrival of winter and/or on the incompetence or cowardice of certain commanders. (It was only a good year later, after the catastrophic defeat in the Battle of Stalingrad during the winter of 1942-43, that the German public, and the entire world, would realize that Germany was doomed; which is why even today many historians believe that the tide turned in Stalingrad.)

On December 7, 1941, Hitler, in his headquarters deep in the forests of East Prussia, had not yet fully digested the ominous news of the Soviet counteroffensive in front of Moscow, when he learned that, on the other side of the world, the Japanese had attacked the Americans at Pearl Harbor. We will soon deal with the background and significance of this attack, which brought the US into the war. At this time it ought to be pointed out that it caused the US to declare war on Japan, but not on Germany, which had nothing to do with the attack and had not even been aware of the Japanese plans. Hitler had no obligation whatsoever to rush to the aid of his Japanese friends, as is claimed by some American historians, just as the Japanese leaders had not felt an obligation to rush to Hitler's side when he went to war against Poland, France, and the Soviet Union. However, on December 11, 1941 — four days after Pearl Harbor — the German dictator suddenly declared war on the US. This seemingly irrational decision must be understood in light of the German predicament in the Soviet Union. Hitler almost certainly speculated that this entirely gratuitous gesture of solidarity would induce his Far Eastern ally to reciprocate with a declaration of war on the enemy of

Germany, the Soviet Union, and this would have forced the Soviets into the extremely perilous predicament of a two-front war. (The bulk of the Japanese army was stationed in northern China and would therefore have been able to immediately attack the Soviet Union in the Vladivostok area.) Hitler appears to have believed that he could exorcize the spectre of defeat in the Soviet Union, and in the war in general, by summoning a sort of Japanese deus ex machina to the Soviet Union's vulnerable Siberian frontier. According to the German historian Hans W. Gatzke, the Führer was convinced that "if Germany failed to join Japan [in the war against the United States], it would . . . end all hope for Japanese help against the Soviet Union."[25] But Japan did not take Hitler's bait. Tokyo, too, despised the Soviet state, but the Land of the Rising Sun, now at war against the US, could afford the luxury of a two-front war as little as the Soviets. Tokyo preferred to put all of its money on a "southern" strategy, hoping to win the big prize of Southeast Asia — including oil-rich Indonesia and rubber-rich Indochina — rather than embark on a venture in the inhospitable reaches of Siberia. Only at the very end of the war, after the surrender of Nazi Germany, would it come to hostilities between the Soviet Union and Japan.

And so, through Hitler's own fault, the camp of Germany's enemies now included not only Great Britain and the Soviet Union, but also the mighty USA, whose troops could be expected to appear on Germany's shores, or at least on the shores of German-occupied Europe, in the foreseeable future. The Americans would indeed land troops in France, but only in 1944, and this unquestionably important event is still often presented as the turning point of World War II. However, one should ask if the Americans would ever have landed in Normandy or, for that matter, ever have declared war on Nazi Germany, if Hitler had not declared war on them on December 11, 1941. And one should ask if Hitler would ever have made the desperate, even suicidal, decision to declare war on the US if he had not found himself in a hopeless situation in the Soviet Union. The involvement of the US in the war against Germany, then, which for many reasons was not in the cards before December 1941, was also a consequence of the German setback in front of Moscow.

Nazi Germany was doomed, but the war was still to be a long one. Hitler ignored the advice of his generals, who strongly recommend trying to find a diplomatic way out of the war, and decided to battle on in the slim hope of somehow pulling victory out of a hat. The Russian counteroffensive would run out of steam, the Wehrmacht would survive the winter of 1941-42, and in the spring of 1942 Hitler would scrape together all available forces for an offensive — code-named "Operation Blue" (*Unternehmen Blau*) — in the direction of the oil fields of the Caucasus. Hitler himself acknowledged that "if he did not get the oil of Maikop and Grozny, then he would have to end this war."[26] However, the element of surprise had been lost, and the Soviets appeared to dispose of huge masses of men, oil, and other resources, as well as excellent equipment, much of it produced in factories that had been established behind the Urals between 1939 and 1941. The Wehrmacht, on the other hand, could not compensate for the huge losses it had suffered in 1941. Between June 22, 1941, and January 31, 1942, the Germans had lost 6,000 airplanes and more than 3,200 tanks and similar vehicles. No less than 918,000 men had been killed, wounded, or gone missing in action, amounting to 28.7 per cent of the average strength of the army, or 3.2 million men.[27] (In the Soviet Union, Germany would lose no less than 10 million of its total 13.5 million men killed, wounded, or taken prisoner during the entire war, and the Red Army would end up claiming credit for 90 per cent of all Germans killed in the Second World War.)[28] The forces available for a push toward the oil fields of the Caucasus were therefore extremely limited. Under those circumstances, it is quite remarkable that in 1942 the Germans would manage to make it as far as they did. But when their offensive inevitably petered out, in September of that year, their weakly held lines were stretched along many hundreds of kilometres, presenting a perfect target for a Soviet counterattack. When that attack came, it caused an entire German army to be bottled up and, ultimately, destroyed in Stalingrad. It was after this great victory of the Red Army that the ineluctability of German defeat in World War II would be obvious for all to see. However, the seemingly minor and relatively unheralded German defeat in front of Moscow in late 1941 had been the precondition for the admittedly more spectacular and more visible German defeat at Stalingrad.

There are even more reasons to proclaim December 1941 as the turning point of the war. The Soviet counteroffensive destroyed the reputation of invincibility in which the Wehrmacht had basked ever since its success against Poland in 1939, thus boosting the morale of Germany's enemies everywhere. The Battle of Moscow also ensured that the bulk of Germany's armed forces would be tied to an eastern front of approximately 4,000 kilometres for an indefinite period of time, which all but eliminated the possibility of German operations against Gibraltar, for example, and thus provided tremendous relief to the British. Conversely, the failure of the blitzkrieg demoralized the Finns and other German allies. And so on and so forth.

It was in front of Moscow, in December 1941, that the tide turned. Indeed, it was there that the blitzkrieg failed and that Nazi Germany was consequently forced to fight, without sufficient resources, the kind of protracted war that Hitler and his generals knew they could not possibly win. It was at that point that the United States entered the war against Nazi Germany.

Chapter 6
THE UNITED STATES AT WAR
WITH JAPAN AND GERMANY

If Hitler had attacked the Soviet Union, the despised homeland of communism, ten years, five years, or even just one year earlier, rather than in June 1941, he would undoubtedly have been loudly cheered by the American media. In 1941 however, this was not the case, as more and more Americans had been switching their allegiance to Great Britain. This also applied to the nation's power elite, previously sympathetic to fascism, but keenly aware that Lend-Lease deliveries to Hitler's British enemy were now good for business and in fact responsible for America's economic revival. There was little or no genuine sympathy for the Soviets, but it was greatly appreciated that a new enemy for the Germans was a boon to the British. The longer the Soviets could resist the Germans, the better for Great Britain. But many Americans were convinced that the Soviets, like the Poles and the French before them, would be unable to resist the onslaught of the Wehrmacht for very long. Even those who did not find Britain's new Soviet ally quite so repulsive — President Roosevelt among them — actually shared this pessimistic opinion. Washington counted on a German victory and made plans to bring a non-communist government to power in any Soviet territories that might possibly escape German occupation, such as Siberia. A signal was flashed to émigré Alexander Kerensky, whose Russian government had been overthrown by the Bolsheviks in 1917, to warm up on the sidelines for this purpose. More importantly, Stalin's urgent request for American supplies did not receive a positive response. After all, in America no credit is given to a customer suspected of teetering on the brink of bankruptcy. The American ambassador to the USSR, Laurence Steinhardt, warned emphatically against sending aid, arguing that in view of the impending Soviet collapse these supplies would fall into German hands.

The situation changed in the late fall of 1941 when it became increasingly clear that the Soviets would not be "crushed like an egg" and that their tough resistance to the Nazis demonstrated that they were likely to be an extraordinarily useful continental ally to the British for some time to come, which of course also benefitted Britain's American partner in the Lend-Lease business. The New York Stock Exchange started to reflect this fact of life: the quotations rose as the Nazi advance into Russia slowed down. Moreover, credit could now be extended to the Soviet Union, and that meant that corporate America could start doing business with the hitherto despised Soviet "Reds." In November 1941, Washington and Moscow concluded a Lend-Lease agreement.[1]

When the Red Army forced the Wehrmacht panzers to shift into reverse gear in front of Moscow in early December, that was particularly good news for corporate America, and particularly for the corporations involved in Lend-Lease. They were not aware of the true importance of the Battle of Moscow, but it was now evident that their British partner, who had survived the adversities of 1940 with some difficulty, could continue to wage war indefinitely, without making it necessary for the Americans themselves to intervene. The Soviet Union made itself useful, then, by contributing mightily to the military and economic survival of America's paramount customer, Great Britain.[2] And when, on December 11, 1941, Hitler declared war on the US, the Soviet Union, as enemy of America's enemy, automatically became a partner, an ally, and a kind of friend — an unloved and temporary friend, but a friend nonetheless.

America thus became closely associated with a state that had earlier been thoroughly despised by Washington and the US power elite. Symptomatic of the new situation was the treatment accorded to Maxim Litvinov, the new Soviet ambassador who arrived in Washington to present his credentials in December 1941. In stark contrast to his predecessor, noted journalist David Brinkley, Litvinov was feted by the social elite, who "now saw Russia as an ally, an enemy of the enemy and therefore a friend."[3] Within the American power elite it was no longer fashionable to express admiration for Hitler, even though with his attack on the USSR the German dictator had done exactly what America's leading circles had long expected of him. By the end of 1941 a Nazi triumph over the Soviets had ceased to be desirable not only because Germany had suddenly become an enemy but also because it would now be a bad thing for business; it would have jeopardized the profits flowing from the cornucopia of Lend-Lease. A German victory over the USSR would have been disastrous in terms of the bottom line of all actuarial calculations — something that is much closer to the hearts of hard-nosed businessmen than any fanciful ideological considerations.

The American elite now wore an anti-fascist hat, but deep in their hearts many, if not most, of its members remained true anti-communists. Those who had earlier hoped that Hitler would destroy the cradle of communism now saw the titanic struggle on the endless Eastern Front in a different light. They wished for no clear victory for either side, but preferred that the antagonists be locked for as long as possible in a war that would debilitate them both. The hope for an extended conflict between Berlin and Moscow was reflected in many newspaper articles and in the much-publicized remark uttered by Senator Harry S. Truman on June 24, 1941, only two days after the start of Operation Barbarossa, the Nazi attack on the Soviet Union: "If we see that Germany is winning, we should help Russia, and if Russia is winning, we should help Germany, so that as many as possible perish on both sides . . . ." Even as late as December 5, 1941, just two days before the Japanese strike against Pearl Harbor, which "formally put Americans in the same anti-fascist boat with the British and the Russians" as the American historians Clayton R. Koppes and Gregory D. Black write, a caricature in Hearst's *Chicago Tribune* suggested that it would be ideal for "civilization [if these] two dangerous beasts [the Nazis and the Soviets] destroyed each other." If this scenario would somehow become reality, then America itself, with Great Britain on its side, would be able to create a new order in Europe. At the end of 1941 it did indeed look as if such a scenario might come to pass.[4]

Militarily and politically, things were going fine for the United States, and economically America's corporations were profiting from the war on the Eastern Front and the market that had opened up with its new Lend-Lease partner. The United States (together with Canada and Great Britain) would supply the USSR far less with weapons than with Studebakers and other trucks, jeeps, clothing, and canned food. Lend-Lease also opened up previously unthinkable prospects for bringing the gigantic Soviet Union into the American economic sphere of influence after the war, a theme that we will cover later.

It is sometimes alleged that the Soviet Union managed to survive the Nazi attack only thanks to American Lend-Lease aid, but for a number of reasons that is extremely doubtful. First, as we have seen, a Lend-Lease agreement with the Soviet Union was concluded only at the end of 1941. For their first deliveries of American weapons and other supplies, the Soviets were required to pay in cash. And these first supplies were very modest, if not insignificant. A German historian, Bernd Martin, actually claims that throughout 1941 American aid to the Soviet Union remained "fictitious." American material assistance became meaningful only in 1942, that is, long after the Soviets had single-handedly put an end to the progress made by the Wehrmacht and turned the tide of the war. Second, American aid never represented more than 4 to 5 per cent of total Soviet wartime production, although it must be admitted that even such a slim margin may possibly prove crucial in a crisis situation. Third, the Soviets themselves cranked out all of the light and heavy high-quality weapons — such as the T-34 tank, probably the best tank of the Second World War — that made their success against the Wehrmacht possible. Fourth, and probably most importantly, the much-publicized Lend-Lease aid to the USSR was to a large extent neutralized by the unofficial, discreet, but very important assistance provided by American corporate sources to the German enemies of the Soviets. In 1940 and 1941, American industry profited primarily from business with Great Britain, but this did not prevent American oil firms and trusts from concluding clandestine yet lucrative business deals with Nazi Germany as well. Huge amounts of oil were delivered to Nazi Germany via neutral states such as Spain, something that was known in the White House. The American share of Germany's imports of vitally important oil products increased rapidly; in the case of motor oil, from 44 per cent in July 1941 to no less than 94 per cent in September 1941. In view of the depletion of their stockpiles of petroleum products at that time, it is fair to say that the German panzers would probably never have made it all the way to the outskirts of Moscow without fuel supplied by American oil trusts.[5] In fact, without US-supplied fuel, neither the German attack on the Soviet Union nor, for that matter, any of the other major German military operations of 1940 and 1941 would have been possible, according to the German historian Tobias Jersak, an authority in the field of American "fuel for the Führer."[6] Finally, it should also be taken into account that, via "reverse Lend-Lease," the Soviet Union also supplied the US with important raw materials, including chrome and manganese ore as well as platinum; on account of this, the US possibly even became a net beneficiary of wartime trade with the Soviets.[7]

Thanks to the war in Europe, America was emerging from the nightmare of the Great Depression. Great Britain and the USSR could henceforth be counted on as markets for American industrial goods. But elsewhere in the world there were other potential markets as well as sources of cheap raw materials, such as rubber and oil, which the United States' booming industry increasingly needed. The US had joined the other great industrial nations in a very competitive worldwide scramble for markets and resources at the end of the nineteenth century, thus becoming an imperialist power like Great Britain and France. Via an aggressive foreign policy, pursued by presidents such as Theodore Roosevelt, a cousin of Franklin Delano Roosevelt, and a "splendid little war" — as John Hay, the United States Ambassador in London, had called it — against Spain, America had acquired control over former Spanish colonies such as Puerto Rico, Cuba, and the Philippines, and also over the hitherto independent island nation of Hawaii. Uncle Sam thus became very interested in the Pacific Ocean, its islands, and the lands on its far shores, the Far East. Particularly attractive over there was China, from a businessman's point of view a "market" with unlimited potential, and a huge but weak country seemingly ready to be penetrated economically by any imperialist country with enough power and ambition to do so.[8] All this, however, did not prevent the United States — a former British colony — from presenting itself everywhere as an opponent of colonialism, as a champion of the cause of freedom, and as a fighter for the rights of oppressed nations. America's brand of imperialism differed from the European variety, as the American historian William Appleman Williams sarcastically notes, in that "we have masked our imperial truth with the rhetoric of freedom." Of this American imperialist expansion, the primary beneficiary had been American business. The success of Dole, for example, the American canned pineapple empire, would not have been possible without the (stolen) land and the (forced) labour of the indigenous Hawaiians, who today count for little on their own islands.

In the Far East, and particularly with respect to China, the US faced the competition of an aggressive rival power that sought to realize its own imperialist ambitions in that part of the world, namely Japan, the Land of the Rising Sun. Relations between Washington and Tokyo had not been good for decades but worsened during the Depression-ridden 1930s, when the competition for markets and resources was heating up. Japan was even more needy for oil and similar raw materials to feed its factories, and also for markets for its finished products and for investment opportunities. Tokyo went so far as to wage war on China and to carve a client state, Manchukuo, out of the northern part of that great but weak country. What bothered the US was not that the Japanese treated their Chinese (and Korean) neighbours as "subhumans" or *Untermenschen*, to use Nazi terminology, but that they appeared determined to turn China and the rest of the Far East, including resource-rich Southeast Asia and Indonesia, into what they called the "Greater East Asia Co-Prosperity Sphere," i.e., an economic bailiwick of their very own, a "closed economy" in with there was no room for the American competition.[9]

American businessmen, and the American power elite in general, were extremely frustrated by the prospect of being squeezed out of the lucrative Far Eastern market by the "Japs," a supposedly inferior "yellow race" many Americans had already started to despise during the nineteenth century.[10] In light of this, we can understand why, in the 1930s, the US military had plans ready for war against Japan. (Plans had also been prepared for war against Mexico, Great Britain, and Canada, but not against Nazi Germany.)[11]

With the eruption of war in Europe, a new factor came into play. The defeat of France and the Netherlands in 1940 at the hands of Nazi Germany raised the question of what would happen to their respective colonies in the Far East: Indochina, rich in rubber, and Indonesia, rich in petroleum. With the mother countries occupied by the Germans, these colonies looked like ripe fruits ready to be harvested by one of the remaining competitors in the ruthless competition among the great powers — but which one? Perhaps the Germans, if and when they would win the war and impose a Versailles-style settlement on the losers. But the prospects of a German triumph were fading fast during the fall of 1941, when it looked increasingly likely that the Wehrmacht faced a long war in Russia. As for the British, they continued to have their hands full with the war against Nazi Germany. A very likely candidate, however, was Japan, a power with great ambitions, especially in its own part of the world, and a keen appetite for rubber and oil. Could the US tolerate a Japanese expansion into Southeast Asia in addition to a Japanese monopoly of the Chinese market? That was unlikely, since it would mean Japanese hegemony in the Far East — and the end of American ambitions and dreams in that part of the world. However, precisely such a scenario seemed to start unfolding when Vichy France's collaborator government transferred control of Hanoi and Saigon to Japan in 1940 and when, the following year, Japan took over all of Indochina.

In the US, the power elite now felt that action was urgently required before oil-rich Indonesia also fell to the Japanese and the entire Far East was lost. During the 1930s, that elite, while mostly opposed to war against Germany, had increasingly looked favourably on the prospect of a war against Japan. The Land of the Rising Sun was perceived as an arrogant but essentially weak upstart country that mighty America could easily "wipe off the map in three months," as Navy Secretary Frank Knox put it on one occasion.[12] As mentioned, plans for war against the Japanese had been ready for quite some time. It was also with such a war in mind that aircraft carriers and strategic bombers had been developed in the 1930s. These weapons provided Uncle Sam with a military arm long enough to reach across the Pacific, where the Philippines, strategically situated close to Japan as well as China, Indochina, and Indonesia, could of course serve as a most useful base of operations.

The US power elite wanted war against Japan, and President Roosevelt, whose family's wealth had been built at least partly in the opium trade with China, revealed himself quite willing to provide such a war. But

Washington could not afford to be seen to start the conflict, for only a *defensive* war could be sold to the reputedly isolationist Congress and to an American public with little appetite for war. An American attack on Japan, moreover, would also have required Nazi Germany to come to the aid of Japan under the terms of their treaties, while a Japanese attack on the US did not do so.[13] (Moreover, since it was already in dire straits in the Soviet Union, Germany was not believed to be keen to take on a new enemy of the calibre of the US. This belief seemed to be confirmed by Berlin's restraint in the face of a string of incidents involving ships and German submarines in the Atlantic in the fall of 1941, the hyperbolically named "undeclared naval war.") In order to conjure up the kind of war that was wanted, that is, a new edition of the "splendid little war" against Spain at the turn of the century — a war against a single and supposedly relatively weak enemy — Japan had to be provoked into an act of aggression.

Having decided that "Japan must be seen to make the first overt move," President Roosevelt made "provoking Japan into an overt act of war the principal policy that guided [his] actions toward Japan throughout 1941." The stratagems used included the deployment of warships close to, and even into, Japanese territorial waters, apparently in the hope of sparking an incident that could serve as a *casus belli*. More effective, however, was the relentless economic pressure that was brought to bear on Japan, a country desperately in need of raw materials and therefore likely to consider such methods to be singularly provocative. In the summer of 1941, the Roosevelt administration froze all Japanese assets in the United States and embarked on a "strategy for frustrating Japanese acquisition of petroleum products." In collaboration with the British and the Dutch, the US imposed severe economic sanctions on Japan, including an embargo on vital oil products, a policy which served to increase the Japanese desire to acquire control over the oil-rich Dutch colony of Indonesia. The situation deteriorated further in the fall of 1941, especially since Washington also challenged Tokyo with respect to its exclusivist policy in China, demanding an "open door" for American business in that country. Tokyo responded by offering to apply in China the principle of non-discriminatory trade relations on the condition that the Americans did the same in their own sphere of influence in Latin America. However, Washington wanted reciprocity only in the sphere of influence of other imperialist powers, and not in its own backyard. The Japanese offer was rejected.

The continuing US provocations of Japan were intended to cause Tokyo to go to war and became increasingly likely to do so. "This continuing putting pins in rattlesnakes," FDR would confide to friends later, "finally got this country bit." On November 26, when Washington sent its "Ten Point Note" demanding Japan's immediate withdrawal from China, the "rattlesnakes" in Tokyo decided they had enough and prepared to "bite."[14] A Japanese fleet was ordered to set sail for Hawaii in order to attack the impressive collection of warships that FDR had decided to station there in 1940 — rather provocatively as well as invitingly, as far as the Japanese were concerned. It was hoped that a deadly strike at the mid-Pacific naval base would make it impossible for the Americans to intervene effectively in the Far East for the foreseeable future. And this would provide Japan with a window of opportunity big enough to firmly establish its supremacy in the Far East, for example by adding Indonesia to its collection of trophies, by taking over the Philippines, et cetera. Thus would be created a *fait accompli* which the US, once recovered from the blow administered at Pearl Harbor, would not be able to undo — especially since the Americans would be deprived of their bridgehead in the Far East, the Philippines. Having deciphered the Japanese codes, the American government and top army brass knew exactly what the Japanese armada was up to but did not warn the commanders in Hawaii, thus allowing the "surprise attack" on Pearl Harbor to happen on Sunday, December 7, 1941.[15] The following day FDR found it easy to convince Congress to declare war on Japan, and the American people, shocked by a seemingly cowardly attack that they could not know to have been provoked, and expected, by their own government, predictably rallied behind the flag.[16] The US was ready to wage war against Japan, and the prospects for a relatively easy victory were hardly diminished by the losses suffered at Pearl Harbor which, while ostensibly grievous, were far from catastrophic. The ships that had been sunk were older, "mostly...old relics of World War I," and far from indispensable for warfare against Japan. The modern warships, on the other hand, including the aircraft carriers, whose role in the war would turn out to be crucial, were unscathed. They had conveniently been ordered by Washington to leave the base just before the attack and were safely out at sea when the Japanese struck.[17]

However, the scheme did not quite work out as anticipated. The reason was that, a few days after Pearl Harbor, on December 11, Hitler unexpectedly declared war on the US, for reasons that have been clarified earlier. Admittedly, US relations with Germany had been deteriorating for some time because of America's Lend-Lease support for Great Britain, escalating to the undeclared naval war of the fall of 1941. However, with his war against Britain unfinished and his crusade against the Soviet Union not going according to plan, Hitler had no desire to take on a mighty new enemy. Conversely, even though there were plenty of compelling humanitarian reasons for crusading against the truly evil "Third Reich," the American power elite had no desire to declare war on Germany. The country's major US corporations were doing wonderful business in and with Nazi Germany and also profiting handsomely from the war Hitler had unleashed via Lend-Lease. And some members of the US elite, unaware of the significance of the battle of Moscow, still hoped that Hitler might eventually destroy the Soviet Union. A war against Germany was not wanted and had not been planned. In the White House, the German declaration of war arrived as a nasty surprise.

America was thus pulled into the war in Europe against its will, which raises an interesting but unanswerable question: When would Washington have entered the war against Nazi Germany if Hitler himself had not declared war on December 11, 1941? Perhaps never? In any event, the Americans unexpectedly found themselves confronting two enemies rather than just one. And they now had to fight a much bigger war than expected, a war on two fronts, a European as well as an Asian war, a genuine *world war*, instead of another splendid little war.

Some American revisionist historians draw attention to the plain but unpleasant and therefore generally ignored fact that the United States did not declare war on Japan because of Tokyo's unprovoked aggression and horrible war crimes in China but because of an attack on an American imperial possession. Howard Zinn, probably America's best-known radical historian, dryly observes that

It was not Hitler's attacks on the Jews that brought the United States into World War II . . . What brought the United States fully into the war was the Japanese attack on the American naval base at Pearl Harbor . . . it was the Japanese attack on a link in the American Pacific Empire that did it.[18]

Chapter 7
CLASS WARFARE ON THE AMERICAN HOME FRONT

If the war in Europe had been good, the world war would prove nothing less than wonderful for American industry, which had to shift into over-drive. The result was a sustained economic boom that saw employment as well as profits soar impressively. The total number of jobless in the United States was to decrease over the war years from more than 8 million in 1940 to 5.5 million in 1941, 2.6 million in 1942, 1 million in 1943, and 670,000 in 1944, with the result that unemployment rates plummeted from almost 15 per cent of the nation's labour force in 1940 to merely 1.2 per cent in 1944. The army alone absorbed millions of men and women who might otherwise have had difficulty finding a job: no fewer than 16 million Americans would join the armed services during the war. The pendulum of employment actually swung from one extreme to the other, and labour shortages soon developed in important sectors such as airplane construc-tion, so that more and more women had to be mobilized for work in the factories. In any event, America's workers now enjoyed ample employment opportunities, higher wages (but also prices), and an unprecedented meas-ure of prosperity. No domestic prescription had brought an end to the Great Depression; instead, the nightmare of the "dirty thirties" was terminated by overseas conflict.[1] "The war was like an alchemist," writes the American author Studs Terkel, "who changed Bad Times into Good Times."[2]

Ordinary Americans did well, but the primary beneficiaries of the wartime boom were unquestionably the nation's entrepreneurs and corporations, who accumulated unprecedented riches. "During the four war years, 1942-45," writes Stuart D. Brandes, the historian of war profits in the United States, "the 2,230 largest American firms . . . reported earnings of $14.4 billion after taxes — an increase of 41 per cent — [in comparison to the pre-war years 1936–39];" he adds that "generous tax amortization rules" caused these figures "to understate [the] actual earnings by about 20 per cent." The relatively low rates of taxation merely served to maximize a wartime profit boom generated primarily by an "enormous rise in sales during the war," itself due to the state's lavish program of defence spending, combined with the absence of meaningful anti-profiteering restrictions and/or effective price controls.[3] "If you are going to try to go to war . . . in a capitalist country," declared Roosevelt's war secretary, Henry Stimson, "you have to let business make money out of the process, or business won't work."[4]

However, while corporate profits (after taxes) in general increased considerably during the war years, by more than 70 per cent according to some estimates, a very restricted corporate elite — big business as opposed to business in general — profited the most from the boom. Fewer than sixty enterprises were to receive 75 per cent of all lucrative military and other government orders and, not surprisingly, the largest corporations turned out to be the "warhogs" (Brandes) that enjoyed privileged access to the trough of the state's wartime spending. IBM was one of the enterprises that knew how to profit from this window of opportunity. Edwin Black writes:

> *War had always been good to IBM. In America, war income was without equal. Within ninety days of Pearl Harbor, [IBM chairman] Watson was able to inform the media that IBM had secured more than $150 million in munitions and other defence contracts. Total wartime sales and rentals tripled from approximately $46 million annually in 1940 to approximately $140 million annually by 1945.*[5]

As for GM, the war blessed that corporation with profits of 673 million dollars on a wave of state orders with a total value of 13.4 billion dollars.[6]

Corporations big and small also benefitted from the fact that during the war, the state financed new technologies and new factories, generously subsidizing private investment and spending more than 17 billion dollars on over 2,000 public defence projects. Private-sector firms were allowed to lease public productive facilities in return for a very modest remuneration, and after the war they would be able to purchase them from the government for "only one-half to one-third of the [original] cost," as Brandes writes. Millions of dollars would thus be made, primarily, of course, by large corporations "swollen with surplus cash," prompting Harry Truman to "denounce this form of gain as 'legal profiteering'."[7] The journalist David Brinkley also refers to this postwar privatization extravaganza, commenting that it was "a remarkable windfall that defenders of 'free enterprise' seldom acknowledged." Indeed, the latter prefer to ignore any evidence that undermines the myth to which they subscribe, namely, that in America most if not all wealth is generated in and by the private sector."[8]

Corporate America made a lot of money during the war, but also profited from the war in other important ways. The enforcement of the so-called "antitrust laws," for example, which had inhibited corporate freedom, was virtually abandoned. It was also during the war that representatives of corporate America took over many important government posts in Washington. There was a "wartime upsurge in business influence in government," writes an American economic historian, Harold G. Vatter, and "Wall Street elements" and "a business stratum" in general acquired increasing influence in public policy, and especially in the State Department and the Pentagon. An intimate partnership thus emerged between big government and big business, of which big business was to continue to profit long after the war was won.[9]

The American state financed its war effort less by means of taxation (approximately 45 per cent) than with loans (approximately 55 per cent). Washington's war bonds, which paid a relatively high interest rate, thus represented a particularly interesting form of investment for banks, insurance companies, and moneyed individuals. Prominent among the buyers of war bonds were the very same shareholders and managers of the large corporations that made a fortune as a result of government orders, and that might otherwise not have found similarly lucrative investment opportunities. To the wealthy Americans, then, normally defenders of private enterprise and enemies of state intervention in economic life, the American state functioned during the war as a generous patron. In any event, the wealthy and powerful Americans unquestionably became even wealthier and more powerful because of the way in which the American government chose to wage war.[10] C. Wright Mills remarks in this respect that while in general "private industrial development of the United States has been much underwritten" by public largesse, "wars have led to many opportunities for the private appropriation of fortune and power." In this respect, Mills continues, the Second World War "[made] previous appropriations seem puny indeed," as "the keys to control of the nation's means of production were given to private corporations."[11]

However, the silver lining of the wartime boom also had its dark cloud. With the end of unemployment and the developing labour shortages, the advantage shifted from the side of the employers to that of the employees in the tug-of-war that in a free labour market determines the price of labour, that is, wage levels and working conditions. For the first time, American workers enjoyed bargaining power vis-à-vis their bosses, as the British historian Arthur Marwick has noted, and they took advantage of this situation to demand higher wages and better working conditions. They did not do so individually, by appearing cap in hand before the boss with their requests, but collectively, by making demands on behalf of the workforce of an entire factory, industrial sector, or union through collective bargaining. American workers had started to understand the advantages of solidarity and organization during the crisis of the "dirty thirties," and during the war they joined the unions en masse to defend the interests of labour. The union ranks would swell from approximately 9 million members in 1939 to almost 15 million in 1945. In the United States, business had already been "big business" for a long time, but now labour was in the process of becoming "big labour," and henceforth big labour was a factor to be taken into account, not only in the boardrooms of America's corporations, but even in the corridors of power in Washington, including the White House, where previously only the voice of big business had commanded attention.

America's employers were unenthusiastic about the prospect of having to forgo even a minor share of their war profits because of collective bargaining. The workers, however, did not hesitate to back up their demands with the tried and tested weapon of the strike, a weapon that revealed itself to be particularly effective at that time. True to its tradition, the American state did intervene in this conflict with measures that favoured the side of business. Shortly after the attack on Pearl Harbor, the Roosevelt administration thus wrested from the big (and conservative) labour unions such as the American Federation of Labor (AFL) a so-called "no strike pledge," a promise not to strike during the war. And in 1943 Congress would make a pro-business contribution in the form of the Smith-Connally Act, which outlawed certain forms of industrial action. But none of this could prevent a wave of strikes from sweeping over the United States during the war. Howard Zinn provides details:

> Despite the overwhelming atmosphere of patriotism and total
> dedication to winning the war, despite the no-strike pledges
> of the AFL and CIO, many of the nation's workers, frustrated
> by the freezing of wages while business profits rocketed
> skyward, went on strike. During the war, there were fourteen
> thousand strikes, involving 6,770,000 workers, more than in
> any comparable period in American history. In 1944 alone, a
> million workers went on strike, in the mines, in the steel mills,
> in the auto and transportation equipment industries.

The keenest strikers were the miners, who were led by John L. Lewis of the United Mine Workers' union. Furthermore, an unusually large number of strikes were wildcat strikes, spontaneous work stoppages not authorized by a union. The labour militancy was such that the employers — and the American state — had to raise the white flag. Wage demands were gradually conceded throughout the country, and as a result of this, the average weekly wage would rise spectacularly during the war, from approximately twenty-three dollars in 1939 to more than forty-four dollars in 1945. (This amounts to an increase of just over 90 per cent; inflation during the same period amounted to only 30 per cent.)[12]

During the Second World War, a bitter class struggle was waged in the United States between labour and capital, and this too is an important part of the history of America's role in that world conflict. This class war was fought on the American home front, and its skirmishes and battles consisted of innumerable strikes, big and small. This war, however, was not a black-and-white conflict between "good" Americans and "evil" Krauts or Japs, but a kind of social civil war among Americans themselves. From this conflict, no clear winners and no clear losers would emerge, and no armistice ever put an end to it. Small wonder that Hollywood has never devoted a film to that dramatic and important but also painful and still ongoing conflict, and that in the United States itself no monument honours its memory. No wonder, likewise, that most Second World War history texts prefer to restrict themselves safely to the battles that were fought on the far sides of the Atlantic and Pacific Oceans.

In the generally ignored class war that raged on the American home front in the forties, the US power elite learned a momentous lesson, namely that forms of collective action such as strikes and demonstrations constituted the most effective weapon available to their employees. It is precisely because of this that Hollywood movies suggest time and again that problems are best solved by means of the heroic stunts of (preferably heavily armed) individuals, stunts which contrast starkly with the supposed apathy and powerlessness of the masses; in action movies the focus is always on individual action, never on collective action. In this manner, Hollywood undermines, among the very people who could benefit from it, interest and confidence in the kind of collective action that caused the American power elite such headaches during the Second World War. On an intellectual level, also, an offensive was launched against collective action. In an influential book, first published by the prestigious Harvard University Press in 1965, the economist Mancur Olson associated the collective action of labour unions with coercion and violence, referring specifically to the growth of unions and the success of strikes and other forms of collective action during the Second World War. Olson's book continues to this very day to be treated at North American universities as an authoritative text in courses in business administration, political science, organization theory, and so on. Finally, the revulsion of the American elites for all kinds of collective action is also clearly mirrored in the sneering remarks frequently made in the media concerning the readiness of the French people to defend their interests by means of strikes and demonstrations.[13]

After Pearl Harbor, the United States found itself formally at war with Japan, a distant and relatively unknown country, and with Nazi Germany, a state about which influential people had told them many positive things only shortly before. Conversely, America was now officially allied not only with Great Britain, but also the Soviet Union, an entity previously portrayed as a pariah. One can understand that the American people were in urgent need of clarification, and clarification was soon forthcoming in the form of a propaganda campaign that explained in black and white how everything made perfect sense.

Posters still constituted an important propaganda medium in those days. In the twenties and thirties, and especially at the time of the Red Scare and the Little Red Scare, they had often taken aim at the godless Bolsheviks, but now they began to portray sadistic "Japs" and haughty, monocled Nazi officers with the helpful explanation "This is the Enemy."[14] The designers were obviously eager to correct the mistake made earlier, when they had depicted the Bolsheviks as the great nemesis. In order to further instruct the public about the enemy, the US government also prevailed on the well-known movie producer Frank Capra to crank out a series of documentaries entitled *Why We Fight*, which portrayed the Nazis as "vicious, diabolical mobsters" determined to enslave all free people and to destroy religion. The first of these films, *Prelude to War*, was described in promotional material as "the greatest gangster movie ever filmed . . . more horrible than any horror movie you ever saw!" and the quest for world power was attributed to "vicious, diabolical mobsters."[15] Hollywood took its cue and proceeded to enlighten Americans about the true nature of fascism by means of films such as *The Hitler Gang*, which also portrayed the Nazis as unscrupulous gangsters, and ridiculed fascism with cartoons such as *The Ducktators*, in which the leading part was played by a despotic bird named "Hitler Duck." American comic-strip heroes such as Captain America, Superman, and Wonder Woman contributed to the propaganda campaign by foiling cunning Nazi agents and spies. Thus was born in America the image of the Nazi as a gangster, a villain, a caricature — an image that has survived to this very day in Hollywood productions of the Indiana Jones type. However, this simplistic propaganda campaign contributed absolutely nothing to a genuine understanding of the complex social phenomenon of European fascism in general and German Nazism in particular.[16]

The Soviets underwent an equally remarkable metamorphosis from godless Bolsheviks to heroic "Russian" patriots. Hollywood, which had shown little interest and even less sympathy for the Soviet Union before the war, set the tone — clearly on a signal from Washington — with pro-Soviet films such as *Mission to Moscow, The North Star,* and *Song of Russia.* America's popular magazines, including *Life, The Saturday Evening Post,* and *Reader's Digest,* which had earlier eagerly disseminated anti-communist and anti-Soviet propaganda and would do so again after the war, "made a turn of 180 degrees," as historians Koppes and Black write, and offered a pro-Soviet contribution of their own. The formerly sinister-looking denizens of the distant workers' paradise were now presented as hard-working, down-to-earth, and decent people, who — so *Life* claimed in 1943 — "look like Americans, dress like Americans, and think like Americans" and who were merely waiting for the end of the war to graduate to capitalism and democracy. (Conversely, the Nazis were henceforth pictured as Teutonic Bolsheviks, who lacked any respect for things Americans held dearly, like religion and private property.) The Soviet leader, Stalin, became the darling of the American magazines; they adopted him, as it were, into the great American family as Uncle Joe, put flattering photos of him on their covers, and in 1943 *Time* proclaimed him "man of the year." Americans were also supposed to be favourably impressed by reports that Stalin had a weakness for American cigarettes such as Camels, Chesterfields, and Lucky Strikes. In the allegedly "Red" thirties, not only America's communists, but also many radical and progressive Americans had romanticized the Soviet Union; in the early forties, the Soviet Union was romanticized in the promised land of capitalism even by Hollywood and the American media.[17]

And so the American people were warmed up to Washington's new course vis-à-vis the USSR, a new course that had considerable advantages as far as American industry was concerned. This did not mean that America's power elite no longer despised the Soviet state and communism, but only that they benefitted from temporarily muting the anti-communist rhetoric. Something analogous occurred in the Soviet Union, where the anti-capitalist slogan of world revolution disappeared from official discourse, and where on May 22, 1943, Stalin dismantled the Comintern — the communist "International" that under Moscow's guidance was supposed to foment proletarian revolutions everywhere on earth; the news was welcomed by the American media as "evidence of the willingness [of the USSR] to play ball with us if we play ball with her."[18]

The kind of collective brainwashing that Washington administered to the American people with regard to the Soviets had important consequences for the class war that was being fought on the US home front during the war. Among the American workers, there was henceforth even more interest in the socialist experiment launched in 1917. They learned, for example, that there was no unemployment in the USSR, and that their Soviet counterparts, who admittedly earned lower wages than American workers, benefitted from considerably lower prices, free education and health care, old age pensions, paid holidays, and other social advantages. More and more Americans — and certainly not only workers — thus began to think that the time had come to introduce an at least equally generous system of full employment and social security for the benefit of ordinary Americans. After all, did the war they were helping to win make any sense if it did not lead to a social "new deal" instead of a return to the misery of the dirty thirties?[19] Confronted with such expectations, America's power elite had reason to be concerned. The business establishment found that it was making more than enough concessions by paying considerably higher wages to employees, and it was not happy with the prospect of having to finance social reforms. As the end of the war approached, it became obvious that something would have to be done in order to prevent America, the homeland of unfettered free enterprise, not from experiencing a Bolshevik revolution, because such a thing was never even a remote possibility, but from being transformed into some kind of welfare state.

Chapter 8
A SECOND FRONT FOR STALIN, OR A THIRD FRONT IN THE AIR?

In the spring of 1942, the *Wehrmacht* launched a new offensive on the Eastern Front. The Soviets had barely survived the Nazi attack of 1941, and the Red Army was again fighting with its back to the wall. Material help was now forthcoming from the United States and Great Britain, but what Stalin really wanted from his allies was effective military assistance; so he asked Churchill and Roosevelt to open a second front in Western Europe. An Anglo-American landing in Western Europe — in France, Belgium, or Holland — would have forced the Germans to withdraw troops from the Eastern Front and would therefore have afforded the Soviets much-needed relief.

In America and Great Britain, the political and military leaders were divided with respect to the possibilities and the merits of a second front. Militarily, it was already possible in the summer of 1942 to open a second front, that is, to land a sizable force in France or elsewhere in Western Europe. The British army had sufficiently recuperated from the troubles of 1940, and large numbers of American and Canadian troops had meanwhile joined their British comrades on the British Isles and were ready for action. From the cliffs of Dover to the highlands of Scotland, tens of thousands of Americans and Canadians were waiting restlessly for the order, which had to be given sooner or later, to tackle the Nazis on the Continent. Meanwhile, they kept busy by chasing the women left behind by Tommies who were defending the interests of the Empire in North Africa and elsewhere. "Overfed, oversexed, and over here," was how the American soldiers stationed in Great Britain were sarcastically described by the locals.

Furthermore, it was not a secret that, on account of their need to scrape their resources together for a desperate new offensive on the Eastern Front, the Germans had relatively few troops available to defend thousands of kilometres of Atlantic coast. And these troops also happened to be of considerably inferior quality compared to their forces on the Eastern Front. On the Atlantic coast, Hitler had about sixty divisions at his disposal, which were generally deemed to be second-rate, while no less than 260 German divisions fought the primordial battle in the east.[2] It is a fact, finally, that on the French coast in 1942 the German troops were not yet as strongly entrenched as they would be later, at the time of the landings in Normandy in June 1944. The order to build the fortifications of the famous Atlantic Wall was given by Hitler only in August 1942, and the construction would drag on from the fall of 1942 until the spring of 1944.[3]

A number of British and American army commanders — including the American chief of staff, George Marshall, as well as General Eisenhower — were well aware of this state of affairs and were therefore in favour of an early landing in France. Such a project also enjoyed the support of President Roosevelt, at least initially. He had promised Churchill that the United States would give priority to the war against Germany, and would settle accounts with Japan later. This decision was known as the "Germany First" principle.[4] Consequently, Roosevelt was eager to deal with Germany right away, and this task required opening a second front. American leaders probably also worried that without the benefit of a second front the Soviets might yet collapse under the Nazi pressure. Yet another factor in the American calculus may have been that immediate military assistance for the Soviets might make it unnecessary to make political concessions to Moscow later on. In any event, in May 1942 Roosevelt promised the Soviet minister of foreign affairs, Molotov, that the Americans would open a second front before the end of the year.[5]

In spite of the Germany First principle, however, Washington could not resist the temptation of committing a high proportion of manpower and equipment to the war against Japan, in which America's own interests were more directly at stake than in Europe. In light of this, rushing in to open a second front in France seemed somewhat imprudent. And then there was the considerable weight of the opinion of the British prime minister, Winston Churchill, who was an outspoken opponent of a second front. He may have feared, as some historians suggest, that a landing in France might lead to a duplication of the murderous warfare associated with the battlefields of northern France in the First World War. Churchill probably also liked the idea that Hitler and Stalin were administering a major bloodletting to each other on the Eastern Front, believing that London and Washington could benefit from a stalemated war in the east. Truman and many other prominent Americans shared this opinion. Since he had three years of war experience, Churchill still had much influence on Roosevelt, a newcomer to the war in Europe. We can understand, therefore, that the opinion of the British leader ultimately prevailed, and that plans for opening a second front in 1942 were quietly discarded.[6]

Once he had been persuaded by Churchill not to rush into a second front, Roosevelt discovered that this course of action — or rather, inaction — opened up attractive prospects. He and his advisors realized that defeating Germany would require huge sacrifices, which the American people would not be delighted to bring. Landing in France was tantamount to jumping into the ring for a face-off with the German enemy, and even if ultimately successful such a contest would unquestionably be a very costly affair. Was it not far wiser to stay safely on the sidelines, at least for the time being, and let the Soviets slug it out against the Nazis? With the Red Army providing the cannon fodder needed to vanquish Germany, the Americans and their British allies would be able to minimize their losses. Better still, they would be able to build up their strength in order to intervene decisively at the right moment, when the Nazi enemy and the Soviet ally would both be exhausted. With Great Britain at its side, the USA would then in all likelihood be able to play the leading role in the camp of the victors and act as supreme arbiter in the sharing of the spoils of the supposedly common victory. In the spring and summer of 1942, with the Nazis and Soviets locked into a titanic battle, watched from a safe distance by the Anglo-Saxon *tertius gaudens*, it did indeed look as if such a scenario might come to pass.[7]

The strategy of sitting on the fence clearly involved some risks, and Washington and London were aware of them. In the spring of 1942 the

Germans had scraped together enough resources to launch a new offensive on the Eastern Front, aimed at the vitally important oil-rich regions of the Caucasus. Looking back, it is clear that the chances of a German success were rather slim, but to contemporaries everything still seemed possible. The possibility of a sudden collapse of the unloved but useful Soviet ally, while increasingly unlikely, could not yet be entirely ruled out by Washington and London. In order to prevent such a scenario, which would have left the Western Allies to face the German Goliath alone, more and more equipment was now shipped to the USSR. For added insurance, contingency plans — code-named "Sledgehammer" — were prepared for a landing in Western Europe in case the Red Army faltered and it became necessary to open a second front to save the skin of the Soviets in extremis. The opposite scenario, a sudden collapse of Germany on the Eastern Front, was theoretically also possible, but in 1942 it seemed so unlikely that no plans were prepared for this contingency. Less than one year later, however, after the battle of Stalingrad, this scenario would start to preoccupy London and Washington. Plans would then finally be made to cross the English Channel in order to open a second front.[8]

The Americans and the British could not, of course, reveal the true reasons why they did not wish to open a second front. Instead, they pretended that their combined forces were not yet strong enough for such an undertaking. It was said then — and it is still claimed now — that in 1942 the British and the Americans were not yet ready for a major operation in France. Presumably, the naval war against the German U-boats first had to be won in order to safeguard the required transatlantic troop transports. However, troops were successfully being ferried from North America to Great Britain, and in the fall of that same year the Americans and British revealed themselves able to land a sizable force in distant North Africa, on the same side of the dangerous Atlantic Ocean. These landings, known as Operation Torch, involved the occupation of the French colonies of Morocco and Algeria.[9]

Stalin, however, who knew that the German defences in Western Europe were weak, continued to press London and Washington for a landing in France. To make things worse, Churchill experienced considerable domestic pressure in favour of a second front, including from members of his own cabinet, such as Richard Stafford Cripps, and particularly from the side of the trade unions, whose members were sympathetic to the plight of the Soviets. Thankfully, relief from this relentless pressure came suddenly to the British prime minister in the form of a tragedy that appeared to demonstrate conclusively that the Western Allies were not yet able to open a second front. On August 19, 1942, a contingent of Allied soldiers, sent on a mission from England to the French port of Dieppe, seemingly in an effort to open some sort of "second front," were tragically routed there by the Germans. The operation was code-named "Jubilee."

Of the 6,086 men who made it ashore, 3,623 — almost 60 per cent — were either killed, wounded, or captured. The British army and navy suffered approximately 800 casualties, and the RAF lost 106 aircraft. The 50 American Rangers who participated in the raid had 3 casualties. But the bulk of the losses were suffered by Canadian troops, with nearly 5,000 men. The majority of the Canadians' entire force, no less than 3,367 of them — 68 per cent — became casualties; about 900 were killed, nearly 600 were wounded, and the rest were taken prisoner. Of losses such as these, it is traditionally expected that they were "not in vain" and, unsurprisingly, it was especially in Canada that the media and the public wanted to know what the objectives of this raid had been, and what it had achieved. However, the political and military authorities provided only rather unconvincing explanations, though they duly found their way into the history books. For example, the raid was presented by Churchill as a "reconnaissance in force," as a necessary test of the German coastal defences. But did one really have to sacrifice thousands of men to learn that the Germans were strongly entrenched in a natural fortress — a seaport surrounded by high cliffs — which is what Dieppe happens to be? In any event, crucial information such as the location of pillboxes, cannon, and machine gun positions could have been gleaned through aerial reconnaissance and through the services of local Resistance fighters.

Talking about the Resistance, the raid supposedly also purported to boost the morale of the French partisans and of the French population in general. If so, it was unquestionably counterproductive. Indeed, the outcome of the operation, an ignominious withdrawal from a beach littered with abandoned equipment and corpses, and the sight of exhausted and dejected Canadian soldiers being marched off to a POW camp, was not likely to cheer up the French. If anything, the affair provided grist for the propaganda mill of the Germans, allowing them to ridicule the incompetence of the Allies, boast of their own military prowess, and thus dishearten the French while giving a lift to Germany's own civilians, who were very much in need of some good news on account of the constant flow of bad tidings from the east.

Last but not least, Operation Jubilee was also claimed to have been an effort to provide some relief to the Soviets. However, it is obvious that Dieppe was merely a pinprick, unlikely to make any difference whatsoever with respect to the titanic fighting on the Eastern Front. It did not cause the Germans to transfer troops from the east to the west; on the contrary, after Dieppe the Germans could feel reasonably sure that in the near future no second front would be forthcoming, so that they could actually feel free to transfer troops from the west to the east, where they were desperately needed. To the Red Army, then, Dieppe brought no relief.

Historians have mostly been happy to regurgitate these rationalizations of Jubilee, and in some cases they have invented new ones. Just recently, for example, the Dieppe raid was proclaimed to have been planned also, if not primarily, for the purpose of stealing equipment and manuals associated with the Germans' Enigma code machine, and possibly even all or parts of the machine itself.[10] But would the Germans not immediately have changed their codes if the raid would have achieved that objective? The argument that the raiders would have blown up the installations prior to withdrawing from Dieppe, thus destroying evidence of the removal of Enigma equipment, is unconvincing because it presupposes that the Germans would have been too stupid or incompetent to find out that their top-secret equipment had disappeared.

After the June 1944 Allied landings in Normandy, code-named "Overlord," an ostensibly convincing rationale for Operation Jubilee could be concocted. The Dieppe raid was suddenly triumphantly revealed to have been a "general rehearsal" for the successful Normandy landings. Dieppe had supposedly been a test of the German defences in preparation for the big landing yet to come. Lord Mountbatten, the architect of Jubilee, who was — and continues to be — blamed by many for the disaster, thus claimed that "the Battle of Normandy was won on the beaches of Dieppe" and that "for every man who died in Dieppe, at least ten more must have been spared in Normandy in 1944." A myth was born: the tragedy of Jubilee as the *sine qua non* for the triumph of Overlord.

A very important military lesson had allegedly been learned in Dieppe: the German coastal defences were particularly strong in and around harbours. It was for this reason, presumably, that the Normandy landings took place on the harbourless stretch of coastline north of Caen, with the Allies bringing along an artificial harbour, code-named Mulberry. However, was it not self-evident that the Germans would be more strongly entrenched in seaports than in insignificant little beach resorts? Had it really been necessary to sacrifice thousands of men on the beaches of Dieppe in order to learn that lesson? And one must also wonder whether information obtained from a "test" of the German coastal defences in the summer of 1942 was still relevant in 1944, especially since it was mostly in 1943 that the formidable Atlantic Wall fortifications had been built. And why would landings for which the "general rehearsal" had taken place in August 1942 be carried out two years later? Is it not absurd to proclaim Jubilee a rehearsal for an operation — Overlord — implemented in June 1944 but not yet conceived two years earlier, in that summer of 1942? Finally, the advantage of lessons learned at Dieppe, if any, were almost certainly offset by the fact that at Dieppe the Germans had also learned lessons, and possibly more useful lessons, about how the Allies were likely — and unlikely — to land troops. The idea that the tragedy of Jubilee was a precondition for the triumph of Overlord, then, is merely a myth. And so, even today, the Dieppe tragedy remains shrouded in disinformation and propaganda.

Perhaps we can catch a glimpse of the truth about Dieppe by finding inspiration in an old philosophical conundrum: If one seeks to fail, and does, does one fail, or succeed? If a military success was sought at Dieppe, the raid was certainly a failure. But if a military failure was sought, the raid was a success. In the latter case, we would have to inquire about the real objective of the raid, or, to put it in functionalist terms, about its latent rather than its manifest function.

There are indications that military failure was intended. First, the town of Dieppe happened to be, and was known to be, an eminently defensible site, and therefore necessarily one of the strongest German positions on the Atlantic coast of France. Anyone arriving there by ferry from England sees immediately that this port, surrounded by high and steep cliffs, known to be bristling with machine guns and cannon, must have been a deadly trap for the attackers. The Germans ensconced there could not believe their eyes when they found themselves being attacked. One of their war correspondents, who witnessed the inevitable slaughter, described the raid as "an operation that violated all the rules of military logic and strategy."[11] Other factors, such as poor planning, inadequate preparations, inferior equipment such as tanks that could not negotiate the pebbles of Dieppe's beach, make it seem more likely that the objective was military failure rather than success.

On the other hand, the Dieppe operation, including its bloody failure, actually made sense — in other words, it was a success — if it was ordered for a non-military purpose. Military operations are frequently carried out to achieve a political objective, and that seems to have been the case at Dieppe in August 1942. The Western Allies' political leaders in general, the British political leadership in particular, and Prime Minister Churchill above all, found themselves under relentless pressure to open a second front, were unwilling to open such a front, but lacked a convincing justification for their inaction. The failure of what could be presented as an attempt to open a second front, or at least a prelude to the opening of a second front, did provide such a justification. Seen in this light, the Dieppe tragedy was indeed a great success, even a double success. First, the operation could be, and was, presented as a selfless and heroic attempt — by all the Anglo-Saxons — to assist the Soviets. Second, the failure of the operation seemed to demonstrate only too clearly that the Western Allies were indeed not yet ready to open a second front.

If Jubilee was intended to silence the voices clamouring for the opening of a second front, it was successful. The Dieppe disaster silenced the popular demand for a second front and allowed Churchill and Roosevelt to continue to sit on the fence as the Nazis and the Soviets were slaughtering each other in the east. While no hard evidence for this hypothesis is available at this stage, it would explain why the lambs that were led to the slaughter of Dieppe were not American or British, but Canadian. Indeed, the Canadians constituted the perfect cannon fodder for this enterprise, because their political and military leaders did not belong to the exclusive club of the British-American top command who planned the operation and who would obviously have been reluctant to sacrifice their own men.

After the tragedy of Dieppe, Stalin stopped asking for a second front. The Soviets would eventually get their second front, but only much later, in 1944, when Stalin was no longer asking for such a favour. However, at that point, the Americans and the British had urgent reasons of their own for landing on the coast of France. Indeed, after the Battles of Stalingrad and Kursk, when Soviet troops were relentlessly grinding their way toward Berlin, "it became imperative for American and English strategy," as two American historians have written, "to land troops in France and drive into Germany to keep most of that country out of [Soviet] hands."[12] When a second front was finally opened in Normandy in June 1944, it was not done to assist the Soviets, but to prevent the Soviets from winning the war on their own. The Soviets got their second front when they no longer wanted or needed it. (This does not mean that they did not welcome the landings in Normandy, or did not benefit from the belated opening of a second front; after all, the Germans remained an extremely tough opponent until the very end.) As for the Canadians, who had been sacrificed at Dieppe, they also got something, namely, heaps of praise from the men at the top of the military and political hierarchy. Churchill himself, for example, solemnly declared that Jubilee, described as "a Canadian contribution of the greatest significance to final victory," had been the key to the success of the landings in Normandy. The Canadians were also showered with prestigious awards, including two Victoria Crosses, and this generosity probably reflected a desire on the part of the authorities to atone for their decision to send so many men on a suicidal mission intended to achieve highly questionable political goals.

A second front would be opened later, when such an operation would suit the purposes of the Americans and the British. In the summer of 1942, then, the Americans remained focused on their war against the Japanese, against whom important battles were won near Midway Islands and on Guadalcanal. However, the United States, in conjunction with their British ally, had more than sufficient resources in men and supplies to also undertake something against Nazi Germany. It was in 1942 that the United States Army Air Force (USAAF) and the British Royal Air Force (RAF) opened the so-called "third front," by bombing German cities and other targets. The aim of this strategic-bombing program was to paralyze German industry, to demoralize the German population, and thus to lay the groundwork for the final victory. The architect of this strategy was the head of the RAF's Bomber Command, a man who exerted a great deal of influence on Churchill, and whose statue was unveiled in London some years ago — not without controversy and protest. His name was Arthur Harris, but his own men called him "Bomber Harris." As for the commanders of the American armed forces, they had already become enchanted with the potential of strategic bombing in the thirties, when they had developed the famous four-engine B-17 Flying Fortress bomber. After the end of the war, the Americans would continue to believe — as recent actions against Iraq, Serbia, and Afghanistan have shown — that wars can be won in the air, by means of manned bombers. And yet, the experiences with strategic bombing during the Second World War were not all that impressive.

The strategic-bombing program required the investment of a disproportionately large amount of human and material resources, which could arguably have been used more efficiently for other purposes, possibly for opening a second front in Western Europe. Furthermore, the USAAF and the RAF would suffer enormous losses in planes and crews. The Americans alone lost 40,000 men and 6,000 airplanes. In one month — July 1943 — the USAAF, which bombed Germany in broad daylight, lost one hundred planes and one thousand crew members. The situation would improve toward the end of 1943 with the introduction of long-range fighters such as the P-51 Mustang, capable of escorting the lumbering giants deep into German airspace. Although the spectacular bombing raids provided perfect grist for the Allied propaganda mill as well as inspiration for later movies such as *Dambusters* and *Memphis Belle*, strategic bombing never produced the expected results, as a thorough official study, the *Strategic-Bombing Survey* of 1946, acknowledged after the war. Strategic bombing was generally very inaccurate, even though the Americans spoke of "precision bombing," and could not prevent the consistent increase in German industrial output, which culminated as late as 1944. As far as the German civilian population was concerned, 300,000 of them would fall victim to Allied bombing during the war. The bombing raids thus earned the Allies the hatred of the German civilians, who were not demoralized at all but became grimly determined to carry on to the "final victory" that Hitler and Goebbels continued to conjure up so convincingly.[13]

The men and supplies that were not used for a second front in Western Europe were squandered, in a sense, on strategic bombing. And precisely because the British and the Americans invested so much military capital in Harris's plan, a second front did indeed become a less and less feasible proposition. However, in November 1942, the Americans landed sizable forces in North Africa. Not without some difficulty, these troops managed to wrest France's colonial possessions from the tutelage of Vichy and then, in cooperation with British forces advancing from Egypt, to eliminate what was left of Rommel's North African army.

Operation Torch, as the North African landings were referred to in military code, offered undeniable benefits. For example, it greatly strengthened the British positions in strategically important Gibraltar, in Egypt with its Suez Canal, and in the oil-rich Middle East. It was probably because British interests were so heavily involved that Churchill had been the greatest champion of Torch and of a Mediterranean strategy in general. Another advantage of this operation was that the Allies now also directly threatened Germany's weak partner, Italy, where they would land troops in the summer of 1943. Churchill firmly believed that it made sense to attack the Nazi monster via its "soft underbelly" in the Mediterranean, rather than via a second front in France. However, the narrow and mountainous Italian peninsula would prove to be a major obstacle, easily defended by relatively few German troops after the fall of Mussolini. The road to Berlin (and/or Vienna) via Italy would reveal itself as an endless *via dolorosa*. The landings in North Africa, then, did not yield significant benefits other than the safeguarding of British interests there and in the neighbouring Middle East. Moreover, Torch also brought a considerable disadvantage.

Now that the British-Americans had shown their strategic hand, the Germans knew that there would be no second front in France (or elsewhere in Western Europe) for the time being. Thus, they could afford to ferry more troops from Western Europe to the Eastern Front. For the Soviets, then, the military situation did not improve at all as a result of Torch.[14] Stalin was extremely disappointed. From the events of late 1942 he drew the conclusion that in the merciless struggle against Nazi Germany he could only count on the Soviet Union's own military strength, on the Red Army, and that he should not have much faith in his allies.

As for the British and the Americans, it is questionable whether the decision not to open a second front earned them any significant advantages. The sacrifices associated with a landing in France, for example, were not avoided, but merely postponed from 1942 until 1944. Moreover, had they opened a second front in France in 1942 instead of investing so much military capital in strategic bombing and in the war in North Africa, their troops might possibly have penetrated much deeper into Western Europe and into Germany than would be the case in 1944 and 1945. At war's end, the Americans and the British might thus have found themselves ensconced in Berlin and perhaps as far east as Warsaw, and this would have given them the kind of advantages vis-à-vis the Soviets that they had sought to attain by *not* opening a second front. However, it is impossible to know with certainty if all this would have happened, because a second front never became a reality in 1942 nor, for that matter, in 1943.

Chapter 9
STALIN'S SOVIET UNION: AN UNLOVED BUT USEFUL PARTNER

Shortly after the Americans had revealed their hand, not only to the Germans but also to the Soviets, with their landings in North Africa, the military situation suddenly changed dramatically on the far side of the European theatre of war. On the distant Eastern Front, in and around the city of Stalingrad, a German army of no less than 300,000 men was routed by the Red Army after a long and murderous battle. The sentimental "Song of the Volga," from an operetta by Franz Lehar, proved to be a major hit in the German *Heimat* during the winter of 1942-43, but what came to pass on the banks of that Russian river amounted to nothing less than a catastrophe for Germany. The failure of Hitler's blitzkrieg in the Soviet Union in December 1941 had been the real turning point of the war, but until the end of 1942 everything still seemed possible. On the banks of the Volga, however, in the vicinity of the city named after the Soviet leader, the tide truly turned in the sense that everybody realized that the German army had received a blow from which recovery was extremely unlikely. When relatively shortly thereafter, in the summer of 1943, a second major Soviet success, this time in the vicinity of Kursk, caused more huge losses to the Wehrmacht, it was clearly only a matter of time before Nazi Germany would founder.[1]

As far as inter-Allied relations were concerned, Stalingrad represented an equally crucial turning point. Churchill's ideal view of what he termed the "Grand Alliance," the anti-Hitler alliance of the United States, Great

Britain, and the Soviet Union, has been described by the British historian Fraser J. Harbutt as "a solid, dominant British-American combination confronting a petitionary Soviet Union." Until the winter of 1942-43, the reality conformed with this image. Indeed, Stalin had hitherto played the role of a mendicant in the fine company of his rich allies, one who constantly begged for the favour of a second front. Washington and London dominated the coalition in the sense that they themselves were not directly threatened by the Nazis and disposed of immense resources of manpower and supplies. The Americans and the British could then still hope that in due course they would be able to intervene on the Continent, like a *deus ex machina*, in order to impose their will on the exhausted Soviets as well as the defeated Nazis.

After Stalingrad, however, the situation was dramatically different. The Red Army was no longer fighting with its back against the wall, was making excellent progress also without the benefit of a second front, and was slowly but surely on its way to Berlin. Within the Great Coalition, Stalin could no longer be dominated; to Roosevelt and Churchill he was henceforth an equal partner, who needed to be treated with respect.[2] From a purely military perspective, Stalingrad had been a boon to the Western Allies, because this defeat had impaired the Nazi war machine to their advantage as well. However, the American and British leaders were not particularly happy with the changed power relations within the anti-Hitler coalition and the implications of this change for the post-war arrangements that would follow the now apparently inevitable defeat of Nazi Germany.

In the United States, the White House was inundated with warnings, produced by the military, the secret services, elder statesmen, and Allied leaders such as Wladyslaw Sikorski, the premier of the Polish government in exile and commander of the Polish forces. These Cassandras lamented the looming occupation of Germany by the Red Army and the possibility of Soviet expansion "perhaps as far west as the Rhine, perhaps even beyond," as William C. Bullitt, former ambassador to the USSR and one of the most vocal doomsayers in this respect, put it in a memorandum to Roosevelt. Great concern also reigned in London. Before the war, Churchill had feared that the attempt by appeasers like Chamberlain to have Hitler eliminate the USSR might backfire and actually permit Soviet communism to expand westward; he now abhorred the thought that the Soviets might possibly win the war without the help of their allies and thus end up dominating Germany and the rest of the European continent.[3]

But things had not yet gone that far. The Red Army was still nowhere near the German capital. Furthermore, on the Eastern Front the Soviets continued to face "the overwhelming bulk" of the German army, as the British historian Clive Ponting has observed, while the Western Allies never engaged more than 10 per cent of the Wehrmacht's total forces. The Soviets would still have their hands full for a long time, and in the meantime all sorts of things could happen in Western Europe. By means of a landing in northern France or Belgium, the Americans and British could themselves invade Germany and possibly reach Berlin before the Red Army. In this sense, a second front in France became increasingly more interesting for the Western Allies. However, having opted for a southern strategy, the British and Americans had their landing equipment tied up in the Mediterranean, so that a second front in Western Europe was no longer an option in 1943.[4]

After Stalingrad, the Western Allies were confronted with three major possible scenarios. In the worst-case scenario, the Soviets would defeat Nazi Germany singlehandedly and thus become the "masters of Europe," as Bullitt warned in January 1943, as soon as the significance of Stalingrad started to reveal itself. However, even the best-case scenario was far from attractive for Washington and London. Even if the Americans and the British would invade Germany via Italy or France and thus manage to win the war together with the Soviets, Stalin would inevitably enjoy considerable input into the post-war rearrangement of Germany and the rest of Europe. The prospect of having to share the guardianship over post-war Europe with the Kremlin was all the more painful because only shortly before it had looked as if at the end of the war the British-Americans would be able to impose their will not only on the Germans but also on the Soviets.

These two scenarios filled the Western leaders with concern for the future. In addition, they found themselves bedeviled by a third unattractive post-Stalingrad scenario, namely, the possibility that Stalin might again make a deal with Hitler. An American expert in the history of the Second World War, Warren F. Kimball, writes:

> *A nagging nightmare for Roosevelt and Churchill through-*
> *out the war was the thought of a Soviet-German deal . . .*
> *Throughout the war, and particularly after the Red Army's*
> *victory at Stalingrad, American intelligence assessments*
> *expressed concern that, once the Germans were pushed out of*
> *the Soviet Union, he [Stalin] would minimize losses and seek*
> *a favorable settlement, leaving his Allies to deal with Hitler.*
> *That concern never left Roosevelt . . .*[5]

Roosevelt and Churchill realized that an encore of the Hitler-Stalin Pact of 1939 was not inconceivable, because for both the Soviets and the Nazis the alternative, continued bloodletting on the Eastern Front, was far from inviting. Furthermore, a post-Stalingrad agreement with Nazi Germany would almost certainly have involved major German concessions to the Soviet Union. In comparison with a possibly very advantageous deal with Hitler, could Stalin be expected to see any merit in a continued alliance with the Americans and the British, whose chestnuts he had hitherto pulled out of the fire, only to be denied relief in the form of a second front? A new non-aggression pact between the Nazis and the Soviets would have ended the war on the Eastern Front and would have enabled Nazi Germany to turn all of its (considerable) remaining might against the Americans and the British. For London and Washington that would obviously have con- stituted a major calamity. There was actually a historical precedent for this kind of scenario: the Russian-German treaty of Brest-Litovsk of early 1918. This settlement had enabled the Germans to launch a major offensive on the Western Front, which nearly permitted them to snatch victory from the jaws of defeat at the end of the First World War.[6]

Stalin did not mind that Washington and London were worried. Quite the contrary. Their concern allowed him to put pressure on his Western partners, obtain more material assistance from them, and make them more inclined to go along with the war aims of the Soviet Union. As the anxiety of Roosevelt and Churchill mounted, Stalin's self-assurance within the coalition increased. To improve his position even further, he may even have spread rumours of negotiations between Soviet and Nazi representa- tives in neutral Sweden. However, there is reason to believe that Stalin did not really think of deserting his British and American allies. In 1941 he had traumatically experienced the unreliability of Hitler, with whom he had concluded an agreement two years earlier. Furthermore, the Nazis' barbarian style of warfare in the east had revealed all too clearly Hitler's true intentions with respect to the USSR, so that the chances of a new pact between Berlin and Moscow were virtually non-existent. Stalin also had to wonder if a new deal with Hitler would benefit the Soviet Union in the long run: would the British-Americans, if ultimately victorious against Germany, not want to exact retribution from the Soviets? Alternatively, would Hitler, after a hypothetical triumph in the West, not come looking for "living space" in the east once more? In view of this, it is understandable that a number of unofficial German "peace feelers" received no response from Moscow.[7] Since on the Eastern Front the Red Army continued to battle the Wehrmacht ferociously after Stalingrad and Kursk, Washington and London would eventually perceive, to their considerable relief, that Stalin would not leave them in the lurch.

In this context, then, we can understand why in the immediate aftermath of Stalingrad, on the occasion of the Casablanca Conference of January 14–25, 1943, Roosevelt proposed that the Allies would promise never to negotiate separately with Nazi Germany and to accept only an *unconditional* surrender from the common Nazi foe. Stalin had declined to attend the meeting in the Moroccan seaport, which had probably intensified American-British concerns about his intentions. And so the Western Allies were greatly relieved when the Soviet leader agreed with the formula of unconditional surrender. Still, Roosevelt continued to fret about the spectre of a new pact between Moscow and Berlin until well into the fall of 1943.[8] As for the formula of unconditional surrender, it has been argued that this demand was unwise, since it seems to have prolonged German resistance. Also, in the spring of 1945, when Nazi Germany was finally ready to submit, the theory of the Casablanca Declaration would not easily be put into practice, as we will see later.

A new pact between Stalin and Hitler, then, did not come about. However, the Americans and the British now started to worry more and more about the rewards that Uncle Joe might claim at the war's end for the Soviet Union's contribution to the victory over Nazism. Stalin entertained certain expectations that his allies could hardly deny him, although they were clearly reluctant to certify them. It was obvious, for example, that the western borders of the Soviet Union would be revised. Soviet intentions in this respect had already been made clear in the summer of 1941 to the British secretary of the foreign office, Anthony Eden. Civil war and foreign intervention had caused the newborn Soviet Union to lose vast territories — in comparison to the western borders of its czarist predecessor-state — to the new Baltic States and Poland in the early 1920s. The border with Poland had moved a considerable distance to the east of the so-called Curzon Line, identified after the First World War on behalf of the Western powers by the British foreign secretary, Lord Curzon, as the ethnically and linguistically optimal border between the USSR and Poland. (Poland, for example, had absorbed much of the western Ukraine). Sadly for Poland and the Baltic states, after the war the USSR's western border would inevitably have to move back further west. Poland, however, could be compensated with German territory east of the rivers Oder and Neisse. This arrangement can hardly be called fair, but it was perfectly rational from the perspective of the punitive principles assiduously practised by all sides in the First World War and again in the Second, including Germany as long as she was victorious. Stalin also made it clear that in neighbouring countries such as Poland he was not prepared to tolerate the kind of virulently anti-Soviet regimes that had ruled there before 1939. This, too, was an expectation against which the Western Allies could hardly raise objections.[9]

Stalin's expectations proved no more unreasonable or extravagant than the analogous expectation on the side of the Western Allies that they themselves would sooner or later recuperate their own lost imperial possessions, such as Britain's very own Hong Kong and Singapore, the French colony of Indochina, Dutch Indonesia and, in the case of the United States, the Philippines. (When he was driven from the Philippines by the Japanese, the American general MacArthur declared that he would return there, and this bold "I shall return" was celebrated in the United States and made him instantly famous; nobody ever bothered to ask if the Philippine people were longing for the return of their American masters.) With respect to the Soviets, the British and the Americans found it much more difficult to validate the same kind of territorial privileges that they considered to be totally fair in their own case and in the case of their Western imperial colleagues. And yet, the colonial privileges they reclaimed clearly contravened not only the basic rules of Western democracy but also the celebrated Atlantic Charter, in that no attention whatsoever was paid to the opinions of millions of colonial subjects and elections were never even considered.

If the Americans and the British found that they could not afford to object to Stalin's expectations, however, it was not because they understood all this, but because they realized only too well that a final victory against Nazi Germany and Japan — the precondition for the recovery of their own imperial possessions — would require many more Soviet sacrifices. Roosevelt was aware that many more such sacrifices would be needed in order to win the war without having to spill much American blood. (In this context it deserves to be mentioned that in the Second World War, for each American who "gave his life," as the saying goes, no less than fifty-three Soviet soldiers gave theirs; while a total of 600,000 British and Americans were killed on all fronts, including the war against Japan, more than 13 million Soviet soldiers were killed on the Eastern Front. The city of Leningrad alone lost more people than the combined losses of the United States and Great Britain in the entire Second World War.) In order to obtain Stalin's authorization for the necessary Soviet bloodletting, it was indeed useful to forget momentarily the interests of the Poles and the Balts. Thus, it can be said that Polish territory and Baltic sovereignty were sacrificed, not on the altar of Soviet ambitions, as the conventional wisdom of the Cold War era had it, but on the altar of American and British interests.[10]

There is one final factor that helps to explain the attitude of the Western Allies with regard to the territorial war aims of the Soviet Union: it was a forgone conclusion that at the end of hostilities the territories in question would be occupied by the Red Army. Any effort to undo this *fait accompli* would have been doomed in advance. For all these reasons, then, neither London nor Washington could afford to deny Stalin his territorial aspirations, no matter how much they would have liked to have done so.

The British had already explicitly or implicitly recognized certain Soviet expectations in 1941 and 1942, for example in the British-Soviet treaty of March 26, 1942. President Roosevelt demonstrated some understanding for the Soviet point of view, and followed the British example. However, in order to protect himself against a potentially negative political back-lash (from Americans of Polish descent, for example) he formulated certain objections and also manoeuvred as much as possible to postpone definitive arrangements until after the end of hostilities — that is, until the Soviets would no longer be needed and it would therefore become possible to antagonize them. In any event, virtually all of Stalin's expecta-tions received approval at the time of the first meeting of the "Big Three," which took place in the Iranian capital, Tehran, from November 28 until December 1, 1943, on which occasion Roosevelt and Stalin turned out to get along very well.[11]

But what was to happen to Germany and to the liberated countries? With regard to some points, at least, unanimity did reign. First, the Nazi regime would have to go, and its protagonists and henchmen would be brought to trial as war criminals; in the liberated countries, similar treatment would be meted out to all Nazis, fascists, and collaborators. Second, just as after the First World War, Germany would be presented with a bill for war dam-ages, and would have to pay reparations. What kind of regimes would be installed in defeated Germany and in the liberated countries of Europe? Clearly, American and British ideas about this differed drastically from those of the Soviets. For the time being, the Allies therefore sensibly limited themselves to pious but vague declarations, such as those of the Atlantic Charter, that everyone could agree with. All Allies, for example, agreed to allow the population of liberated countries, and of Germany, to restore "democratic" forms of government under Allied supervision. For Roosevelt, democracy meant American-style democracy; in Churchill's mind the term conjured up fine British democratic traditions; and to Stalin, democracy amounted to the Bolsheviks' democracy of and for workers, peasants, and soldiers, to be known later in Eastern Europe as "people's democracy." Everybody was aware of these differences, but nobody was prepared to raise this sensitive issue, because doing so might have jeopardized the cooper-ation on which an Allied final victory still depended.

In Tehran, Roosevelt, who was very relieved that no new Hitler-Stalin pact had come about, actually found Stalin's demands to be reasonable and moderate. Furthermore, he was delighted that Uncle Joe readily com-plied with an important American request. Stalin promised to declare war on America's enemy in the Far East, Japan, shortly after Germany's defeat.[12] Roosevelt was gratified. However, when in the spring of 1945, after the defeat of the Nazis, Stalin prepared to keep his promise, Roosevelt's successor in the White House would prove far from ecstatic with the prospect of sharing the glory — and the benefits — of victory over Japan, as we will see later.

Chapter 10
THE LIBERATION OF ITALY:
A FATEFUL PRECEDENT

Whatever would happen to the borders of the liberated countries, Germany, and all of Europe after the war would in theory be determined by the agreements concluded by the Allies in Tehran and elsewhere. On the other hand, much would also depend on the way the war would develop militarily, and specifically on two factors. First, the respective military successes (and possibly failures) of the Western Allies and of the Red Army in the final phase of the war might create certain *faits accomplis,* which in turn might influence both the interpretation of the often vaguely formulated earlier agreements and the details of possible new agreements. A second important factor might be the actual circumstances of liberation, that is, the way in which the Allies would conduct themselves in liberated countries and in Germany, thus potentially creating momentous precedents.

As far as the Western Allies were concerned, it was clearly important to at least match the military performance of the Red Army in the final phase of the war, to liberate as much European territory as possible and, if at all possible, to arrive in Berlin before the Soviets. However, because of their landing in North Africa in 1942, the Americans and the British had no choice but to continue along the path of the Mediterranean strategy, at least for the time being. The next move dictated by that strategy was the leap from North Africa to Sicily and southern Italy, which took place in the summer of 1943. On the other hand, plans were now finally prepared for a second front in

France, although this was clearly not done in order to be of service to Stalin. The Soviets would of course inevitably benefit from such an operation, which would finally force the Wehrmacht to transfer sizable forces from the Eastern Front to Western Europe, but they were no longer desperate for this sort of relief, for which they had begged only shortly before. A second front in Western Europe, however, was becoming more and more vital for the Western Allies themselves. They had come to the realization that via the Mediterranean they would certainly reach Germany far too late to prevent the Soviets from taking Berlin unassisted, and thus to prevent them from reaping the prestige and all or most of the benefits of victory over the common Nazi enemy. Only by means of a landing in Western Europe, which, unlike Italy, was not separated from Germany by a screen of mountains, could the American and British armies still hope to compete with the Red Army in the undeclared race to Berlin, and possibly to win that race. In a memorandum to Roosevelt and other Allied leaders, the American air force general Henry Arnold thus warned in the spring of 1943 that a second front needed to be opened soon, since otherwise "we could still be discussing [a cross-channel operation] while the Russians [are] marching into Berlin."[1] However, considerable time would still elapse before the required landing equipment could be transferred to England from the Mediterranean theatre, where it was still needed for the operations in Italy in the summer of 1943. Only in the spring of 1944 would the Western Allies finally be poised to leap across the English Channel, a leap that would go down in history as Operation Overlord.

In the meantime, the Western Allies also derived certain advantages from their presence in the Mediterranean area. While the Red Army continued to fight in its own country, the Americans and the British had the opportunity to knock Italy out of the war. They thus enjoyed the prestige but also the responsibility of being the first to bring down a fascist regime and of restoring democracy to a European country, a large and important one. Unfortunately, it cannot be said that in that respect the Western Allies did a wonderful job.

From a military perspective, the Italian campaign was hardly successful: after the Italians themselves threw in the towel, the Germans were able to put up an effective resistance with relatively few troops until the very end of the war, so that there was never any hope of an Allied advance from Italy to distant Berlin. However, much more important is the fact that the Allies bungled politically. Their course of action during the liberation of Italy put an additional strain on relations with their Soviet partner, and created a fateful precedent that would come back to haunt Washington and London when Stalin later followed it in Eastern European countries liberated by the Soviets.

Mussolini's brutal and corrupt fascist regime was thoroughly despised by the majority of Italians, and they welcomed his fall in the summer of 1943 with relief and enthusiasm. Their liberators, the Americans and the British, now had an opportunity to help the Italians replace Il Duce's fascist regime with a democratic system of government. (Incidentally, Canadian troops also played an important role in the Italian campaign, but Washington and London did not involve Ottawa in the least in the political decision-making process.) A significant anti-fascist resistance movement had been politically and militarily active in Italy. This movement enjoyed wide support among the population and it claimed a leading role in the reconstruction of the country. However, the Allies refused to cooperate with this anti-fascist front: it was too left-wing for their taste, and not only because the Communists played an important role in it. It was obvious that the overwhelming majority of Italian anti-fascists favoured radical social, political, and economic reforms, including the abolition of the monarchy. Churchill, in particular, was allegedly obsessed by the spectre of such radical reforms on the other side of the Alps, reforms that in the eyes of this conservative statesman amounted to the "Bolshevization" of Italy. And so neither the plans and wishes of the Italians themselves nor the merits and aspirations of their anti-fascist resistance movement carried any weight. Instead, a deal was made with officers and politicians who represented the traditional Italian power elite, such as the monarchy, the army, the great landowners, bankers and industrialists, and the Vatican. It did not seem to bother the Allies that it was precisely this elite that had made it possible for Mussolini to come to power in 1922 and that had profited enormously from his regime, for which it was despised by the majority of Italians. The Italian partisans were disarmed militarily and neutralized politically, except of course behind German lines in northern Italy, where they were and remained a force to be reckoned with. Marshal Badoglio, a former collaborator of Mussolini's, who had been responsible for terrible war crimes in Ethiopia,[2] was allowed to become the first head of government of post-fascist Italy. In the liberated part of Italy the new system looked suspiciously like the old one and was therefore dismissed by many as *fascismo senza Mussolini*, or "fascism minus Mussolini."[3]

In Italy in general, and in Sicily in particular, the Americans also collaborated intimately with the Mafia, which they perceived as an "anti-communist bastion." The protagonists in this Operation Mafia included the notorious New York gangster Lucky Luciano and, ironically, J. Edgar Hoover of the FBI. This Sicilian initiative inaugurated an inglorious yet intimate and lengthy post-war cooperation between America's secret services and the international criminal underworld, above all in the lucrative field of drug trafficking. During many decades, the CIA would be able to use the money generated by this collaboration to finance counter-revolutionary activities all over the world, either without, or more likely, with the knowledge of presidents such as Ronald Reagan. Two examples: the attempts on the life of Fidel Castro, planned in direct collusion with the Mafia, and the secret war against Nicaragua's Sandinistas. These were so-called "covert operations," which violated American legislation, so that they could not have been financed through allocations approved by Congress.[4]

What the Western Allies did in Italy after the fall of Mussolini's fascist regime was certainly not entirely correct. However, it is also instructive to note *how* they went to work there. The British and the Americans did not allow their Soviet partner any input, in fact they barely bothered to consult him. Moscow was entitled to a voice in the Italian debate, because Italian troops had fought alongside the Nazis on the Eastern Front. Moreover, the admittedly vague inter-Allied agreements provided for the creation of "Allied Control Councils," and in theory these councils were supposed to enable the three Allies *together* to guide liberated countries on the road back to democracy. This theoretically noble principle was first implemented in Italy. The British-Americans did create an Allied Control Council there, and a Soviet representative was allowed to join it, but in reality the Soviets were allowed no say whatsoever. The Americans and the British clearly viewed post-fascist Italy as their own exclusive sphere of influence and, as the American historian Warren F. Kimball dryly observes, "excluded the Russians from any meaningful role in the occupation of Italy." It was in this manner, then, that fascism was eradicated and that democracy was restored in the first country to be liberated by the Allied powers.[5]

Stalin had undoubtedly observed developments on the other side of the Alps with great interest. He cannot have been very pleased with the way in which the British-American liberators had pushed aside not only the Italian communists and other left-wing anti-fascists but also their Soviet ally. However, Stalin did not want to risk a feud with his Western partners over distant Italy, so he resigned himself to a *fait accompli,* and to the consternation of the Italian Communists he even officially recognized the Badoglio regime in March 1944. Stalin viewed the events in Italy not without reason as a precedent that showed how the inter-Allied agreements were to be put into practice. "The Russians accepted the [Italian] 'formula' without much enthusiasm," writes Kolko, "but carefully noted the arrangement for future reference and as a precedent."[6] Later, in 1944 and 1945, when the Red Army liberated the countries of Eastern Europe, Stalin would proceed there in the same manner and he expected that this time the Americans and the British would resign themselves. However, the Western Allies were to complain bitterly when the Soviets forced their will on Eastern Europe and proceeded to eradicate fascism as they saw fit and to introduce their own brand of democracy. The Americans and the British forgot all too lightly that they themselves had already given the example for this sort of behaviour in 1943 in Italy, and that they had continued to act this way in other liberated countries of Western Europe. Everywhere, in the western as well as the eastern part of Europe, the liberators were to construct a political, social, and economic system that was to their liking, and in doing so they showed little or no regard for the opinion of the liberated population or the interests of their own allies. According to Milovan Djilas, a former high-ranking Communist official and political writer from Yugoslavia, Stalin would formulate in words the principle that had first been put into practice by the British and the Americans:

This war is not like the wars of the past. When one occupies
a territory, one introduces one's own social system. Everybody
introduces his own system into the lands controlled by his own
army. There is simply no other way.[7]

In sixteenth-century Europe, during the troubled times of the Protestant Reformation and the Catholic Counter-Reformation, kings and other crowned heads forced their own religion on their subjects — a particularly undemocratic practice which became known as the principle *cuius regio eius religio*. At the time of the liberation of Europe, from 1943 to 1945, an analogous and equally undemocratic principle determined that each liberated country was saddled with the political, social, and also economic system of its liberator.

The military situation of the Western Allies in Italy in early 1944 was hardly wonderful. The Germans put up a very effective resistance, and the long and murderous fighting around Monte Cassino, between Naples and Rome, could be compared to the terrible battles of the First World War. As it was now obvious that by way of the Italian boot Berlin could never be reached before the Red Army, preparations were accelerated for Operation Overlord, the landings on the French Atlantic coast. The urgency of this task increased rapidly as the Red Army advanced systematically along the entire length of the Eastern Front and was poised in the spring of 1944 to invade Hungary and Romania. "When Russian troops began to push the Germans back," write two American historians, Peter N. Carroll and David W. Noble, "it became imperative for American and English [sic] strategy to land troops in France and drive into Germany to keep most of that country out of Communist hands."[8] The Americans and the British also worried about the possibility that Nazi Germany might suddenly collapse before they could have opened a second front in France. In this case, the Soviets would occupy all of Germany, liberate even Western Europe, and would be able to do there as they pleased, exactly as the British-Americans had done in Italy. "The possibility of a complete Russian victory over Germany before American forces landed on the Continent," writes the American historian Mark A. Stoler, was "nightmarish" for Washington, and of course also for London, but this scenario had to be envisaged.[9] Contingency plans were therefore prepared for an emergency landing on the coast of France and the subsequent use of airborne troops combined with a rapid overland push by armoured units in order to occupy as much territory as possible in Western Europe and Germany before the arrival of the Soviets. This operation was code-named Rankin, and troops were kept in a state of preparedness for Rankin until three months after the landings in Normandy.[10]

Chapter 11
THE LONG SUMMER
OF 1944

Operation Overlord, the long-awaited landing of the Western Allies in France, became reality on June 6, 1944, on the beaches of Normandy. This particularly spectacular operation was already celebrated by Hollywood in the sixties with the blockbuster *The Longest Day* and it was commemorated in 2014, seven decades after the fact, with plenty of fanfare, suggesting that during the entire Second World War no more dramatic or decisive event had taken place. That Operation Overlord had involved not only purely military objectives, but that it was also supposed to enable the Americans and the British to compete with the Soviets in an undeclared race to Berlin, remained unmentioned in the many speeches that punctuated those commemorative ceremonies.

At first things did not go very smoothly in Normandy for the Western Allies. The actual landings were carried out satisfactorily and a considerable beachhead was established, but the Germans eventually managed to bring it under control and to prevent its further enlargement. However, in the first days of August 1944 the German resistance in Normandy suddenly collapsed after heavy fighting in the Caen-Falaise sector. Consequently, the Americans, British, and Canadians were able to push forward much faster than even the most optimistic plans had dared to forecast. Paris was liberated on August 25, and a few days later British tanks rolled into Belgium, where they were hindered more by the country's infamous cobblestones than by their German enemies. Brussels, the Belgian capital, regained its

THE MYTH OF THE GOOD WAR

freedom, and the country's great seaport of Antwerp fell undamaged into the hands of the liberators. These successes appeared to make it possible for the Western Allies to finish the war before the end of the year by means of a Rankin-like rapid push into the heart of Germany. In this case the Americans and the British would hold the best cards in the coming poker game with the Soviets over the post-war reorganization of Germany and Europe.

Thus originated Market Garden, the spectacular British-American attempt, in September 1944, to cross the great rivers of the Netherlands, including the Rhine at Arnhem near the German border, by means of airborne landings (Market) and a fast push overland (Garden). The purpose of this operation was nothing less than to open the way to Germany's industrial heartland, the Ruhr area, and hence to Berlin. Market Garden was to provide Hollywood with inspiration for a swashbuckling super-production, *A Bridge Too Far*. From Tinseltown's all-important box-office point of view, the movie was spectacularly successful, but in the fall of 1944 the ambitious operation in the Dutch lowlands actually ended in dismal failure. And so dissolved the short-lived dream of a speedy final offensive in Western Europe in 1944.

On the Eastern Front, in the meantime, the Red Army had not rested on its laurels. On June 22, 1944, shortly after the landings in Normandy, the Soviets launched an offensive, code-named Bagration, which prevented the Germans from transferring troops from the east to face the British-Americans in France; General Eisenhower himself later acknowledged that this had been a necessary precondition for the success of Operation Overlord. Once again the Wehrmacht was mauled by the Red Army, and the Soviets achieved an advance of more than 600 kilometres, all the way from deep in Russia to the suburbs of the Polish capital, Warsaw, into Romania and Bulgaria, and to the borders of Hungary and Yugoslavia.[1]

In order to prevent the Soviets from acting unilaterally in the countries they were liberating, or would soon liberate, from doing there what the Western Allies had already done in Italy, Churchill took the trouble to visit Stalin in Moscow in the fall of 1944. With Roosevelt's consent, he offered the Soviet leader a deal settling the respective degree of influence of the Soviets and the Western Allies in each liberated country of the Balkans.

The Western Allies, and above all the British, who believed themselves to have a special interest in that part of Europe, had reason to be pleased. For Stalin actually did agree to the deal, which was to be officially approved in October 1944. The British-Americans did have to allow the USSR a much higher percentage of influence in Romania, Bulgaria, and Hungary, but Great Britain obtained 50 per cent of influence in Yugoslavia and no less than 90 per cent of influence in Greece. What the people of these countries thought about this arrangement played no role, neither for Stalin, about whom we are told time and again that he was a dictator, nor for Churchill, allegedly one of the greatest democrats of the twentieth century. Afterwards Roosevelt also gave his blessing to the agreement. In any event, many possibilities remained open for the future, because in spite of the extremely precise percentages, it was absolutely unclear how this deal would later be put into practice.[2]

In Greece, a key country in the Mediterranean Sea, where Churchill planned to have Great Britain emerge after the war as "the leading power," the British would operate as they had done in Italy, only much more ruthlessly. The Greek anti-fascist resistance movement enjoyed wide popular support, but was too leftist to the taste of London and was therefore brushed aside by the British liberators, who installed an authoritarian right-wing regime featuring many former collaborators and fascist elements, in other words, Greek versions of Badoglio. Stalin cannot have been very happy that the communists were the prime target of British repression in newly liberated Greece, but he did nothing to help his Hellenic comrades; instead, he carefully observed the agreement he had concluded with Churchill. On the other hand, Stalin now undoubtedly felt free to pursue Soviet interests all the more energetically in countries liberated or conquered by the Red Army and therefore situated within the Soviet sphere of influence. Even so, for the time being Stalin proceeded with great caution in these countries; it was only later that he would install communist regimes in their capitals.[3]

In the late summer of 1944 it was the turn of France and Belgium to be liberated. The Americans and their British partner now had the opportunity to help decide which kind of political and socio-economic systems would emerge in these countries. Their attention naturally focused on France, a country that only a few years earlier had still loomed as a major power of the calibre of the United States and Great Britain. In France, however, the situation was extremely complex. In Vichy, Marshal Pétain presided over a collaborator regime that cultivated the conservative traditions of Ancien-Regime France, in other words of France before the Great Revolution of 1789, and which considered itself, and was considered by many Frenchmen, to be the legitimate government of the country. In London, however, a certain Charles de Gaulle, also a conservative man, fulminated as much against Vichy as against the Germans and in French-language BBC broadcasts spoke eloquently of a rebirth of France that could and would become reality under his authoritarian leadership. In occupied France itself, a variety of resistance groups were active. The Resistance Front, a broad movement in which the communists played an important role although they did not control the leadership, was determined that after the war the clock would not simply be turned back to 1939; in contrast to both Pétain and de Gaulle, the rank and file as well as Resistance leaders dreamed of more or less radical social and economic reforms that were eventually codified in the "Charter of the Resistance" of March 1944. (This charter called for "the introduction of a genuine economic and social democracy,involving the expropriation of the big economic and financial organizations" and "the socialization [le retour à la Nation] of the [most important] means of production such as sources of energy and mineral wealth, and of the insurance companies and great banks.")[4] Virtually all members of the Resistance despised Pétain and many of them found de Gaulle not only politically too authoritarian but also socially too conservative. The personality of de Gaulle, then, definitely did not dominate the Resistance, as many would learn to assume after the war, and in France itself the Gaullists remained a minority for the duration of the war. "Although precise figures do not exist," writes Kolko, "within France itself the Resistance groups that were Gaullist in ideology were always in a small minority [and] in many key parts of France they hardly existed at all."[5]

In spite of this, de Gaulle enjoyed considerable influence on the Resistance, mainly because of his contacts in Great Britain, which controlled the supply of weapons to the patriots in France. Churchill hoped to manipulate de Gaulle for his own purposes: not only to eliminate communist influence in France itself but also to integrate France into a post-war block of Western European countries that, under Great Britain's leadership, might be able to pit itself against the United States and the USSR, the two countries whose emergence as superpowers Churchill foresaw and feared.[6]

As for American leaders, including President Roosevelt, they had little feeling and even less understanding for the French imbroglio. They found it mystifying that the French patriots appeared to long for more than just the withdrawal of the Germans from their country and the return of the political, social, and economic status quo. The US authorities were as concerned as Churchill about the radical tendencies in general, and the communist influence in particular, within the Resistance and about this movement's relatively radical socio-economic plans for the future. Such plans might have enjoyed wide popular support within France itself, but they did not fit into the conservative vision of the liberators. The Roosevelt administration actually preferred the collaborator Pétain over a resistance that turned out to be so left-oriented, and also over de Gaulle, perceived as a chauvinistic Frenchman who was insufficiently subservient to London and Washington. In the White House the latter was considered almost intolerable, and not without reason he was also seen as a potential puppet of Churchill, who would favour British rather than American interests in post-war France.[7]

Washington would have preferred to be rid of de Gaulle, so at one point Roosevelt proposed to Churchill to arrange for the French general's appointment as governor of Madagascar! At the time of the landings in French North Africa, which caused Vichy to break off diplomatic relations with Washington, the Americans did not even inform de Gaulle about their plans. They negotiated a ceasefire with the Pétainist French commander in North Africa, François Darlan, and appeared ready to recognize the latter as head of state of liberated French colonies. De Gaulle was furious, and within the United States itself there was a public outcry against such cooperation with a former collaborator. The problem was conveniently resolved when Darlan was assassinated in Algiers, possibly by Gaullist agents. Washington came to understand only very slowly that there could be no place for the collaborator regime of Vichy in post-war France. Consequently, the Americans procrastinated very long before they finally gave their support to de Gaulle. They had no sympathy whatsoever for him, as little, in fact, as he had for them, and they would continue to have problems with him.[8]

Not without reason, the Americans considered de Gaulle an arrogant megalomaniac. "A narrow-minded French zealot with too much ambition for his own good," as Secretary of War Henry L. Stimson wrote in his diary, echoing the view of President Roosevelt. However, de Gaulle offered Washington two advantages: first, his reputation was not soiled by collaboration, as was the case for Pétainists such as Darlan; second, his plans for post-war France did not call for radical, possibly even revolutionary, social and economic experiments akin to those of the leftist Resistance. The first quality made him acceptable to the French themselves, the second quality made him acceptable to the Americans and the British. "De Gaulle is bad," Stimson confided to his diary, "but not to deal with him is worse." Indeed, unlike the ultra-conservative, reactionary Pétainists, the non-Gaullist Resistance loomed as a threat to US interests. Its plans for socio-economic reforms, outlined in the Charter of the Resistance, were perceived in Washington as communist-inspired, and the prospect of a Red revolution in France deeply troubled many American leaders, including President Roosevelt, as Stimson reported.[9] Another perceived threat to American interests was that the communist and other leftist partisans of France aimed to cultivate friendly relations with the Soviet Union. From an American intelligence station in Berne, Switzerland, which monitored developments in German-occupied Europe, came urgent warnings that the non-Gaullist National Committee of Liberation "had a dangerous tendency to strengthen pro-Russian sentiment among the French." Someone was needed, observes Kolko, "who could save France from the Left," someone who was "qualified to control" the influential communists within the Resistance, and the disagreeable de Gaulle revealed himself to be the only one who could and would take on this mission. Kolko dryly concludes: "If the Americans did not like de Gaulle they preferred [French] Bolsheviks even less."[10]

And so from the summer of 1944 Washington gradually followed Great Britain's example and helped to support de Gaulle's ambition of becoming the leader of post-war France. On October 23 of that same year, Washington finally recognized him as the legitimate head of the French government.

Shortly after the landings in Normandy, de Gaulle was repatriated to his homeland for the purpose of presenting him to the French people as hero and leader of the Resistance and to have him acclaimed as the head of government of a liberated and rejuvenated France. But in France itself, and particularly within the Resistance, there was far less enthusiasm for this fabricated coronation ceremony than one generally assumes today. Alternative plans were concocted. In Paris, for example, the Resistance took up arms against the German garrison as the Allied armies advanced to the French capital. This initiative would cost the lives of many partisans. Why did these patriots not simply wait a few days until the Germans had withdrawn and the Allied tanks rolled into town, so that the liberation party could start? For many Frenchmen it was of course very important that they themselves liberated their capital, the heart and symbol of the nation. In addition, they may have wanted to prevent Hitler's infamous order for the destruction of Paris from being implemented. That this was all that the Parisian partisans had in mind was wrongly suggested in a much-publicized movie released in the sixties, *Is Paris Burning?* However, particularly the most radical Resistance fighters took up arms in Paris, and that was no coincidence. They knew that together with the Allied armies the conservative and authoritarian de Gaulle was on his way, and they understood only too well that the British and the Americans planned to bring him to power, to eliminate the left-wing Resistance leaders politically, and thus to stave off their plans for post-war reform. The leftist, radical members of the Resistance had aspired to grab power quickly in Paris, the city that controls the heavily centralized network of the French state apparatus, in a way that the Western Allies, and their protegé de Gaulle, would have found very difficult to nullify.[11]

Polish resistance fighters similarly tried to liberate Warsaw in August 1944 before the arrival of the Red Army, but the uprising of the Polish capital was smothered in blood by the Nazis. A major determinant of this fiasco was the fact that the Soviets did not come to the rescue. Stalin knew that in marked contrast to the Resistance fighters in Paris, the Polish resistance fighters were anti-communist and anti-Soviet, and that they envisaged an outcome in Warsaw that would be unfavourable for the Soviets. He was therefore certainly not troubled by the fact that the Nazis ruined the Polish partisans' scenario. However, it is far from certain that the Red Army would have been able to intervene successfully in Warsaw, even though its vanguards were already positioned in the eastern suburbs, separated from the city itself by the Vistula River. Soviet military strategy after Stalingrad was characterized by gargantuan offensives along an extremely wide front, extending from the Baltic to the Black Sea. Such offensives, exemplified by "Bagration," produced huge territorial gains, and were typically alternated with very long pauses, urgently needed not only to permit the exhausted troops to rest but also to strengthen the stretched supply lines between the front and the industrial production centres deep in the Soviet Union. The Warsaw rising took place during such a pause. For the Red Army, an intervention would have been in many ways a risky undertaking, which might have offered the weakened but still very dangerous Wehrmacht an opportunity for a counter-stroke.[12]

In Paris the Western Allies were too fast for the Red partisans. The Sherman tanks rolled into the City of Light before the Germans had been driven out entirely. And so a triumphant entry could be contrived for de Gaulle after all, a spectacle that served to create the impression that he was the saviour for whom patriotic France had been waiting impatiently for four long years. It is said that the general himself ensured that during his march down the Champs Elysees the local Resistance leaders were prevented from walking alongside him, as they had intended to do, but were made to follow him at a respectful distance. The authoritarian de Gaulle — a "general who had never conducted a battle and a politician who had never presented himself at an election," as the British historian A. J. P. Taylor has cynically noted[13] — was thus foisted upon the French people by their American and British liberators. De Gaulle would have to allow the communists and other left-wing groups of the Resistance a measure of political input, and would have to introduce certain political reforms, but without him a much more radical government would have certainly come to power in France and the reforms envisaged in the Charter of the Resistance might perhaps have become reality.

As had already been the case in Italy, the conduct of the Americans and their British partner in France was far from unimpeachable, at least in the sense that it could hardly be reconciled with the accepted principle that the liberators were to permit liberated peoples themselves to restore democracy to their country. It is true that the Western Allies did not act as crudely in France as they did in Italy and Greece, but this was due far less to British and American tact than to the fact that after the liberation of Paris the French Communists revealed themselves to be particularly docile. It is virtually certain that they behaved this way on instructions from Stalin, who did not want to see his good relations with the United States and Great Britain jeopardized as a result of the ambitions of the communists in France. In any event, the Soviet Union was again denied any form of input into the affairs of the newly liberated country.[14]

In Belgium the Western Allies proceeded in a similar fashion. With the return of the Belgian government from its exile in London the political and socio-economic clock was simply turned back four years. The resistance groups that had planned to carry out more or less radical reforms after the liberation, in the first place the local communists, were forced by the liberators to lay down their weapons and were politically checkmated. Since Belgium was seen by London as a small yet important part of the future British sphere of influence in Europe, as a kind of British beachhead on the Continent, it was primarily the British who restored the old order in the country. They did so, however, "with strong American approval," because the US authorities were also keen to prevent the dialectic of occupation and liberation from leading to radical political, social, and economic change in Belgium. With the eager assistance of the national elites and the established political parties, the desire for change in Belgium would be emasculated and displaced, eventually degenerating into the "royal question," that is, the relatively unimportant issue of whether the monarchy would have to yield to republican institutions or not.[15]

Chapter 12
THE SUCCESSES OF THE RED ARMY AND THE YALTA AGREEMENTS

The events of the years 1943 and 1944 in countries such as Italy, Greece, and France had shown all too clearly that it was the liberators who determined how the local fascists were chastised or spared, how democracy was restored, how much input the anti-fascist resistance movements and the local population in general were permitted in the reconstruction of their own country, and whether political, social, and economic reforms were introduced or not. The unsubtle conduct of the Western Allies implicitly gave Stalin carte blanche to proceed similarly in countries liberated by the Red Army. However, this symmetry was far from perfect. First, until the summer of 1944 the Soviets continued to fight almost exclusively in their own country. It was only in the fall of that same year that they liberated neighbouring countries such as Romania and Bulgaria, states which could hardly rival Italy and France. Second, the sphere-of-influence formula agreed upon between Stalin and Churchill afforded the Western Allies a small but possibly important percentage of input in some countries of Eastern Europe, which the Soviets did not enjoy anywhere in Western Europe. With regard to their prospects for influence in the post-war reorganization of Europe, then, the situation of the Americans and the British did not look bad at all toward the end of 1944. And yet, there were also reasons for concern.

After Market Garden it had become obvious that the war in Europe was far from over. A considerable part of the continent still awaited liberation, and Nazi Germany itself had yet to be conquered. In the meantime, it was evident that Poland would be liberated in its entirety by the Soviets, a prospect that alarmed many Poles, in particular the conservative and strongly anti-Soviet Polish government-in-exile in London. This government, incidentally, did not consist of devoted democrats, as is too often taken for granted, but represented the autocratic Polish regime of the pre-war period, a regime that had connived with Hitler himself and that on the occasion of the Munich Pact had followed his example by pocketing a piece of Czechoslovakia.[1] Furthermore, by the start of 1945 at the latest it was as good as certain that the prestige of marching victoriously into Berlin would fall to the Red Army, and not to American or British troops. The advance of the British-Americans in the direction of the German capital was first checked in the Netherlands at the time of Market Garden and was strongly impeded again between December 1944 and January 1945 by Field Marshal von Rundstedt's unexpected counteroffensive in the Ardennes. The latter episode was destined to enter the American collective consciousness as well as American history books as a gigantic and heroic clash, the Battle of the Bulge, and was celebrated in due course in an eponymous Hollywood production. In reality, however, the confrontation in the Ardennes represented a serious setback for the Americans. Von Rundstedt's counteroffensive did eventually end in failure, but initially the German pressure was considerable. The Americans battled back heroically on many occasions, for example at Bastogne, but there were also cases of panic and confusion, and the danger would not be fully averted before the end of January 1945.[2]

It was therefore decided to call once again on the useful Soviet partner. Responding to an urgent American request, the Red Army unleashed a major offensive in Poland on January 12, 1945, one week earlier than originally planned. Forced to face a new threat in the east, the Wehrmacht had to divert resources from its project in the Ardennes, thus relieving the pressure on the Americans. But on the Eastern Front the Germans could not stop the Soviet steamroller, which forged ahead so quickly that in a few weeks it reached the banks of the Oder. In early February, the Soviets arrived in Frankfurt-on-the-Oder, a town situated less than one hundred kilometres from the German capital. The Americans had reason to be grateful for the military favour rendered by Moscow, but they were far from happy that in the undeclared inter-Allied race to Berlin the Soviets had thus taken a huge lead over their Western partners, who had not even reached the banks of the Rhine and were still separated from Berlin by more than 500 kilometres.[3]

Already after the failure of Market Garden, it became apparent to the American and British leaders that they would lose the race to Berlin and that the Red Army would eventually control the lion's share of German territory, so that in keeping with precedents set by the liberators in Italy and elsewhere, the Soviets would be able to impose their will on post-war Germany. This produced much pessimism, and doomsayers like General MacArthur, who opined in November 1944 that all of Europe would inevitably fall under Soviet hegemony, undoubtedly gained additional credibility at the time of the setback suffered in the Battle of the Bulge.[4] It was true that if military developments alone would be allowed to determine things, the eventual outcome would be very unfavourable to the Western Allies. However, the end result might be different if the Soviets could be talked into agreements which would be binding regardless of military developments.[5] Precisely this is what the British and the Americans hoped to achieve in a series of meetings with Soviet representatives in London in the fall of 1944. They proposed to divide Germany into three roughly equal occupation zones regardless of the position of each ally's army at the end of the hostilities. (A fourth occupation zone would be assigned to the French much later.) This arrangement was clearly in their own interest, but Stalin accepted the Western proposal. It was a major success for the British-Americans, which must have dumbfounded pessimists such as MacArthur. "In brief," writes Kolko, "the Russians agreed not to run Germany unilaterally despite every indication of an imminent military victory that would permit them to do so."[6]

An additional unexpected bonus for the Western Allies turned out to be the fact that the Soviets also agreed that the capital, Berlin, like Germany as a whole, would be divided into three occupation zones, even though it was obvious that the Red Army would take the city and that Berlin would be situated deep in the occupation zone assigned to the USSR. That a "West Berlin" could later exist in the heart of East Germany was due to the accommodating attitude displayed by Stalin in the fall of 1944 and again during the winter of 1944-45. Indeed, the London Agreements regarding the future occupation zones in Germany, and the agreements reached by the Big Three (Roosevelt, Churchill and Stalin) at the Yalta Conference between February 4 and 11, 1945, can be properly understood only from the perspective of the conundrum of the Western Allies at the time of the setbacks of their own armed forces and the simultaneous successes of the Red Army in 1944-45.

It has often been said that in the Crimean resort of Yalta the shrewd Stalin managed to dupe his Western colleagues, and above all President Roosevelt, who was already a very sick man at the time. Nothing could be further from the truth. First of all, it was the British and Americans who had nothing to lose, and everything to gain, from such a meeting. The reverse applied to the Soviets, who might arguably have been better off without this conference. Indeed, the Red Army's spectacular advance deep into the German heartland put more and more trumps into Stalin's hands. On the eve of the conference General Zhukov stood on the banks of the Oder River, a mere stone's throw from Berlin. This is why Washington and London, and not Moscow, insisted on a meeting of the Allied leaders. Precisely because they were so desperate to meet Stalin in order to reach binding agreements, Roosevelt and Churchill also proved willing to accept his precondition for a conference, namely, that it be held in the USSR. The American and British leaders had to undertake an inconveniently long voyage, allowing the Soviets a kind of "home-game advantage" during the tug-of-war that the conference promised to be. But these were minor imperfections compared to the advantages that a conference might bring and compared to the huge disadvantages certain to be associated with the anticipated occupation of most of Germany by the Red Army. Stalin had not needed or wanted a meeting of the Big Three at this stage of the war. However, as we will soon see, he had reasons of his own for agreeing to hold such a conference, from which he of course also expected to derive certain advantages for the Soviet side, and he also had good reasons to reveal himself accommodating vis-à-vis his Western partners.[7]

Second, the agreements which eventually resulted from the Yalta Conference were indeed favourable to the Western Allies. Roosevelt's secretary of state, Edward Stettinius, who was present at the Crimean resort, later wrote that in this conference "the Soviet Union made more concessions to the [west] than were made to the Soviet Union."[8] And the American historian Carolyn Woods Eisenberg emphasizes in a relatively recent book that the US delegation left Yalta "in an exultant spirit," convinced that thanks to the reasonableness of the Soviets not only the Americans but mankind in its entirety had "won the first great victory of the peace."[9]

With regard to Germany, the London Agreements were officially confirmed in Yalta by the Big Three. As mentioned, the division of Germany into occupation zones was advantageous to the Americans and the British, because already in the fall of 1944 and even more so at the time of the Yalta Conference it appeared likely that the Red Army, which stood in Frankfurt-on-the-Oder in the east, might find itself in Frankfurt-on-the-Main in the West when the hostilities came to a conclusion. Furthermore, the British and Americans were assigned the bigger and richer western part of Germany; more will have to be said about this later on. It was also agreed in principle on the Crimean peninsula that after the war Germany would have to make reparation payments, as had been the case after the First World War. Both Roosevelt and Churchill found it justified and reasonable that half of these payments, then roughly estimated at 20 billion dollars, would go to the Soviet Union, where the Nazi vandals had conducted themselves in a particularly barbarous and destructive manner. (The amount of 10 billion dollars assigned to the USSR has been considered by some to be too high. In reality it was "very moderate," as the German historian Wilfried Loth has put it. A few years after the Yalta Conference, in 1947, the total war damage suffered by the Soviet Union was conservatively calculated at no less than 128 billion dollars.) To Stalin the issue of reparation payments was crucially important. It is very likely that he revealed himself to be so accommodating toward his Western partners regarding the division of Germany into occupation zones because he craved their cooperation in the matter of reparations.[10] Conversely, in order to obtain the Soviet leader's ratification of Germany's division into occupation zones and his acceptance of other arrangements that were advantageous to themselves, the Americans and the British also indulged Stalin in some respects. In return for Stalin's renewed commitment to eventually declare war on Japan, for example, Roosevelt offered American assent to the Soviet recuperation of

Far Eastern territories that czarist Russia had lost as a result of the Russian-Japanese War of 1904-05.[11]

No definitive decisions for Germany's future were arrived at in Yalta, even though particularly the Americans, and to a certain extent also the Soviets, showed some interest at the time in the widely publicized plan of the American secretary of the treasury, Henry Morgenthau. Morgenthau reportedly proposed to solve the "German problem" by simply dismantling the country's industry, thereby transforming Germany into a backward, poor, and therefore harmless agrarian state. In reality, this plan amounted to not much more than a rather vague and incoherent series of proposals, far less draconian than its opponents claimed and many Germans still believe. [12]

What was not properly realized at the time, neither in Washington nor in Moscow, was that not only major moral but also serious practical objections could be raised against the Morgenthau Plan. For example, the plan could hardly be reconciled with the expectation that Germany was to pay huge reparations; this presupposed a certain measure of wealth, and for such wealth there was no room in Morgenthau's scenario. "The logical inference of the Morgenthau Plan," writes the German historian Jörg Fisch categorically, "was that there could be no question of reparations payments."[13] Moreover, as the American historian Carolyn Woods Eisenberg points out, Morgenthau's plans for a "pastoralization" of Germany were totally "out of step with the thinking of the most important US . . . policymakers," who had good reasons for favouring the alternative option, "the economic reconstruction of Germany." Certain American politicians feared that the Plan would drive Germany into the arms of anarchy, chaos, and possibly Bolshevism. Businessmen realized that one would not be able to do any profitable business with a poor Germany. And influential Americans worried about the possibly extremely negative implications of the Morgenthau Plan regarding the fate of Opel and other German subsidiaries of American corporations. It was not a coincidence that precisely the representatives of firms with huge investments in Germany — such as Alfred P. Sloan, the influential chairman of the board of GM, the parent firm of Opel — were most categorically opposed to the Morgenthau Plan. (The Soviet ambassador to the US, Andrei Gromyko, was not far off the mark when he remarked that the opposition against the Morgenthau Plan was spearheaded by America's "imperialist circles.") The Plan would thus gradually and quietly disappear from the scene during the months that followed the Yalta Conference. Morgenthau himself, a good friend of Roosevelt, would be dismissed from his high-ranking government position on July 5, 1945, by the new president, Truman.[14]

From the perspective of the Western Allies, then, the sometimes vaguely formulated agreements concluded in Yalta with regard to Germany were important and advantageous. In addition, Stalin was prepared to discuss the future of the Eastern European countries liberated by the Red Army, such as Poland, even though the Big Three had never discussed the post-war fate of Western European countries such as France, Italy, and Belgium. Stalin had no illusions with regard to Western Europe, and he did not want to jeopardize the relationship with his British and American allies for the sake of countries that happened to be far away from the borders of the Soviet Union, the "socialist fatherland" whose survival and security had obsessed him since the beginning of his career. With respect to Eastern Europe in general, however, and with Poland in particular, the situation was very different. The Soviet Union was keenly interested in the post-war makeup of neighbouring countries whose governments had formerly been unfriendly and sometimes totally hostile to the USSR, and whose terri-tories formed the traditional invasion road to Moscow. As for the postwar reorganization of Poland and other countries of Eastern Europe, Stalin had good reasons and, in the form of the Red Army's presence in these coun-tries, effective means to demand for the Soviet Union at least the same kind of input that the Americans and the British had permitted themselves in Western Europe. Stalin had not challenged the Western Allies' modus oper-andi in Western Europe; it may be supposed that he felt that it was now the turn of his Western partners to give him a free hand in Eastern Europe.[15]

In spite of all this, however, in Yalta Stalin was prepared to discuss the fate of Poland and the rest of Eastern Europe, even though the topic of Western Europe remained unmentioned. In addition, the actual Soviet demands turned out to be minimal and far from unreasonable, as Churchill and Roosevelt could hardly deny: the so-called Curzon Line should form the border between Poland and the Soviet Union (for which Poland would receive compensation in the form of German territory to the east of a line formed by the Oder and Neisse rivers) and no anti-Soviet regimes would be tolerated in Poland and other neighbouring states.[16] In return for their agreement to these demands, the Americans and the British received from Stalin what they wanted in the liberated countries of Eastern Europe, namely, no social and economic changes along communistic lines, free elections, and continuing input for themselves — together with the USSR, of course — in the future affairs of these countries. This kind of formula was far from unrealistic, and variations of it were to be implemented successfully after the war in Finland and Austria. The Yalta Agreements, then, did not award the Soviet Union the monopoly of influence in Eastern Europe, that is, the kind of exclusive influence that the Americans and the British already enjoyed, with Stalin's silent approval, in Western Europe, even though they assigned "controlling influence" in Eastern Europe to the USSR.

The Yalta Agreements thus represented a considerable success for the Western Allies. It has often been said of Churchill that he had grave misgivings about the "concessions" that Roosevelt allegedly had made in the Crimean resort. In reality he was totally euphoric when the conference ended,[17] and with good reason, since the British and Americans had fared far better at Yalta than they would have dared to hope when it started. The allegation that in the Crimean resort the shrewd Stalin wrung all sorts of concessions from his Western colleagues is therefore totally false. It is true that afterwards the Yalta Agreements would not be properly implemented, for example with regard to Poland and the rest of Eastern Europe. This had a lot to do with Stalin's reaction to America's "atomic diplomacy" of the summer of 1945, which will be analyzed later, but also with the irreconcilable, and totally unrealistic, anti-Soviet attitude of the Polish government-in-exile in London. The London Poles did not even want to recognize the Curzon Line as the future eastern border of their country, which had been acknowledged by Roosevelt and Churchill as both fair and inevitable, and which had been officially accepted in Yalta.[18] Owing to the intractability of the London Poles, Stalin increasingly played the card of a communist and pro-Soviet Polish government-in-exile, the "Lublin Poles," and this would eventually lead to the installation of an exclusively communist regime in Warsaw. The Americans, like the British, would complain loudly about this, but their protest was hardly reconcilable with the uncontested fact that after the war they themselves would install or support dictatorial regimes in many countries, such as Greece, Turkey, and China, and that in those dictatorial client states they never insisted on the kind of free elections that they urged Stalin to organize in Poland and elsewhere in Eastern Europe.

Stalin was a realist. On the occasion of the London Agreements and the Yalta Conference he proved to be accommodating vis-à-vis Churchill and Roosevelt not because he wanted to be so, but because he correctly calculated that he could hardly afford not to be. The war in which the USSR had suffered grievously and had just barely escaped total destruction was not yet over. The Soviets' military situation in early 1945 was excellent, of course, but all sorts of disagreeable things could still come to pass. As the end approached for the Third Reich, for example, the propaganda machine of Goebbels aggressively pursued an ultimate rescue scenario for the Nazi state, namely, the project of a separate armistice between Germany and the Western Allies, followed by a common crusade against the Bolshevik Soviet Union. This plan was not nearly as naive and unrealistic as one might assume, because Goebbels knew only too well that leading circles in Great Britain and virtually everywhere else in the Western world had considered Bolshevism as the "natural" enemy, and simultaneously viewed Nazi Germany as the spearhead in the coming anti-Soviet crusade. The Nazi propaganda minister was also keenly aware that during the war quite a few Western leaders found the Soviets a useful ally but continued to despise the communist state and were determined to eliminate it sooner or later.

As for the USSR, all this meant that after years of superhuman efforts and huge losses, when victory seemed tantalizingly near, the order of the day continued to be survival — the survival of the country and the survival of "socialism in one country," which had always been Stalin's great obsession. The Soviet leader worried about Goebbels' scenario, and not without reason. In the camp of the Western Allies a number of leading personalities, generals as well as statesmen, found this scenario quite attractive. After the war some of them would openly express regret that the American and British armies had not continued to march eastward in 1945, preferably all the way to Moscow. Churchill himself flirted with the thought of this kind of initiative, which was known as the "German alternative" or the

"German option."Stalin harboured no illusions with respect to the true Western feelings for the Soviet Union. His diplomats and spies kept him well-informed about opinions and developments in London, Washington, and elsewhere. For the Soviet leader, who remembered the historical precedent of the Allied intervention in the Russian Civil War, the possibility of a reversal of alliances, a combined German-Western undertaking against the Soviet Union, was a genuine nightmare. He tried to exorcize it by not giving Churchill and Roosevelt the slightest excuse to undertake something against the USSR. Thus it becomes possible to understand why he refrained from criticizing their conduct in Western Europe and in Greece, and why he revealed himself to be so accommodating at Yalta.[19]

Chapter 13
DRESDEN: A SIGNAL FOR UNCLE JOE

By the end of January 1945, the Western Allies were still recuperating from the perils of the Battle of the Bulge, and they had not yet reached, let alone crossed, the Rhine. At the same time, the Soviets were penetrating deep into Germany, had reached the Oder, and found themselves within striking distance of Berlin. This situation caused some discomfort to Churchill and Roosevelt, who were about to leave for Yalta and could have no idea that at that conference Stalin would turn out to be a complaisant host. Considering the spectacular recent successes of the Red Army, they probably expected him to be cocky and difficult to deal with. In order to bring him down to earth somewhat and thus to make him more manageable at Yalta, the British and American leaders were eager to make it clear to him that in spite of recent setbacks their military prowess was not to be underestimated. The Red Army admittedly disposed of huge masses of infantry, excellent tanks, and a potent artillery. The Western Allies, however, held in their hands a military trump for which the Soviets had no equivalent, a trump that enabled the Americans and the British to strike a devastating blow even at a great distance from their own lines. That trump was their air force, the most impressive fleet of bombers the world had ever seen. Washington and London wanted to ensure that Stalin was aware of this.

During the night of February 13-14, 1945, which happened to be the night between Shrove Tuesday and Ash Wednesday, Dresden, the capital of Saxony and a famous art city, was attacked by RAF bombers not once, but twice. And the next morning, the city was raided by a fleet of American air force bombers. The consequences of this triple raid, which involved a total of well over 1,000 bombers, were catastrophic. The historical nucleus of the "Florence on the Elbe River" was incinerated. Particularly devastating was the fact that the intensive use by the RAF of incendiary bombs — allegedly a total of 750,000 — intentionally triggered a "firestorm," described by the British journalist and historian Phillip Knightley as

> *an artificial tornado, whereby the air gets sucked faster and faster into the fire. In Dresden, winds of more than 150 kilometres per hour drove people and rubble into a flaming oven with temperatures of more than one-thousand degrees centigrade. The flames devoured all organic matter, anything that could burn. Thousands of people died — burned, incinerated, asphyxiated.*[1]

A huge number of city residents as well as refugees, of whom tens of thousands happened to be in Dresden, lost their lives. Precise information about the casualties is not available; we do not know exactly how many people lost their life in the flames that night. In the past, huge figures tended to be cited, some as high as 300,000. The comparatively low figure of approximately 30,000 dead has often been mentioned, but it appears to refer to identified bodies, a small fraction of the total number of victims, which according to a secret report of the local police may have been somewhere between 200,000 and a quarter of a million. For many reasons we will probably never know the exact number. However, the majority of those who are considered experts in the matter now seem to agree on a minimum of 25,000 and a maximum of 40,000.[2] These statistics really do not matter all that much. It suffices to know that in Dresden a huge number of people died a terrible death.

The death and destruction inflicted on the city are generally believed to have been senseless. The main raison for that is that the beautiful "Florence on the Elbe" was an industrially and militarily unimportant city, and therefore not a target worthy of the considerable common American and British effort involved in the raid. From a military and strategic standpoint,

Dresden with its "marginal war industries, [which] were not even targeted" was too insignificant an objective to justify such an inordinate American-British undertaking, was the conclusion reached by the American historian Michael S. Sherry, writing in the late 1980s.[3] Neither did the attack on Dresden make sense as retribution for earlier German bombing raids on cities such as Rotterdam and Coventry. For the destruction of these cities, which had been bombed ruthlessly by the Luftwaffe in 1940, Berlin, Hamburg, Cologne, and countless other German towns big and small had already paid dearly in 1942, 1943, and 1944. By the beginning of 1945, the British and American commanders also knew perfectly well that even the most ferocious bombing raid would not succeed in "terrorizing [the Germans] into submission,"[4] so it is not realistic to ascribe this motive to the planners of the operation. The bombing of Dresden, then, seems to have been a senseless slaughter.

In recent years, however, the bombing of countries and of cities has become a regular occurrence, rationalized not only by our political leaders but also presented to us by our media as an effective military undertaking and as a perfectly legitimate means to achieve supposedly noble objectives. In this context it has been easier for certain historians to claim that the bombing of cities during World War II was also justified and effective. In his book *Why the Allies Won*, published in 1995, for example, Richard Overy argued against hitherto prevailing opinion that bombing played a significant role in the defeat of Nazi Germany.[5] In this new climate, even the terrible attack on Dresden has been rehabilitated. In *Dresden: Tuesday, February 13, 1945*, published in 2004, the British historian Frederick Taylor argued, first, that the huge destruction wreaked in the Saxon capital had not been intended by the planners of the attack but was the unexpected result of a combination of unfortunate circumstances. These included the increasing effectiveness of the strategy of "area bombing," developed by the British Bomber Command under the leadership of Arthur Harris — a.k.a. Bomber Harris — in response to earlier German air attacks on Britain; the perfect weather conditions; and the city's hopelessly inadequate defences against (and preparations for) air attacks. While many earlier air raids on German cities had caused less damage than expected, the raid on Dresden happened to cause much more damage than expected. At least, this is the way Taylor sees things, and he concludes that Dresden was the attack in "which every-thing went horribly right."[6] In addition, against the conventional view, Taylor argues that Dresden did constitute a legitimate target, since it was not only an important military centre but also a first-rate turntable for rail traffic as well as a major industrial city, where countless factories and work-shops produced all sorts of militarily important equipment.

Taylor's claim that the degree of destruction was greater than expected, however, is contradicted by a fact that he himself refers to in his book, namely, that approximately forty "heavies" of the USAAF strayed from the flight path and ended up dropping their bombs on Prague instead of Dresden.[7] If everything had gone according to plan, then, the destruction in Dresden would surely have been even bigger than it already was. An unusually high degree of destruction was obviously intended, and that is the reason why an unusually high degree of destruction, though not quite as high as intended, was in fact achieved.

More convincing seems to be Taylor's argument that Dresden was an important nodal point of railway lines, and that the city contained cer-tain military installations as well as numerous factories and workshops which produced weapons and other military materiel, making Dresden a worthwhile and legitimate target for a major air raid. However, a string of facts indicate that the presence in the city of all sorts of things worth bombing hardly played a role in the calculations of the planners of the raid. First, the only truly significant military installation, the Luftwaffe airfield a few kilometres to the north of the city, was not attacked at all during the raid. Second, the presumably crucially important railway sta-tion was not marked as a target — with green flares called "Christmas trees" by the German population — by the British pathfinder aircraft that preceded the bombers. The crews were instructed to drop their bombs on the inner city, situated to the north of the railway station. Consequently, even though countless people perished in it, the station suffered relatively little structural damage — so little, in fact, that it was again able to handle trains transporting troops within days of the bombing. Third, the great majority of Dresden's militarily important industries were not located downtown but in the suburbs, where no bombs were dropped, at least not deliberately.[8]

It cannot be denied that Dresden, like any other major German city, contained militarily important industrial installations, and that at least some of these installations were located in the inner city and were therefore wiped out in the raid. But this does not logically lead to the conclusion that the attack was planned for this purpose. Hospitals and churches were also destroyed, but nobody argues that the raid was organized to bring that about. A number of Jews and members of Germany's anti-Nazi resistance, awaiting deportation and/or execution, were able to escape from prison during the chaos caused by the bombing,[9] but no one claims that this was the objective of the raid. Finally, numerous Allied POWs who happened to be in the city at the time were killed in Dresden on February 13–14, 1945, but would anybody want to suggest that this is why the city was obliterated? There is no logical reason, then, to conclude that the destruction of an unknown number of industrial installations, of greater or lesser military importance, was the *raison d'être* of the raid, that — like the liberation of a handful of Jews and German anti-Nazis — this destruction was anything more than an unplanned spin-off of the operation.

An explanation frequently offered by historians, including Taylor, echoes what was already said to the RAF and USAAF crews who were sent on the mission to Dresden — that the bombing of the Saxon capital was intended to facilitate the advance of the Red Army. It is alleged that the Soviets asked their Western partners during the Yalta Conference (February 4–11, 1945) to weaken the German resistance along the Eastern Front by means of air raids and thus to enable the Red Army to advance more easily into the heart of Germany. However, there is no evidence whatsoever that confirms such allegations. The possibility of Anglo-American air raids on targets in eastern Germany was indeed discussed at Yalta, but during these talks the Soviets expressed the concern that their own lines might be hit by the bombers, so they requested that the RAF and USAAF not operate too far to the east.[10] (The Soviets' fear of being hit by what is now called "friendly fire" was not unwarranted, as was demonstrated during the raid on Dresden itself, when, as we already know, a considerable number of planes went astray and bombed Prague, situated about as far from Dresden as the Red Army lines.) It was in this context that a Soviet general by the name of Antonov showed a general interest in "air attacks that would impede enemy movements," but this can hardly be interpreted as a request to mete out to the Saxon capital — which he did not mention at all — or to any other German city, the kind of treatment that Dresden received on February 13–14. Neither in Yalta, nor on any other occasion, did the Soviets ask their Western allies for the kind of air support that presumably materialized in the form of the obliteration of Dresden. Moreover, they never gave their approval to the plan to bomb Dresden, as is often claimed.[11] It should also be noted that the Soviets did not provide their Western allies with precise information about the direction of their troop movements, so that it would not have been easy to know which cities to bomb in order to facilitate their advance.

The Soviets did not ask for Dresden to be bombed. In addition, the question should be asked whether, even *if* Moscow would have asked for such assistance at Yalta, the political and military authorities in London and Washington would have responded immediately — Dresden was bombed only days after the end of the Crimean Conference — by unleashing the unusually mighty fleet of bombers that happened to raid Dresden. The answer to this question is undoubtedly negative. The Americans, British, and Canadians had not yet crossed the Rhine, and their lines were still separated from Berlin by more than 500 kilometres. On the Eastern Front, meanwhile, the Red Army had launched a major offensive on January 12 and advanced rapidly to the banks of the Oder River, in some places reaching locations within 100 kilometres of the centre of the German capital. The resulting virtual certainty that the Soviets would not only take Berlin but penetrate deep into Germany's western half before the war ended greatly perturbed many American and British military and political leaders. Is it realistic to believe that, under those circumstances, Washington and London would have been eager to enable the Soviets to achieve even greater progress? Even if Stalin had asked for Anglo-American assistance from the air, Churchill and Roosevelt would undoubtedly have concocted an excuse for *not* providing it. They might have provided some token assistance, but they would never have launched the massive and unprecedented combined RAF-USAAF operation that the bombing of Dresden revealed itself to be.

Moreover, attacking Dresden required hundreds of big bombers to fly more than 2,000 kilometres through enemy airspace in order to approach the lines of the Red Army so closely that they would run the risk of being fired at by Soviet anti-aircraft artillery or, conversely, that they might have dropped their bombs on the Soviets. Could Churchill or Roosevelt be expected to invest such huge human and material resources, and to run such risks, in an operation that would make it easier for the Red Army to take Berlin and possibly reach the Rhine before they got there? Absolutely not. The American-British political and military leaders were undoubtedly of the opinion that the Red Army was already advancing fast enough.

The bombing of Dresden was planned before the Yalta Conference, where, it was believed, the Soviet leader would be cocky and difficult to deal with. It is in this context that a demonstration of the military might of the Western Allies, and especially of the might of their air forces, was perceived to be useful. It was felt that Stalin had to know that the Americans and British held in their hands a military trump which the Soviets were unable to match: the most impressive collection of bombers the world had ever seen — a weapon that made it possible to launch devastating strikes even on the most distant targets. If Stalin could be made aware of this, would he not prove easier to deal with during — and after — the meeting at Yalta?

It was Churchill who decided that the total obliteration of a German city, under the noses of the Soviets, so to speak, would send the desired message to the Kremlin. The RAF and USAAF had been able for quite some time already to strike a devastating blow against any German city, and detailed plans for such an operation, known as "Operation Thunderclap," had been meticulously prepared. However, during the summer of 1944, at the latest, when the rapid advance from Normandy made it seem likely that the war would be concluded victoriously before the end of the year, and thoughts were therefore turning to postwar reconstruction, a Thunderclap-style operation had started to loom useful as a way to intimidate the Soviets. In August 1944, an RAF memorandum thus pointed out that

> *a spectacular and final object lesson to the German people…*
> *would be of continuing value in the postwar period…The*
> *total devastation of the centre of a vast city…would offer*
> *incontrovertible proof to all peoples of the power of a modern*
> *air force…[It] would convince the Russian allies…of the*
> *effectiveness of Anglo-American air power.*[12]

For the purpose of defeating Germany, Thunderclap was no longer considered necessary by early 1945. However, toward the end of January 1945, i.e., while preparing to travel to Yalta, Churchill suddenly showed great interest in this project, insisted that it be carried out *tout de suite*, and specifically ordered Bomber Harris to wipe out a city in Germany's east, in other words, a city in the line of advance of the Red Army.[13] A string of cities qualified, but in the end Dresden was chosen, probably by Churchill himself. Indeed, on January 25 the British prime minister indicated where he wanted the Germans to be "blasted," namely, somewhere "in their [westward] retreat from Breslau [now Wroclaw in Poland]."[14] In terms of urban centres, this was tantamount to spelling D-R-E-S-D-E-N.

That Churchill himself was behind the decision to bomb a city in Germany's east, which ended up being the capital of Saxony, is also hinted at in the autobiography of Bomber Harris, who wrote that "the attack on Dresden was at the time considered a military necessity by much more important people than myself."[15] It is obvious that only personalities of Churchill's calibre were able to impose their will on the czar of strategic bombing. As the British military historian Alexander McKee has written, Churchill "intended to write [a] lesson on the night sky [of Dresden]" for the benefit of the Soviets. However, since the USAAF also ended up being involved in the bombing of Dresden, we may assume that Churchill acted with the knowledge and approval of Roosevelt. Churchill's partners at the top of the United States' political as well as military hierarchy, including General Marshall, shared his viewpoint; they too were fascinated, as McKee writes, by the idea of "intimidating the [Soviet] communists by terroris-ing the Nazis."[16] The American participation in the Dresden raid was not really necessary, because the RAF was undoubtedly capable of wiping out Dresden in a solo performance. But the "overkill" effect resulting from an intrinsically redundant American contribution was perfectly functional for the purpose of demonstrating — to the Soviets — the lethality of Anglo-American air power. It is also likely that Churchill did not want the respon-sibility for what he knew would be a terrible slaughter to be exclusively British; it was a "crime" for which he needed a "partner."

A Thunderclap–style operation — large-scale by definition — would of course do damage to whatever military and industrial installations and communications infrastructure were housed in the targeted city, and would therefore inevitably amount to yet another blow to the already tottering German enemy. But when such an operation was finally launched, with Dresden as the target, it was done far less in order to speed up the defeat of the Nazi enemy than in order to intimidate the Soviets. Using the terminology of the functional analysis school of American sociology, hitting the Germans as hard as possible was the "manifest function" of the operation, while intimidating the Soviets was its far more important "latent" or "hidden" function. The massive destruction inflicted on Dresden was not the result of an unfortunate combination of circumstances. It was planned — in other words, was "functional" — not for the purpose of striking a devastating blow to the German enemy, but for the purpose of demonstrating to the Soviets that their Western allies had a weapon which the Red Army, no matter how mighty and successful against the Germans, could not match, and against which it had no adequate defences.

Many American and British generals and high-ranking officers were undoubtedly aware of the latent function of the destruction of Dresden, and approved such an undertaking. And this knowledge also reached the local commanders of the RAF and USAAF as well as the "master bombers." (After the war, two master bombers claimed to remember that they had been told clearly that this attack was intended "to impress the Soviets with the hitting power of our Bomber Command.")[17] But the Soviets, who had hitherto made the biggest contribution to the war against Nazi Germany, and who had thereby not only suffered the biggest losses but also scored the most spectacular successes, e.g., in Stalingrad, enjoyed much sympathy among low-ranking American and British military personnel, including bomber crews. This constituency would certainly have disapproved of any kind of plan to intimidate the Soviets, and most certainly of a plan — the obliteration of a German city from the air — in which they would have to participate. It was therefore necessary to camouflage the objective of the operation behind an official rationale. In other words, because the latent function of the raid was "unspeakable," a "speakable" manifest function had to be concocted.And so the regional commanders and master bombers were instructed to formulate other, and hopefully credible, objectives for the benefit of their crews. In view of this, we can understand why the instructions to the crews with respect to the objectives differed from unit to unit and were often fanciful and even contradictory. The majority of the commanders emphasized military objectives and cited undefined "military targets," hypothetical "vital ammunition factories" and "dumps of weapons and supplies," Dresden's alleged role as "fortified city," and even the existence in the city of some "German army headquarters." Vague references were also frequently made to "important industrial installations" and "marshalling yards." In order to explain to the crews why the historical city centre — rather than the industrial suburbs — was targeted, some commanders talked about the existence there of a "Gestapo headquarters" and of "a gigantic poison gas factory." Some speakers were either unable to invent such imaginary targets or were for some reason unwilling to do so; they laconically told their men that the bombs were to be dropped on "the built-up city centre of Dresden," or "on Dresden" *tout court.*[18]

To destroy the centre of a German city, hoping to cause as much damage as possible on military and industrial installations and on communications infrastructure, happened to be the essence of the Allied, or at least Britsh, strategy of "area bombing."[19] The crew members had learned to accept this nasty fact of life, or rather of death, but in the case of Dresden many of them felt ill at ease. They questioned the instructions with respect to the objectives, and had the feeling that this raid involved something unusual and suspicious, that this mission was certainly not a "routine" affair, as Taylor presents things in his book.[20] The radio operator of a B-17, for example, declared in a confidential communication that "this was the only time" that "[he] (and others) felt that the mission was unusual."[21] The anxiety experienced by the crews was also illustrated by the fact that in many cases a commander's briefing did not trigger the crews' traditional cheers but was met with icy silence.[22]

Directly or indirectly, intentionally or unintentionally, the instructions and briefings addressed to the crews sometimes revealed the true function of the attack. A directive of the RAF to the crews of a number of bomber groups, for example, dated on the day of the attack, February 13, 1945, unequivocally stated that it was the intention "at the same time to show the Russians, when they reach the city, what our Bomber Command is capable of doing."[23] Under these circumstances, it is hardly surprising that many crew members understood clearly that they had to wipe Dresden from the map in order to scare the Soviets. A Canadian member of a bomber crew, for example, replied as follows when, many years after the war, he was questioned by an oral historian about the goal of this mission:

> What really happened, I think, is the following: The Russians made very good progress, and the [Western] Allies decided that they would show the Russians that we not only had a mighty army, but also a fantastic air force. This way it was made clear to the Russians that they had to behave themselves, otherwise we would show them what we could also do to Russian cities. [Dresden] was an idea of men like Churchill; it was a deliberately arranged bloodbath — I have no doubt about that.[24]

The news of the particularly awful destruction of Dresden also caused great discomfort among British and American civilians, who also had much sympathy for the Soviet ally and who, upon learning the news of the raid, likewise sensed that this operation exuded something unusual and suspicious. The authorities felt the need to exorcize the public's unease, and they did so with a kind of "flight to the front." The raid was explained to the public, as it had been earlier to the crews, as an effort to facilitate the advance of the Red Army. This was done at an RAF press conference, held in liberated Paris on February 16, 1945. The journalists who attended were told that the destruction of this "communications centre" situated close to "the Russian front" had been inspired by the desire to make it possible for the Russians "to continue their struggle with success." That this was merely a rationale, concocted after the facts by what are called "spin doctors" today, was revealed by the military spokesman himself. In response to questions from journalists, who were then (in contrast to now) still capable of challenging the official version of events, he lamely acknowledged that he merely "thought" that it had "probably" been the intention to assist the Soviets.[25]

The hypothesis that the attack on Dresden aimed first and foremost to intimidate the Soviets explains not only the magnitude of the operation

— a triple raid, and an unprecedented common undertaking of the RAF and USAAF — but also the choice of target. For the planners of Thunderclap, Berlin had always seemed to be the perfect target. However, by the time Churchill revived the project, in January 1945, the German capital had already been bombed repeatedly. Could it be expected that yet another bombing raid, no matter how devastating, would have the desired effect on the Soviets when they would fight their way into the city? Destruction unleashed within 24 hours would surely loom considerably more spectacularly if a compact and "virginal," i.e., not yet bombed, city was the target. Dresden, fortunate not to have been bombed before and therefore known as "the Reich's air-raid shelter" (*Reichsluftschutzkeller*), was now unfortunate enough to meet all these criteria. Moreover, the British-American commanders expected that the Soviets would reach the Saxon capital within days, so that they would be able to see very soon with their own eyes what the RAF and the USAAF could achieve in a single operation. It was for this reason that Dresden was selected as the target. However, the Red Army was to enter Dresden much later — May 8, 1945 — than the British and the Americans had expected. In spite of this, in some ways the destruction of Dresden did have the desired effect. The Soviet lines were situated only a couple of hundred of kilometres from the city, so that the men of the Red Army could admire on the nocturnal horizon the glow of the Dresden inferno, which was allegedly visible up to a distance of three hundred kilometres.

When intimidating the Soviets is viewed as the "latent," in other words, the *real* function of the destruction of Dresden, not only the magnitude, but also the *timing* of the operation makes sense. The attack was supposed to have taken place, at least according to some historians, on February 4, 1945, but had to be postponed on account of inclement weather to the night of February 13–14.[26] February 4 was the day on which the Yalta Conference got under way. If the Dresden fireworks had taken place on that day, they might have provided Stalin with some food for thought at a critical moment. It was hoped that the Soviet leader, buoyed by the recent successes of the Red Army and enjoying the "home game advantage" vis-à-vis his Western partners, would be sobered by the ominous writing on the wall by the RAF and the USAAF, and would therefore turn

153

out to be a less confident and more agreeable interlocutor at the conference table. This expectation was clearly reflected in a comment made by
the American general David M. Schlatter, member of the SHAEF (Supreme
Headquarters Allied Expeditionary Force), one week before the start of the
Yalta Conference:

> I feel that our air forces are the blue chips with which we will
> approach the post-war treaty table, and that this operation
> [the planned bombing of Dresden and/or Berlin] will add
> immeasurably to their strength, or rather to the Russian
> knowledge of their strength.[27]

The bombing had to be postponed, but it was not cancelled. This kind
of demonstration of military potency retained its psychological usefulness
even after the end of the conference on the Crimea. It was still expected
that the Soviets would soon enter Dresden and thus be able to see what
horrible destruction the Anglo-American air forces were able to inflict, on a
city far removed from their bases, in one night. Afterwards, when the vague
agreements made at Yalta would have to be put into practice, they would
surely remember what they had seen in Dresden and draw useful conclusions from their observations. Toward the end of the hostilities, American
troops had an opportunity to reach Dresden before the Soviets. Churchill
urged Eisenhower not to permit this; even at that late stage the British
prime minister apparently still wanted the Soviets to benefit from the
demonstration effect of the bombing of Dresden. Although he was eager
for the Anglo-Americans to occupy as much German territory as possible,
Churchill insisted that Dresden be occupied by the Soviets.

Dresden was not just bombed, not even just heavily bombed, but obliterated — virtually wiped off the face of the earth — in order to intimidate
the Soviets with a demonstration of the enormous firepower that permitted
the bombers of the RAF and the USAAF to unleash death and destruction
hundreds of kilometres away from their bases. All to show that, if deemed
necessary, they could do the same behind Red Army lines and in the Soviet
Union itself. The bombing of Dresden was a show of force that purported
to demonstrate that in their air force the Western Allies had a weapon

154

which the Red Army, no matter how strong and successful against the Germans, could not match, and against which it had no adequate defences.

This interpretation explains the many peculiarities of the bombing of Dresden, such as the magnitude of the operation, the unusual participation of both the RAF and the USAAF in a joint raid, the choice of the target, the (intended) enormity of the destruction, the timing of the attack, and, last but not least, the fact that the supposedly crucially important railway station and the suburbs with their factories and Luftwaffe airfield were not targeted. The bombing of the Saxon capital had little or nothing to do with the war against Nazi Germany, which was virtually over at that time. It had nothing to do with the German men, women, old folks, and children of Dresden itself or with the countless German and Eastern European refugees who had sought shelter in, or who were simply passing through, that city — but who became the victims of the operation. The destruction of Dresden was simply an American-British signal for the benefit of Uncle Joe.

During the Cold War era it was often suggested that at the end of the Second World War the Red Army was poised to overrun all of Europe, and that it would certainly have done so had the Americans and their British partner not prevented such a scenario. Nothing could be further from the truth. The Soviet Union had only survived the Nazi attack on its territory thanks to superhuman efforts and huge sacrifices. According to the most recent estimates, almost 30 million Soviet soldiers and civilians — approximately 15 per cent of the pre-war population — lost their lives during the Second World War, and much of the country was totally destroyed.[28] With their country in such condition, it would have amounted to absolute insanity for its leaders to immediately unleash a new war, a war of conquest no less, to be fought thousands of kilometres away from home base, and this against former allies whose air force alone could have done ten times as much damage to the USSR as it had done to Dresden.

Stalin was not insane. There is overwhelming evidence that the Soviet leader was keenly aware that it was already an enormous achievement for his country to have survived the Nazi aggression and to have emerged from a terrible war with an enlarged territory, as well as unprecedented influence and prestige. He understood only too well that the Red Army was no match for the combined forces of the British and the Americans with their powerful air weapon, and a little later with their nuclear bomb, so that it was far better not to antagonize them at all, but instead to seek their favour by being accommodating and by making concessions. The Americans themselves actually knew very well that militarily the Soviets constituted no real threat to themselves. In early 1945, their army's Joint Chiefs of Staff (JCS) reported that the Soviet Union had overwhelming reasons to "avoid conflict with Great Britain and the United States." The proposition that in 1945 the Soviets stood ready to overrun all of Europe is nothing but a fairy tale, one of the many fables of the lush mythology of the Cold War era.[29]

AMERICANS
will <u>always</u> fight for liberty

On this poster the Second World War was presented as a "fight for liberty," similar to the American War of Independence. In reality, the leaders of America had their own economic interests in mind. (National Archives, Washington, DC)

In the Atlantic Charter of August 14, 1941, Roosevelt and Churchill declared that the struggle against Nazi Germany was fought for the sake of "four freedoms," freedom of speech, freedom of religion, freedom from want, and freedom from fear. This poster with a sentimental illustration by Norman Rockwell was used to spread the word that this was really what the war against Nazi Germany was all about. (National Archives, Washington, DC)

OURS...to fight for

Freedom of Speech

Freedom of Worship

Freedom from Want

Freedom from Fear

America's most notorious anti-Semite was the industrialist Henry Ford, who admired Hitler, supported him financially, and inspired him with his anti-Semitic book, The International Jew, which had been published in the early twenties. A copy of the German edition, read eagerly and approvingly by Hitler, is shown here. (Wikimedia Commons)

On July 30, 1938, on the occasion of his 75th birthday, Henry Ford received the highest medal Nazi Germany could bestow on a foreigner; it was offered to him on behalf of Hitler by the German consul in Cleveland. (Detroit Free Press)

In 1918-1920 the Wilson Administration sent troops to Russia to assist the "white" troops in their fight against the "red" Bolsheviks during the Civil War. The picture shows US troops parading in Vladivostok. (National Archives, Washington, DC)

During the 1930s, Ford's German branch plant, the Ford-Werke in Cologne, made a lot of money thanks to Hitler's elimination of trade unions and his rearmament program. Hitler himself came to admire new Ford models at the 1936 Berlin Auto Show. (Informations- und Beratungsstelle für NS-Verfolgte, Cologne)

Lend-Lease supplies of all sorts of war equipment provided much-needed support to Great Britain but also helped to pull the US out of the Great Depression. Here bombers are being loaded onto a ship in an American port. (Franklin D. Roosevelt Library, Hyde Park, NY)

Ford produced thousands of airplanes, including huge Liberator-bombers like this one, in the gigantic Willow Run Factory. (Franklin D. Roosevelt Library, Hyde Park, NY)

During the war, Opel, the German branch plant of General Motors, mass-produced planes and trucks for Nazi Germany. Hitler showed his appreciation by honouring Opel in 1943 with the prestigious title of "exemplary war enterprise" (Kriegsmusterbetrieb), which was proudly announced on the front page of the firm's publication, Der Opel Kamerad. (Stadtarchiv Rüsselsheim)

Oil already played a very important role in World War II. American firms such as Standard Oil and Texaco supplied the US air force, but they also supplied Hitler with the fuel he needed to wage war against Poland, France, and the Soviet Union . . . (National Archives, Washington, DC)

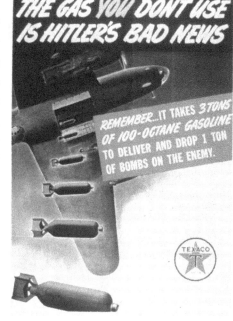

In wartime America, the Nazis and the Japanese leaders were typically portrayed as gangsters. General Motors, whose German branch plant, Opel, actively helped Hitler to wage war, financed this poster purporting to show how America was threatened by bloodthirsty villains. (National Archives, Washington, DC)

Let us hope that these two dangerous beasts, Nazism and Soviet Communism, will kill each other, was the comment of the author of this caricature in the Chicago Tribune of Decemberr 4, 1941, the very day on which the Red Army "turned the tide" of the war by counter-attacking in front of Moscow. (From Roeder, The Censored War)

Washington financed the war primarily by means of loans, and millions of Americans invested their modest savings in war bonds, which paid a handsome interest. But the war bonds mostly proved to be a lucrative form of investment for banks, insurance companies, and wealthy Americans. (National Archives, Washington, DC)

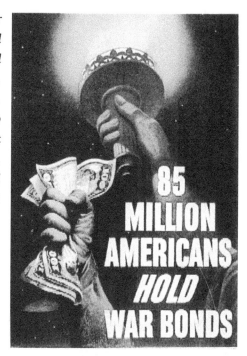

To crush America's enemies required a major industrial effort, such was the message of this poster. But this effort also pulled the country out of the economic crisis that had ravaged the country during the "dirty thirties." (National Archives, Washington, DC)

At the end of August 1944 American and French troops and resistance fighters liberated Paris. American soldiers check to make sure that it is indeed the French tricolore that is waving on top of the Eiffel Tower. (Franklin D. Roosevelt Library, Hyde Park, NY)

During the "Battle of the Bulge" in the Belgian Ardennes from December 1944 to January 1945, the Americans were temporarily pushed into the defensive. Here we see GIs in action in a snowy landscape near the town of Bastogne on December 27, 1944. (National Archives, Washington, DC)

In the night of February 13-14, 1945, Dresden was destroyed in an unprecedented combined British and American bombing raid whose main purpose was to intimidate the Soviets with a demonstration of "fire power." The picture shows piles of corpses and destroyed buildings of the city centre. (German Bundesarchiv)

In March to April 1945 the Germans virtually ceased to resist the Americans and British, whom they hoped to involve in a common "crusade" against the Soviets. The Americans were thus able to advance rapidly eastward. A tank crew takes a break in the main square of the town of Coburg. (National Archives, Washington, DC)

On the western front in March-April 1945, hundreds of thousands of Germans capitulated. British and American leaders such as Churchill and Patton dreamed of using them in a common crusade against the Red Army. Here we see German POWs in a roadside camp in the Ruhr Region. (Franklin D. Roosevelt Library, Hyde Park, NY)

On April 25, 1945, American scouts encountered a vanguard of the Red Army in the vicinity of the town of Torgau, on the banks of the Elbe River. A cordial fraternisation ensued. (National Archives, Washington, DC)

During the Potsdam Conference of July 1945, President Harry Truman finally received the news that the first atom bomb had been tested successfully at Alamogordo in New Mexico on the 16th of that month. Thus was initiated America's fateful "atomic diplomacy" vis-à-vis the Soviet Union. (National Archives, Washington, DC)

On September 2, 1945, General MacArthur accepted the official Japanese surrender on board of an American battleship. Representatives of the Soviet Union, Great Britain, and other allied countries were allowed to be present as extras, but in defeated and occupied Japan the US would not allow them any input whatsoever. (National Archives, Washington, DC)

When the war came to an end and the Red Army was no longer needed, the Soviets were proclaimed by America's leaders and media to be the new enemy. Stalin, until then the popular "Uncle Joe," is portrayed here as a student and imitator of Hitler. (St. Louis Post-Dispatch)

Chapter 14
FROM ROOSEVELT'S "SOFT LINE" TO TRUMAN'S "HARD LINE" TOWARD STALIN

Of all the British and American leaders who in early 1945 sought to intimidate Stalin by means of rumours of a possible Western deal with Nazi Germany and/or cruder stratagems, such as the bombing of Dresden, Churchill was unquestionably the *primus inter pares*. President Roosevelt went along with this policy, but on the other hand he also displayed a measure of understanding for the Soviet standpoint. Already in 1942, he had been inclined to respond positively to Stalin's urgent request for a second front in Europe. Based on his experiences at the Tehran meeting, the American president personally believed that it was possible to do business with the Soviet leader. He also understood very well what the USSR had achieved in the titanic struggle against Nazism, so that after the common victory Stalin would be entitled to more input than anybody else in the decision-making process that would determine the postwar fate of Germany and Europe. Roosevelt's attitude in this respect is often contrasted to that of his successor, Harry Truman, who would reveal himself to be a champion of the Churchillian tough line vis-à-vis Stalin. However, the obvious differences in the Soviet policies of the two American presidents were not really a function of personality, as is usually suggested in books of the "Great Men of History" genre. The main determinants were drastic changes in the circumstances of war and other developments that confronted Washington's decision-makers after Roosevelt's death, including not only the new president, but also senior advisors who had earlier helped to shape his predecessor's foreign policy and who also switched to the Churchillian hard line. They faced an entirely new situation, with totally different difficulties and opportunities. Inexorably, this new constellation of circumstances produced a new course with regard to American foreign policy in general, and with respect to American relations with the USSR in particular. How, then, did the circumstances of war change, and what were the new developments that emerged at the time of Roosevelt's death and Truman's entry into the White House?

First, until the beginning of 1945 Roosevelt worried deeply about a problem that would soon cease to dog his successor, namely, the war against Japan. We have seen that this was really the war which Roosevelt and the American power elite had wanted and even provoked. From the start, the war against Japan had been a greater concern for the American leaders than the conflict in Europe, even though Washington agreed with London that they would first settle accounts with the European enemy, Germany. In the war fought in and around the Pacific Ocean, the United States experienced serious difficulties during the months following the Japanese attack on Pearl Harbor. The Japanese had been seriously underestimated and revealed themselves to be particularly tough opponents. After Pearl Harbor they occupied Indonesia, and they even chased the Americans out of the Philippines, Uncle Sam's bridgehead in the Far East. This meant that the Americans would have to do a lot of "island-hopping" across the Pacific before the real war against Japan could begin and American hegemony could be established in the Far East, which is what, from the perspective of the US power elite, this war was all about. Japan proved a much harder nut to crack than expected, even though the main body of their land army was committed in distant China and was therefore hardly involved in battles against the Americans. The bulk of the Japanese forces was in China not only to fight the Chinese, who resisted Tokyo's continuing encroachments, Mao's communists, and Chiang Kai-Shek's nationalists, but also to guard the border of their vassal state, Manchukuo, along the far eastern reaches of the Soviet Union. Tokyo and Moscow had actually fought a brief border war there in 1939, which had not been a success from the Japanese point of view. Numerous observers believed that these hostilities might flare up again, especially since Tokyo might be tempted to take advantage of the fact that, as of the early summer of 1941, the Red Army had its hands full with the Germans. In Tokyo some political and military leaders had indeed argued for a "northern strategy" directed against the Soviet Union. However, in view of its great need for the rubber and oil of Southeast Asia, Tokyo had finally settled on a "southern strategy," involving a confrontation not with the Soviet Union but with the US. Even so, the bulk of the Japanese army continued to be based in China.

Given these unforeseen complications and difficulties, in Washington it looked as if the war against Japan could be a very costly affair that might last a long time, and this was of course a major cause of concern for Roosevelt. For the Americans it would have been extremely advantageous if the Soviet Union declared war on Japan and then attacked the Japanese army in northern China. Such a scenario had been out of the question as long as the Soviets were fighting with their backs against the wall but started to appear feasible when, in the fall of 1942, the German offensive in the direction of the Caucasian oil fields petered out and a big German army was bottled up around Stalingrad. It was then that Roosevelt let it be known to Stalin that, in return for Lend-Lease aid to the Soviets in their struggle against the Nazis, he expected that the Soviet Union would enter the war against Japan as soon as possible. However, the USSR could still hardly afford the luxury of a two-front war. Its predicament was similar to that of Japan. In December 1941 Tokyo had failed to declare war on the Soviets, as Hitler had hoped it would. The Japanese realized only too well that they would have their hands more than full in the struggle against the Americans and their allies, such as Australia, in the Pacific Ocean. Stalin could similarly ill afford to declare war on Japan as long as the Red Army was locked in a life-or-death struggle with the Nazi war machine.

As mentioned earlier, Roosevelt was pleased with the promise he received from Stalin at the Teheran Conference in 1943: the Soviet Union would declare war on Japan three months at the latest after the end of the war in Europe. However, FDR worried that Stalin might not keep his word. It was mainly in order to avoid giving the Soviet leader a pretext for not keeping his promise regarding the war against Japan that Roosevelt had been accommodating toward the Soviet leader at Yalta, promising him certain territories in the Far East. Stalin had reciprocated not only by reiterating his promise to declare war on Japan but also by ratifying the division of Germany into occupation zones.

As far as Roosevelt was concerned, then, a soft-line policy vis-à-vis Stalin appeared to pay handsome dividends. Even so, Roosevelt's goodwill toward the Soviet ally should not be overestimated. Churchill's arguments in favour of a hard line enjoyed the approval and support of a considerable number of the president's own advisors, and these arguments probably did not fail to leave an impression on him. There are two ways to entice a stubborn donkey to work: with a carrot or with a stick. Roosevelt preferred to use the carrot, but was also prepared to reach for the stick, or at least to threaten with it. America's participation in the Dresden bombing, an enterprise that could also have been carried out by the RAF alone, demonstrated that Roosevelt had no objections to the occasional use of intimidation stratagems typical of the hard line advocated by Churchill.

Roosevelt died on April 12, 1945, and was succeeded by Harry Truman, a resolute champion of the hard line with regard to Stalin. "If Truman brought anything to the White House," writes Michael Parenti, "it was an urgency 'to get tough' with the Kremlin." The new president would indeed soon openly get tough with the Soviets, but this abandonment of Roosevelt's more subtle policy toward Moscow was determined primarily by the fact that the circumstances of war as well as the options of American foreign policy had changed drastically during the couple of months which had elapsed between the Yalta Conference and Roosevelt's death.

Dialogue and cooperation with Stalin had always enjoyed the favour of the Western Allies when the Red Army made good progress and achieved territorial gains, especially when the Western Allies were not doing very well. Roosevelt's most recent preference for the soft line toward the Soviets, exemplified by the Yalta Agreements, has to be viewed in light of a series of important military successes for the Red Army and virtually simultaneous military setbacks for the British-American troops. At the time of the Yalta Conference, General Zhukov stood already at the Oder, less than one hundred kilometres from Berlin, while the Americans were still licking the wounds they had suffered during von Rundstedt's counteroffensive in the Ardennes. Afterwards, however, the Red Army made no further moves for weeks on end, as had been the case after previous major Soviet offensives.

At the time of Roosevelt's death Zhukov's troops could still be found paus-
ing on the muddy banks of the Oder.

In the meantime, the situation had changed dramatically on the Western
Front. In early February the Americans, British, and Canadians had gone
over to the offensive in the Rhineland. At first things did not go smoothly,
but then the Rhine was crossed, first by the Americans in Remagen near
Koblenz on March 7, and then by the British farther north, near the town
of Wesel, on March 23. Excellent progress was made from then on.[1] "This
is the greatest armoured joyride in history," proclaimed war correspond-
ent Hal Boyle, who accompanied US spearheads as they rolled virtually
unopposed eastward toward Berlin.[2] Indeed, on the Western Front the
German resistance was melting away like snow in the spring sunshine, as
more and more troops were transferred to the Eastern Front, where the Red
Army was expected to launch on attack on nearby Berlin at any time. By the
end of March, less than thirty German divisions were facing the Americans
and British, while more than 150 divisions were confronting the Soviets in
the east. This opened the possibility of an Allied race across Germany and
the chance for the Western powers to occupy much more German territory
than they could have dreamed of only a few months earlier. At the time of
Roosevelt's death, the Americans found themselves at the same distance
from Berlin as the Soviets, who were now finally ready to resume their own
advance.[3]

Elsewhere too it became evident that the Soviets would no longer be able
to achieve sizable territorial acquisitions. Only shortly before, it had been
feared in the West that the Red Army would also liberate Denmark, so that
after the war the Soviets might dominate Scandinavia. However, such a
scenario was prevented by an extremely rapid British advance to the Baltic
coast in the vicinity of Lübeck, made possible by the absence of serious
German resistance. Farther south the Americans registered good progress
in the direction of Pilsen and Prague in Czechoslovakia, another piece of
European real estate about which they and the British had not dared to
entertain any ambitions a few months earlier.

In the end, the Red Army was the first to enter Berlin after all. The Soviets
opened fire on the German capital on April 20. They closed the ring around
the city on April 25, the same day on which their vanguard encountered

American scouts farther southwest, in the town of Torgau on the Elbe. Berlin capitulated on May 2, 1945, but the capture of the German capital cost the Red Army no less than 100,000 men. This price was almost as high as the American losses on all European battlefields during the Second World War.[4]

Toward the end of the war in Europe, then, the strategic situation of the Western Allies, when compared with that of the Soviets, had improved drastically during a mere two months. The Red Army was admittedly ensconced in Berlin, but the Americans, the British, and their Canadian and French allies had conquered a much bigger and much more important part of Germany than they would have dared to dream of at the time of Yalta. In some areas American troops had even crossed to the east of the demarcation line between the occupation zones that had been ratified in Yalta, a demarcation line that had seemed so advantageous to the Western Allies at the time of the Crimean conference. Vanguards of the American army occupied the city of Leipzig, located in the middle of the occupation zone reserved for the Soviets.

Now that American and British troops had conquered the most important and the biggest part of Germany and had penetrated deep into Central Europe, the soft line toward Stalin suddenly enjoyed far less favour. Neither Churchill nor certain American leaders (such as General Patton) relished the idea of evacuating this territory in favour of the Soviets, and "cold warriors" would later frequently bemoan the fact that the views of these hawks had not been allowed to prevail. However, such a gross violation of the Yalta Agreements would have been counterproductive, since the Soviets would then certainly have refused to make room in Berlin for a western sector, which was to become West Berlin, likewise agreed upon at Yalta.[5] It was because of this that around the middle of June 1945, after much procrastination, President Truman reluctantly issued an order for the American troops to withdraw behind the demarcation line that would later constitute the border between West and East Germany.[6]

The brand-new American president, an unsophisticated politician from the not very cosmopolitan state of Missouri, had hitherto not been involved in the delicate negotiations of the Big Three. Furthermore, Truman had little or no understanding of the concerns and aspirations of Stalin, the leader of a country that had pulled the chestnuts out of the fire on behalf of all the allies, but which Truman, like countless other representatives of the US power elite, nonetheless despised because it was the Mecca of communism. The circumstances of war had taught Roosevelt to appreciate the advantages of the carrot in his dealings with the Soviets. The changed circumstances of war now gave Truman reasons to believe in the potential of the stick.

Truman's hand had been strengthened, and his confidence boosted, by the military successes of the American and British troops in March-April 1945, leading to the occupation of the greater part of Germany. Moreover, shortly after his arrival in the White House, the man from Missouri learned that within the foreseeable future he would probably have at his disposal an entirely new means to force the will of Washington on the Soviet Union. This was the atomic bomb, but in the spring of 1945 the A-bomb did not yet play a significant role in American diplomacy. Only during the last months of the war, that is, in the summer of 1945, would Truman be able to play the card of nuclear diplomacy.

Chapter 15
AN ANTI-SOVIET CRUSADE?

The Western Allies were mesmerized for a while by the seductive possibility of a separate armistice with Germany. Such an arrangement offered the prospect of British-American cooperation with the Germans for the purpose of chasing the Red Army out of Eastern Europe, and possibly even of wiping out the Soviet state, a thorn in the side of the capitalist world order, or at least of its leaders, since 1917. Even in mere theory, the possibility of such a reversal of alliances was useful for the Americans and the British, because it provided Stalin with some food for thought, just as the Dresden demonstration of British-American air superiority had done, and thus kept him accommodating even at the time of the greatest successes of the Red Army. The so-called German Option, the possibility of an alliance between the Americans and the British on the one side and the Germans on the other, thus constituted an important element of the hard line vis-à-vis the USSR, the "stick" for which the Americans and British increasingly opted in the spring and early summer of 1945. Furthermore, such a scenario paradoxically became more realistic during the final days of the war in Europe.

That Washington and London might make a deal *with the Nazis* was simply unthinkable. On the other hand, the American secret service, the OSS (Office of Strategic Services, predecessor of the Central Intelligence Agency or CIA) had already for some time considered the possibility that in Berlin men might come to power who, in contrast to the Nazis, would in fact be acceptable partners for the Americans and the British. This might happen by means of a *coup d'etat*, perhaps engineered by Wehrmacht generals. With such interlocutors, then, the Americans could hope to talk about things such as a German capitulation at least on the Western Front; the rapid occupation of German territory by the Western Allies after such a capitulation; the possibility that the Wehrmacht might continue to fight on the Eastern Front; and eventually also a common undertaking against the Soviets.

It was not a coincidence that the OSS was interested in such a scenario. According to the German historian Jürgen Bruhn, this secret organization was

> *socially speaking, a mixture of top managers of US indus-*
> *try, Wall Street brokers and lawyers, scientists, high-ranking*
> *military men, politicians, and so-called "defence intellectuals."*
> *The OSS obviously represented the ruling circles of America*
> *. . . The men of the OSS were still preoccupied with the job of*
> *defeating National Socialism, but they were already planning*
> *to "liquidate" the Soviet Union as a political entity or at least*
> *to reduce its influence in post-war Europe to a minimum.*[1]

The policy of the OSS was greatly influenced by a group of American businessmen, lawyers, and politicians who had already been known for their anti-Bolshevik and pro-fascist attitude long before the outbreak of the Second World War, and who continued throughout this war to cultivate close connections with "respectable" Germans via neutral countries. The OSS had thus established contact with certain German military and political leaders who constituted what has gone down in history as the anti-Nazi "opposition," even though the majority of these men had supported Hitler with great enthusiasm at the time of his triumphs. The members of this heterogeneous group had been given the code name "breakers" by Allen Dulles, the OSS agent in Switzerland. Dulles had been a partner in the New York law firm of Sullivan & Cromwell, specializing in US-German business relations. But he had given up his lucrative legal practice to join the OSS and become its agent in neutral Switzerland, whence he could and did remain in touch with his old contacts in Germany. (The head of the OSS, William Joseph — but better known as "Wild Bill" — Donovan, was also a former Wall Street lawyer with excellent German connections.)[2]

Quite a few "breakers" had invested high hopes in their own version of the American "German Option." Their scenario called for the replacement of Nazi rule by a military junta, followed by the conclusion of an anti-Soviet agreement with the Western Allies. Thus they hoped to secure for Germany as many as possible of the territorial gains achieved by Hitler in Eastern Europe. However, the contacts between the OSS and the breakers had not yet produced any concrete results and the prospects for such a German-American deal looked virtually nil after most leaders of the German opposition were eliminated by the Nazis as a result of the failed attempt on Hitler's life on July 20, 1944.[3]

After Hitler's suicide on April 30, 1945, the Americans and the British were presented with a new and possibly ultimate opportunity to find respectable partners in Germany. Nazis such as SS boss Heinrich Himmler also eagerly offered their services, but they failed to meet the crucial criterion of respectability. On the other hand, generals of the traditional aristocratic Prussian Junker type — high-ranking Wehrmacht officers such as von Rundstedt, who in the Western world have rightly or wrongly enjoyed a reputation of integrity until the present day — could perhaps have provided the Western Allies with conservative German partners, and with Prussian versions of Badoglio it might have been possible to conclude an armistice and undertake a common crusade against the Red Army. In any event, the so-called Junker Option was suddenly a realistic proposition for American policy during the final days of the war in Europe, when Hitler's successor turned out to be not another fanatical Nazi but a seemingly respectable man in uniform, Admiral Dönitz. It is not impossible that Hitler had wanted to make such a scenario possible, and had therefore chosen the admiral, and not one of the Nazi Party bonzes, as his successor.

It never did come to a monster alliance between the British-Americans and the Germans and to a common crusade against the Soviets. However, the interest displayed by Washington and London in such an undertaking was certainly not just theoretical: practical preparations were in fact undertaken — "just in case." For example, it is a fact that many captured German units were secretly kept in readiness for possible use against the Red Army. Churchill, who not without reason had a high opinion of the fighting quality of the German soldiers,[4] gave Field Marshal Montgomery an order to that effect during the last days of the war, as he was to acknowledge publicly much later, in November 1954. He arranged for Wehrmacht troops who had surrendered in northwest Germany and in Norway to retain their uniforms and even their weapons, and to remain under the command of their own officers, because he contemplated their potential use in hostilities against the Soviets. In the Netherlands, German units that had surrendered to the Canadians were even allowed to use their weapons on May 13, 1945, to execute two of their own deserters. Interned generals such as Kesselring received permission from the Americans to remain at the head of their captured troops and to move freely among their soldiers. The same unusual treatment was enjoyed in the British sector by the successor of the Führer himself. Admiral Dönitz had declared in a radio broadcast on the occasion of his inauguration that henceforth Germany wanted to wage war only against "Bolshevism." He clearly viewed himself as a potential German partner of the Western Allies against the Soviets. The British — with their weakness for Navy men — probably believed that they recognized in the admiral the kind of respectable German leader with whom anti-Soviet business could be done. In any event, Hitler's successor and his colleagues were initially treated with kid gloves by the British. Dönitz and his entourage were officially put under arrest only on May 23, 1945, two weeks after the German capitulation, and only after General Eisenhower had issued a specific order to that effect.[5]

German soldiers were kept aside with a view to their possible use against the Red Army, but that was not all. Imprisoned German officers were also instructed to write comprehensive reports about the lessons they had learned on the Eastern Front concerning warfare against the USSR. These reports featured titles such as "Battles in Russian Forests and Swamps" and "Warfare in Extreme Northern Territories." The information gleaned from such debriefings was particularly captivating for the American army command because a new version of Operation Barbarossa, Hitler's attack on the Soviet Union, was being contemplated. In order to avoid a repetition of the fiasco of the original Barbarossa, the American authorities were clearly determined to use every possible advantage. They even shamelessly used Nazi spies, such as Reinhard Gehlen, and high-ranking SS personnel, who were prepared to share their expertise in warfare against the Soviet Union with the American information services, and to put these information services into contact with Nazi agents behind the lines of the Red Army. Even many notorious war criminals (such as Josef Mengele and Klaus Barbie) were thus taken under the protection of the Americans; after being debriefed they were routinely provided with false papers and sent off to a secure new life in South or North America.[6]

This American exfiltration of all sorts of war criminals from Central and Eastern Europe — not only from Germany but also from Croatia, the Ukraine, and elsewhere, and usually by way of Italy — enjoyed the particularly active cooperation of the Vatican, which had sympathized with the fascist powers before and also during the war, and which was now eager to save the Nazis and the collaborators from whose war crimes Pope Pius XII had diplomatically averted his gaze.

However, it was extremely doubtful whether contemporary public opinion in the United States, and more particularly in the liberated countries of Europe, would have tolerated such an anti-Soviet crusade undertaken in conjunction with the Germans. The historical precedent of the anti-Bolshevik intervention in the Russian civil war directly after the First World War, for example, had to be considered. This intervention was abandoned due to a total lack of popular support in all Western countries. Moreover, from the end of 1941 onward the government as well as the American media had convinced the people that the enemy was not the Soviets but the Nazis, and that the men of the Red Army fought shoulder to shoulder with the GIs and their British comrades for justice and freedom. It is true that in the United States a silent signal would soon be given for a kind of collective brainwashing aimed at refamiliarizing the population with the opposite image, namely the pre-1941 picture in which the Soviets and not the Nazis functioned as the villain. In the spring of 1945, however, the Soviet ally still enjoyed much goodwill among the people of America, and among the American soldiers stationed in Europe and elsewhere.[7]

A Gallup poll of March 1945 thus revealed that no less than 55 per cent of Americans wanted their country to retain the USSR as an ally after the war.[8] As for the American soldiers, including the GIs in Europe who would have had to be used in a crusade against the Soviets, virtually without exception they displayed sympathy, admiration, and respect for their comrades in the Red Army. Looking back at that era, an American war veteran later echoed this sentiment:

> We were aware that the Russians had taken enormous losses
> on the eastern front, that they really had broken the back of
> the German army. We would have been in for infinitely worse
> casualties and misery had it not been for them. We were well
> disposed toward them. I remember saying if we happen to link
> up with 'em, I wouldn't hesitate to kiss 'em. I didn't hear any
> anti-Russian talk. I think we were realistic enough to know
> that if we were going to fight them, we would come out second
> best . . . In the final campaign down through Bavaria, we
> were in Patton's army. Patton said we ought to keep going [to
> Moscow]. To me, that was an unthinkable idea. The Russians
> would have slaughtered us . . . I don't think the rank of the
> GIs had any stomach for fighting the Russians. We were
> informed enough through press and newsreels to know about
> Stalingrad.[9]

The positive feelings of the GIs toward the Soviets were reflected only too clearly in the results of opinion polls to which the American political and military authorities appear to have paid much attention in the spring of 1945. Washington was very keenly aware of the mood of the population and of the army. Moreover, at the end of the war the GIs in, for example, Manilla, Honolulu, Seoul, London, Frankfurt, Paris, and Reims would make it abundantly clear by means of petitions and demonstrations — in other words, by means of the feared weapon of collective action — that they were not prepared to let themselves be used for anti-Soviet or other military undertakings in Europe or elsewhere. And stateside, the solidarity of workers with the soldiers wanting to return home was reflected in numerous strikes. Under these circumstances, then, an anti-Soviet crusade in conjunction with the Nazis, or with whoever succeeded them in Berlin, proved an impossible dream in the spring of 1945, no matter how attractive such an undertaking may have been in the eyes of certain American and British leaders.[10]

The British-American leaders revealed themselves to be fascinated by the proposals for a surrender on the Western Front only, proposals made time and again by the Germans on the condition that the Wehrmacht would be permitted to continue to fight the Soviets on the Eastern Front, which was now rapidly moving westward. Such a capitulation clearly violated inter-Allied agreements, but its potential advantages were particularly attractive for the Americans and the British. It would have meant, for example, that many more Wehrmacht units would have ended up in British or American, rather than in Soviet captivity, and would therefore have been available for possible use in a Western-German crusade against the Red Army. Such a scenario was the object of the hopes not only of Dönitz and many other German commanders, but also of numerous high-ranking officers on the side of the Western Allies, who dreamed aloud of a push toward Moscow shoulder-to-shoulder with the Wehrmacht.[11] In a telephone conversation with General Joseph T. McNarney, Eisenhower's deputy, General Patton reportedly made this statement:

> We are going to have to fight them [the Soviets] sooner or later . . . Why not do it now while our army is intact and the damn Russians can have their hindends kicked back into Russia in three months? We can do it ourselves easily with the help of the German troops we have, if we just arm them and take them with us; they hate the bastards. In ten days I can have enough incidents happen to have us at war with those sons of bitches and make it look like their fault. So much so that we will be completely justified in attacking them . . .[12]

Patton was not the only American leader who saw things that way. The American historians Russell D. Buhite and William Christopher Hamel emphasize that many other military and political leaders "had begun to consider preventive war [against the USSR] in 1945."[13]

From the perspective of the Western Allies, the Germans' offers to surrender on the Western Front were enticing even when it would not come to a common anti-Soviet crusade. While the Soviets might possibly have to fight for many extra days in order to overcome the final pockets of resistance of the Wehrmacht or the Waffen-SS, the Americans and the British could already start to recuperate from their efforts. The weaker the Soviets would emerge from the hostilities, the better for Washington and London. Even if Moscow would remain a partner, a weak partner was preferred over a strong one, because from a weak partner it would be easier to wrest concessions during the coming negotiations about delicate topics such as the modification of national borders, the Polish problem, German reparations, and so forth.

A general German surrender could not be accepted by the Americans and the British without the presence of their Soviet partner, because this would have constituted an all too blatant violation of inter-Allied agreements. On the other hand, nothing could prevent the Americans or the British from accepting "local" or "individual" — and presumably purely "military" — German capitulations, from which they could derive certain benefits. The Americans did not wait until the last days of the war to talk with the Germans about such local surrenders. As early as March 1945, for example, negotiations took place in Berne, the capital of Switzerland, between the American secret service agent Allen Dulles and the SS general (and notorious war criminal) Karl Wolff. The negotiations in Berne, authorized by Washington and known in code language as Operation Sunrise, concerned the possibility of a German capitulation on the Italian front. The Americans were seeking twin advantages, which they were understandably keen to keep secret from the Soviets, and for which Wolff expected a quid pro quo for himself from the American side in the form of immunity for his war crimes. (As commander of an SS-*Einsatzgruppe* in the Soviet Union, Wolff had been responsible for the deaths of approximately 300,000 people.) The two benefits pursued by the Americans were, first of all, that in case of a German surrender in northern Italy the influential communist partisans could be eliminated as a military and political factor with German assistance; and second, that a German capitulation would allow the American and British armies in Italy to advance rapidly in a northeastern direction in order to put a stop to the progress made by Tito's communist Yugoslav partisans in the direction of the Italian and Austrian borders.

The Soviets were eventually informed about the events in Berne, but their request to participate in the negotiations was turned down. A distrustful

Stalin protested sharply, and Roosevelt did not want to risk a confrontation with Moscow over this issue. As some doubts had already arisen concerning the usefulness of Dulles's contacts anyway, Operation Sunrise was quietly terminated. In the meantime, however, Dulles and Wolff had become good friends, and Dulles would help to ensure that after the war the SS general was hardly bothered as a result of his war crimes. The net result of the Berne initiative was that relations between the Western Allies and their Soviet partner were thoroughly spoiled. From then on the Soviets were to be particularly suspicious whenever the topic of local surrenders was raised. Even so, the British-Americans proved unable to resist the temptation of responding to such German offers behind the back of their Soviet ally. The more the end approached for the Germans, the more offers of capitulation arrived at the headquarters of the British and Americans.[14]

During the first days of May 1945, an American commander thus accepted a local surrender of the Germans on the banks of the Elbe. Its result was that the bulk of General Wenck's Twelfth Army, which had hitherto been battling the Soviets, could slip away behind the American lines. This American indulgence provided much relief for America's German enemies, who could escape Soviet captivity by the thousands, but created problems for America's Soviet ally, who for three more days had to face the determined resistance of Wenck's rearguard. The capitulation, or rather, the rescue of Wenck's army was not an isolated incident. According to the German general Kurt von Tippelskirch, "entire German armies were able to disappear at the very last moment behind American lines" during the final days of the war. This reportedly involved hundreds of thousands of German soldiers, amounting to approximately half of all Wehrmacht troops fighting on the Eastern Front. It has been suggested that the American commanders who accepted such local German surrenders were motivated mostly by humanitarian considerations, namely, by the desire to allow German civilian refugees to escape the Soviet thirst for revenge. However, this argument is unconvincing for a number of reasons. First, the terms of individual surrenders usually gave priority to the German military, so that fleeing civilians were often unable to slip through the American lines in time. Second, German refugees sometimes had to endure a worse fate as a result of local surrenders. For example, once the Soviets understood what was happening, they showered the escape routes with extra artillery fire. In the case of the rescue of Wenck's army, not only German civilians but also a number of GIs thus perished on the banks of the Elbe. Third, while it is true that the Soviets had wreaked a terrible retribution during the winter of 1944-45 when they invaded East Prussia and exacted revenge on civilians, discipline had afterwards been restored in the Red Army. In the spring of 1945, the Soviet conquest of Germany was generally proceeding without atrocities, so that an American "humanitarian" intervention on behalf of German civilians was not required. Fourth, such American humanitarianism did perhaps bring some relief to the Germans, that is, the enemies of the Americans, but also caused unnecessary losses to the allies of the Americans, the Soviets. The German author of a study of the affair of Wenck's army thus emphasizes that the American role in this surrender "[was] unquestionably incorrect vis-à-vis the Soviet ally."[16] If there was any humanitarianism involved, it would appear to have been a very selective humanitarianism, which happened to be extremely functional for unspoken anti-Soviet purposes. One final factor must be considered. While it may well be true that innocent civilians could escape all sorts of undeserved retributions thanks to local surrenders, such surrenders may also have allowed war criminals to evade the punishment they so amply deserved, since from the Soviets the Mengeles and Barbies could not expect to receive a ticket for South America.

Finally, an observation is in order concerning the hundreds of thousands of German soldiers who did not manage to escape to the West, or who had been captured by the Soviets much earlier. The Soviets undoubtedly sensed that the individual surrenders on the Western Front were not really about selfless humanitarianism, but a deliberate manoeuvre aimed (among other things) at obtaining as many German army units as possible for possible use in a common Western-German enterprise against the USSR. At that time already, and also much later, for example at the time of the remilitarization of West Germany, Moscow had to consider the possibility that militaristic and revanchist German circles might attempt a new edition of Operation Barbarossa under Western auspices. In light of this, we can see why the Soviets long hesitated to liberate their own German POWs, who might likewise have been used in a new anti-Soviet crusade. (But there were of course also other reasons for keeping them; for example, in the absence of meaningful post-war reparations from Germany, the labour of German POWs was viewed as some form of compensation for war damages in the Soviet Union.) The hundreds of thousands of Germans who perished in Soviet captivity or who could only return to their country many years after the end of the war, then, have in some way paid the price for the fact that in the spring of 1945 many of their comrades were allowed to disappear behind British-American lines.

Chapter 16
THE WINDING ROAD TO THE GERMAN SURRENDER(S)

More or less secret negotiations with the Germans were of interest to the Americans and British in many respects, and they did take place in Berne and elsewhere. Discussed were issues such as local surrenders, ways for Wehrmacht units to avoid ending up in Soviet captivity and to be made available in good order to the Western Allies, prospects for a common undertaking against the Soviets, strategies for eliminating radical and therefore obnoxious resistance groups behind German lines (as for example in Italy) before the arrival on the scene of the American or British liberators, and so forth. Such contacts obviously violated the spirit of the inter-Allied agreements dating back to the time of the Casablanca Conference, stipulating that there would be no separate negotiations with the Germans.

However, an unconditional German capitulation vis-à-vis America, Great Britain, and the Soviet Union would eventually have to be concluded somewhere. If only for reasons of prestige, the Western Allies preferred that this would happen on the Western Front. British-American contacts with the Germans were therefore of interest not only with an eye on possible local surrenders, but also in view of the coming general and supposedly unconditional capitulation, of which intriguing details, such as the venue of the ceremony, might possibly be determined in advance and without input from the side of the Soviets. There were many possibilities in this respect, because the Germans themselves kept approaching the Americans and the British in the hope of concluding a separate armistice with the Western powers or, if that would prove impossible, of steering as many Wehrmacht units as possible into American or British captivity by means of individual surrenders.

The Great War of 1914–18 had ended with a clear and unequivocal armistice, namely in the form of an unconditional German surrender, which everybody knows went into effect on the eleventh hour of the eleventh day of the eleventh month of 1918. The Second World War, on the other hand, was to grind to a halt, in Europe at least, amidst intrigue and confusion, so that even today there are many misconceptions regarding the time and place of the German capitulation. The Second World War was to end in the European theatre not with one, but with an entire string of German capitulations, with a veritable orgy of surrenders.

It started in Italy on April 29, 1945, with the capitulation of the combined German armies in southwestern Europe to the Allied forces led by Alexander, the British field marshal. Signatories on the German side included SS General Karl Wolff, who had earlier conducted shady negotiations with American secret agents in Switzerland about sensitive issues such as the neutralization of the kind of Italian anti-fascists for whom there was no room in the American-British post-war plans for their country. Stalin had again expressed misgivings about the arrangement that was being worked out between the Western Allies and the Germans in Italy, but in the end he gave his blessing to this capitulation after all.

Many people in Great Britain firmly believe even today that the war against Germany ended with a German surrender in the headquarters of another British field marshal, namely Montgomery, on the Lüneburg Heath in northern Germany. Yet this ceremony took place on May 4, 1945, that is, at least five days before the guns finally fell silent in Europe, and this capitulation applied only to German troops that had hitherto been battling Montgomery's British-Canadian 21st Army Group in the Netherlands and in northwest Germany. Just to be on the safe side, the Canadians actually accepted the capitulation of all German troops in Holland the next day, May 5, during a ceremony in the town of Wageningen in the eastern Dutch province of Gelderland.[1] In the United States and also in Western Europe the event on the Lüneburg Heath is rightly viewed as a strictly local capitulation, even though it is recognized that it served as a kind of prelude to the definitive German capitulation and resulting ceasefire. As far as the Americans, French, Belgians, and others are concerned, this definitive German surrender took place in the headquarters of General Eisenhower, the supreme commander of all Allied forces on the Western Front, in a shabby school building in the city of Reims on May 7, 1945, in the early morning. But this armistice was to go into effect only on the next day, May 8, and only at 11:01 p.m. It is for this reason that even now, commemoration ceremonies in the United States and in Western Europe take place on May 8.

However, even the important event in Reims was not the final surrender ceremony. With the permission of Hitler's successor, Admiral Dönitz, German spokesmen had come knocking on Eisenhower's door in order to try once again to conclude an armistice only with the Western Allies or, failing that, to try to rescue more Wehrmacht units from the clutches of the Soviets by means of local surrenders on the Western Front. Eisenhower was personally no longer willing to consent to further local surrenders, let alone a general German capitulation to the Western Allies only. But he appreciated the potential advantages that would accrue to the Western side if somehow the bulk of the Wehrmacht would end up in British-American rather than Soviet captivity. And he also realized that this was a unique opportunity to induce the desperate Germans to sign in his headquarters the general and unconditional capitulation in the form of a document that would conform to inter-Allied agreements; this detail would obviously do much to enhance the prestige of the United States.

In Reims it thus came to a Byzantine scenario. First, from Paris an obscure Soviet liaison officer, Major General Ivan Susloparov, was brought over in order to save the appearance of the required Allied collegiality. Second, while it was made clear to the Germans that there could be no question of a separate capitulation on the Western Front, a concession was made to them in the form of an agreement that the armistice would only go into effect after a delay of forty-five hours. This was done to accommodate the new German leaders' desire to give as many Wehrmacht units as possible a last chance to surrender to the Americans or the British rather than the Soviets. This interval gave the Germans the opportunity to transfer troops from the east, where heavy fighting continued unabatedly, to the West, where after the signing rituals in Lüneburg and then Reims hardly any shots were being fired anymore. The Germans, whose delegation was headed by General Jodl, signed the capitulation document at Eisenhower's headquarters on May 7 at 2:41 a.m.; but as mentioned earlier, the guns were to fall silent only on May 8 at 11:01 p.m. Local American commanders would cease to allow fleeing Germans to escape behind their lines only after the German capitulation actually went into effect. It can be argued, then, that the deal concluded in the Champagne city did not constitute a totally *unconditional* capitulation.[2]

The document signed in Reims gave the Americans precisely what they wanted, namely, the prestige of a general German surrender on the Western Front in Eisenhower's headquarters. The Germans also achieved the best they could hope for, since their dream of a capitulation to the Western Allies alone appeared to be out of the question: a "postponement of execution," so to speak, of almost two days. During this time, the fighting continued virtually only on the Eastern Front, and countless German soldiers took advantage of this opportunity to disappear behind the British-American lines.[3]

However, the text of the surrender in Reims did not conform entirely with the wording of a general German capitulation agreed upon previously by the Americans and the British as well as the Soviets. It was also questionable whether the representative of the USSR, Susloparov, was really qualified to co-sign the document. Furthermore, it is understandable that the Soviets were far from pleased that the Germans were afforded the possibility to continue to battle the Red Army for almost two more days while on the Western Front the fighting had virtually come to an end. The impression was thus created that what had been signed in Reims was in fact a German surrender on the Western Front only, an arrangement that violated the inter-Allied agreements. In order to clear the air, it was decided to organize an ultimate capitulation ceremony, so that the German surrender in Reims retroactively revealed itself as a sort of prelude to the final surrender and/or as a purely military surrender, even though the Americans and the Western Europeans would continue to commemorate it as the true end to the war in Europe.[4]

It was in Berlin, in the headquarters of Marshal Zhukov, that the final and general, political as well as military, German capitulation was signed on May 8, 1945, or, put differently, that the German capitulation of the day before in Reims was properly ratified by all the Allies. The signatories for Germany, acting on the instructions of Admiral Dönitz, were the generals Keitel, von Friedeburg (who had also been present in Reims), and Stumpf. Since Zhukov had a lower military rank than Eisenhower, the latter had a perfect excuse for not attending the ceremony in the rubble of the German capital. He sent his rather low-profile British deputy, Marshal Tedder, to sign, and this of course took some luster away from the ceremony in Berlin in favour of the one in Reims.[5]

As far as the Soviets and the majority of Eastern Europeans were concerned, the Second World War in Europe ended with the ceremony in Berlin on May 8, 1945, which resulted in the arms being laid down the next day, on May 9. For the Americans, and for most Western Europeans, "the real thing" was and remains the surrender in Reims, signed on May 7 and effective on May 8. While the former always commemorate the end of the war on May 9, the latter invariably do so on May 8. (But the Dutch celebrate on May 5.) That one of the greatest dramas of world history could have such a confusing and unworthy end in Europe was a consequence, as Gabriel Kolko writes, of the way in which the Americans and the British sought to achieve all sorts of big and small advantages for themselves — to the disadvantage of the Soviets — from the inevitable German capitulation.[6]

The First World War had ended de facto with the armistice of November 11, 1918, and de jure with the signing of the Treaty of Versailles on June 28, 1919. The Second World War came to an end with an entire string of surrenders, but it never did come to a peace treaty à la versaillaise, at least not with respect to Germany. (Peace treaties were in due course concluded with Japan, Italy, and so on.) The reason for this is that the victors — the Western Allies on the one side and the Soviets on the other side — were unable to come to an agreement about Germany's fate. Consequently, a few years after the war two German states emerged, which virtually precluded the possibility of a peace treaty reflecting an agreement acceptable to all parties involved. And so a peace treaty with Germany, that is, a final settlement of all issues that remained unresolved after the war, such as the question of Germany's eastern border, became feasible only when the reunification of the two Germanies became a realistic proposition, namely, after the fall of the Berlin Wall. That made the "Two-plus-Four" negotiations of the summer and fall of 1990 possible, negotiations whereby on the one hand the two German states found ways to reunify Germany, and whereby on the other hand the four great victors of the Second World War — the United States, Great Britain, France, and the Soviet Union — imposed their conditions on the German reunification and cleared up the status of the newly reunited country, taking into account not only their own interests but also the interests of other concerned European states such as Poland. The result of these negotiations was a convention that was signed in Moscow on September 12, 1990, and which, *faute de mieux*, can be viewed as the peace treaty that put an official end to the Second World War, at least with respect to Germany.[7]

Chapter 17
AMERICA BETWEEN
CONFIDENCE AND CONCERN

Once Nazi Germany collapsed, everybody knew that the war against Japan could not last much longer. In America, thoughts were therefore turning increasingly to the post-war world. Contemplating the future, the leaders of the United States were optimistic and full of confidence, but they also found that there were some reasons for concern.

It was then already more than obvious that the United States would emerge from the tribulations of worldwide conflict in far better shape than any other country. "When [the war] ended," writes the American economic historian Richard B. Du Boff, "America's enemies were crushed, its allies economically prostrate."[1] Germany and Japan were vanquished and lay in ruins, France was merely a shadow of the former *grande nation*, and exhausted and virtually bankrupt Britain had exchanged its earlier status of world power for the role of junior partner in a close but very asymmetrical British-American alliance. As for the Soviet Union, which had suffered grievous losses, it did not look like a world power or a potential rival of the United States at war's end. The Gross National Product (GNP) of America was three times bigger than that of the USSR and five times bigger than that of Great Britain. The United States had suffered relatively little — just over 300,000 killed and 1 million injured — and had at its disposal not only fantastic military might, but also an unmatched industrial potential. And America was the envy of the entire world because of its enormous reserves in dollars and capital in general, including two-thirds of all gold reserves and three-quarters of all invest-ment capital on earth![2]

America was the great victor, had become the greatest world power, and was really the only "superpower." The Americans found themselves on top of the world, and they knew it. They could face the future with confi-dence, knowing that nothing and nobody could prevent them from doing whatever they wanted to do. In the United States it was generally expected that the twentieth century would turn out to be "the American century," as the publisher of *Life*, Henry Luce, had already predicted in 1941. As many Americans saw things, humanity had escaped the twin threat of European fascism and Japanese militarism thanks to their country, and now they felt called upon to promote their own ideas about freedom, justice, and dem-ocracy everywhere; in other words, to create a new world according to their own vision. An American writer and the editor of *Harper's Magazine*, Lewis Lapham, has commented in this respect that "the United States inherited the earth" and that the Americans believed at the time "that they had been anointed by God."[3]

The spring of 1945 found US leaders and the American people in gen-eral in an optimistic mood, yet not entirely free of worries. The economic crisis of the thirties — essentially a crisis of overproduction — now lay behind them. During the war, the state had eliminated the key problem, the weakness of economic demand, by means of Lend-Lease orders as well as orders from America's own war department. The nation's military expenditures already multiplied sixfold from 1940 to 1941, and between 1940 and 1945 the American state spent no less than 185 billion dollars on tanks, planes, ships, and all sorts of other war supplies.[4] This provided a "mighty stimulus," as Du Boff writes, to the economy of the country.[5] The military expenditures' share of the American GNP — which increased between 1939 and 1944/1945 from approximately 90 billion to around 200 billion dollars — rose from an insignificant 1.5 per cent in 1939 to roughly 40 per cent in 1944/1945. In order to make this growth possible, the nation's industrial capacity had been expanded in the form of countless new, bigger, more modern, and therefore even more productive factories. The aggregate value of all American factories and other productive facilities had increased from 40 billion dollars in 1939 to 66 billion dollars in 1945.

In this way the American economy actually developed a dangerous dependency during the war years, namely, a dependency on the drug of military state expenditures.[6]

Not without reason, post-war "cold turkey" was a serious concern. With the end of the war in sight, the prospect loomed that the fountainhead of military orders would soon run dry. Precisely at the moment when the total supply of industrial goods was higher than ever before, the demand threatened to collapse. Unavoidably, countless factories would have to close their doors and release their employees at a time when hundreds of thousands of demobilized GIs would return home and look for civilian jobs. The kind of unemployment that would result from this fateful constellation would undermine the purchasing power of Americans, thus further decreasing the slumping demand.[7] Kolko writes in this respect:

> Concern over large post-war unemployment was widespread among economic planners from 1942 onward, and a Niagara of pessimistic studies and speeches on the dangers of insufficient post-war trade, access to raw materials, and investment opportunities gushed forth from official and private agencies and personalities.[8]

Paul Samuelson, then a "young Turk" economist — but predestined to become a Nobel Prize winner in his field in 1970 — was one of the experts troubled by dark forebodings. He predicted "that 5 million Americans would lose their jobs or at least suffer greatly reduced work time as a result of government cutbacks" after the end of the hostilities.[9] For the American power elite, and for corporate America in particular, the coming reconversion of the American economy to the conditions of peace threatened to put an abrupt end to the wartime boom, which had brought them a cornucopia of profits and a proliferation of their assets. The return to a peace economy might confront them with the problems associated with widespread unemployment, including demands for radical and even revolutionary change. America appeared poised to enter a crisis that might well reveal itself to be even more traumatic than the Great Depression of the "dirty thirties."[10]

However, there existed means to prevent this daunting scenario from becoming reality. For example, the economic boom could be prolonged if American industry might find ways to market its products all over the world, thus nullifying the threat of a collapse of demand. Dean Acheson, the deputy secretary of state at the time and a very influential statesman, had already emphasized in November 1944 in a speech to a congressional committee that the United States "cannot have full employment and prosperity . . . without the foreign markets."[11] The majority of the political and industrial leaders of America shared this opinion. Some mouthpieces of the American power elite even went so far as to declare dramatically that the preservation of the capitalist system in America depended on a considerable expansion of overseas trade.[12]

In the 1930s every country had sought to protect its sickly industry by means of high tariffs and other protectionist measures. A good example was provided by the British imperial preference tariffs, which have already been mentioned. However, with the *Hawley-Smoot Act* of 1930 the United States itself had increased its tariffs by no less than 50 per cent.[13] If it might prove possible to eliminate such practices after the war, and if instead the principle of free trade might find general acceptance, then it would be possible for American industry to do wonderful business all over the world. One reason for this was that the industry of the United States enjoyed the major competitive advantages associated with economies of scale. In addition, the modernization and rationalization required during the war had made American industry super efficient and therefore extremely competitive.

In the nineteenth century the British Empire had actively propagated the principle of free trade, because as the strongest industrial power it stood to benefit from the implementation of this principle. It was for exactly the same reason that one hundred years later, at the end of the Second World War, the American government, exemplified above all by the secretary of state, Cordell Hull, eagerly preached the gospel of universal free trade. Free trade was presented by the Americans as the remedy against all the economic and even political evils that plagued the world. Somewhat simplistically, free trade was equated with peace among nations, while protectionism was associated with conflict, crisis, and war.[14]

The Americans did not wait for the end of the war to lay the foundations for a new, "Hullian" economic world order based on free trade. Lend-Lease aid to Great Britain had been tied to certain conditions that purported to open up the closed economy of the British Empire as a market for the export goods of American industry in the long run. Similar expectations applied to the Lend-Lease arrangements with the Soviet Union. Many other countries that found themselves, like Britain, in an uncomfortable economic position during the war and were therefore dependent on American assistance, were persuaded to accept the rules of the future economic world order.[15] Historian Howard Zinn writes the following:

> Quietly behind the headlines in battles and bombings, American diplomats and businessmen worked hard to make sure that when the war ended, American economic power would be second to none in the world . . . The Open Door policy of equal access would be extended from Asia to Europe . . . [16]

The principle of the open door — a new policy of free trade, which would open all doors for American products and for American investment capital — was ratified at a conference in Bretton Woods, New Hampshire, in the summer of 1944, which was attended by representatives of no less than forty-four countries. This conference created the institutional mechanisms that would put the principles of the new economic policy into practice, above all the International Monetary Fund (IMF) and the World Bank, so-called international organizations that have always been dominated by the United States and continue to be so today.[17] For very similar economic as well as political reasons, the American government also energetically pursued the creation of the United Nations (UN) and arranged for the headquarters of this international organization to be established in New York, but that is a history that goes beyond the scope of this study.[18]

From the countries that had been liberated by America, Washington expected grateful cooperation with regard to free trade and an open door for American investment capital. It is fair to say that the Americans made sure that only governments that were in favour of the open door came to power in countries they had already liberated. The Americans hoped, moreover, that in the other countries of Europe, namely Germany and the Eastern European states, governments would come to power after the war that displayed a positive attitude toward the kind of liberal economic policies from which the United States expected such high dividends. Above all, the reconstruction of the defeated German nation promised to generate unprecedented business opportunities, and American industry was determined to profit gloriously from the coming gold rush between the Rhine and the Oder. In the nineteenth century, the frontier with the Wild West had functioned as the economic and social dynamo of America; after the Second World War it looked as if Providence was conjuring up a new, eastern frontier for America in Europe, and above all in Germany — a frontier that would provide America with a cornucopia of unlimited economic opportunities.[19]

Fabulous business prospects might possibly also open up because of the reconstruction of the USSR. American participation in this Herculean task still remained possible, and "the prospect of lucrative large-scale trade with Russia" caused many American industrial tycoons to lick their lips. This also applied to those who shortly before had not made any secret of their hatred for the Soviet system. It was estimated that the value of future annual exports to the Soviet Union would amount to between 1 and 2 billion dollars.[20]

America's leaders were determined to inundate the world not only with American export products but also with the concomitant American world view, which carried individual freedom, democracy, free enterprise, and free trade in its banner. It was an ideology that was used to promote America's new economic order in Europe and everywhere on earth and, last but not least, in the United States itself. That some people had other ideas, for example European resistance fighters who dreamed of a social and economic "new deal" that was radically different from America's raw capitalist system, US leaders found simply unthinkable. They had little or no understanding for radical, progressive socio-economic programs, such as those of the Charter of the Resistance in France, which called for the socialization of some firms or industrial sectors and which therefore offended the principles of free enterprise. Equally distasteful to them were the moderate but more or less left-wing ideas of the European socialists or social democrats. However, the most abhorrent credo in American eyes was communism. The reason: it was a revolutionary ideology that rejected capitalism *in toto*, an ideology, furthermore, whose adherents had been preoccupied since 1917 in the Soviet Union with the construction of a radically different socio-economic system, thus providing capitalism with the unwanted competition of a counter-system.

In the twenties and thirties the American political and industrial elites had been anti-communist and therefore sympathetic to fascism. After Pearl Harbor, however, the fascists had become America's enemies, while the Soviet Union had been metamorphosed by the quirks of war into an ally of Uncle Sam. It was only for this reason that during the war the formerly blazing lights of anti-communism had been dimmed. Even so, the majority of America's religious, political, and also military leaders continued to consider communism as the true enemy. Even after Pearl Harbor, Catholic journalists, for example, tended to remain loyal to the pre-war orthodoxy, which had preferred fascism, approbated by the Vatican, to "godless" communism. Many leading Americans lamented publicly that the United States found itself at war with "the wrong enemy," and Senator Taft warned loudly that "a victory of communism would be much more dangerous for the United States than a victory for fascism."[21] At the military academy of West Point, where America's martial elite is schooled, a handful of generals in a fit of candour openly complained that America had stumbled into the war on the wrong side; the blame for this blunder was put squarely on the shoulders of President Roosevelt, condescendingly referred to as "the Jew Franklin D. Rosenfeld," almost exactly as Hitler put it. "We ought to be fighting the commies, not Hitler," was the generals' conclusion.[22]

All this meant in practice that also during the war real or imaginary communists were systematically harassed by the American authorities. The hunt for communists had long been, and continued to be, a specialty of J. Edgar Hoover's FBI, but during the war the FBI faced increasing competition in this respect from the so-called House Un-American Activities Committee (HUAC), a supposedly anti-fascist committee of the Congress. It is "one of the great ironies of [US] history," writes an American scholar, Noah Isenberg, that the FBI and HUAC specifically targeted Germans who had fled the Nazi dictatorship "on political as well as racial grounds" and had settled in the United States, such as Thomas and Heinrich Mann, Erich Maria Remarque, and Bertolt Brecht. The G-men of J. Edgar Hoover, Isenberg writes, "the self-appointed protector of the nation from the threat of foreign communist infiltration," spied upon these German refugees and frequently harassed them, not because they were suspected of being Nazi agents, but because their political leanings were too leftist for the taste of the authorities.[23]

In his famous oral history of the Second World War, *The Good War*, Studs Terkel cites a member of the American Red Cross who remarked that, as far as America's leaders were concerned, the wartime alliance with the USSR was simply never "a thing of the heart."[24] It was a very defensible statement. For the American power elite the war against Nazi Germany was indeed nothing more than an anomaly, an unplanned, unwanted, and unexpected interlude that temporarily interrupted their deeply rooted anticommunist thoughts and plans, but which would not prevent them from refocusing on these thoughts and plans as soon as the conflict with "the wrong enemy" was over. As the Italian historian Filippo Gaja has put it:

> *The focus remained on the struggle against Bolshevism and against a transformation of the world along socialist lines. In this sense, the Second World War had been a phonomenon of secondary importance, a mere digression within a much wider scheme, namely the planned destruction of Bolshevism.*[25]

With the defeat of fascism in Europe in the spring of 1945, then, the conditions were created for a revival of anti-communism in America. At that time communism was all the more detested because it was seen as the only remaining ideological competitor with the American ideology and as the arch-enemy of democracy, of individual freedom, of private property and, last but certainly not least, of the kind of international free trade in which American industry, and the American power elite, had invested such high hopes. In the brave new world that was to arise under American auspices from the ashes of the Second World War, the American Century of which 1945 was supposed to be year zero, there was no room for communism.

Chapter 18
NUCLEAR DIPLOMACY AND THE ONSET OF THE COLD WAR

With the German capitulation in early May 1945 the war in Europe was over. The victors, the Big Three, now faced the complex and delicate problem of the post-war reorganization of Europe. In Western Europe the Americans and the British had already created a new order almost one year earlier, and Stalin had accepted that arrangement. In Eastern Europe, on the other hand, the Soviet leader clearly enjoyed the advantage thanks to the presence of the Red Army. Even so, at that time the Western Allies could still hope that they would be able to provide a measure of input into the reorganization of this part of Europe as well. Stalin had manoeuvred there to the advantage of the communists and their sympathizers, and to the disadvantage of all those who were rightly or wrongly suspected of being anti-Soviet or anti-communist, but everything was still possible.[1] Furthermore, with respect to Eastern Europe the Western outsiders had a foot in the door, so to speak, thanks to previous agreements such as those concluded at Yalta and Churchill's sphere-of-influence formula. As for Germany, the Western Allies actually enjoyed a light advantage over their colleague in the Kremlin, because as a result of earlier agreements ratified in Yalta, the Americans and the British together occupied a much bigger and much more important part of Germany as well as the lion's share of Berlin real estate.

In Western Europe everything had already been settled, but in Eastern Europe and in Germany everything remained possible. It was far from unavoidable that Germany would long remain divided in occupation zones and that Eastern Europe would linger for half a century in the iron grip of the Soviets. Stalin, who was to receive most of the blame for all this unpleasantness later on, actually had good reasons to be accommodating with respect to Germany and Eastern Europe. He was aware that unreasonable demands or recalcitrance vis-à-vis the British-Americans involved great risks. As Dresden had clearly shown, such conduct might be ruinous for the Soviet Union. In addition, Stalin hoped that goodwill and cooperation, in combination with his promise to declare war on Japan, might bear rich fruit in the form of American assistance in the virtually superhuman task that the reconstruction of the Soviet Union was certain to be.

Motivated by a combination of fear and hope, Stalin was prepared to cooperate with the Americans and the British, but of course he also fully expected to reap some of the benefits to which the victors felt entitled. For example, he looked forward to certain territorial gains (or compensation for earlier territorial losses of the Soviet Union or its predecessor, czarist Russia); considerable reparations from Germany; recognition of his right not to have to tolerate anti-Soviet regimes in neighbouring countries; and, last but not least, the opportunity to continue to build a socialist society in the USSR. His American and British partners had never indicated to Stalin that they found these expectations unreasonable. On the contrary, the legitimacy of these Soviet war aims had been recognized repeatedly, either explicitly or implicitly, in Tehran, Yalta, and elsewhere.

It was possible to talk with Stalin, but such a dialogue also required patience and understanding of the Soviet viewpoint, and had to be carried out in the knowledge that the Soviet Union was not prepared to leave the conference table empty-handed. Truman, however, had no desire to engage in such a dialogue. He had no understanding for even the most basic expectations of the Soviets, and he abhorred the thought that the Soviet Union might receive reparations for its sacrifices and might thus be offered the opportunity to resume work on the project of a communist society. Like numerous other leading Americans, the president hoped that it would actually be possible to squeeze the Soviets out of Germany and Eastern Europe without compensation, and even to somehow put an end to their communist experiment, which remained a source of inspiration for Reds and other radicals and revolutionaries everywhere on earth, even in the United States itself.[2]

Like Churchill, Truman found the "stick" of the hard line vis-à-vis Stalin much more promising than the "carrot" of the soft line. We have already seen that this had a lot to do with the fact that the military situation of the Western Allies in Germany had improved dramatically in March and April of 1945. However, this turned out to be only a minor advantage in comparison to a potentially fantastic trump the new American president could soon hope to play in the card game with Stalin. On April 25, 1945, Truman was briefed about the secret Manhattan Project or S-1, as the atomic bomb project was referred to in code language. American scientists had been working on this potent new weapon for years; it was almost ready, would soon be tested, and would shortly thereafter be available for use. The atomic bomb was to play an enormously important role in the new course taken by American policy in the spring of 1945 in Europe and also in the Far East. Truman and his advisors fell under the spell of what the renowned American historian William Appleman Williams has called a "vision of omnipotence." They were totally convinced that the atomic bomb would enable them to force their will on the Soviet Union.[3] The atomic bomb was "a hammer," Truman himself stated, which he would wave over the heads of "those boys in the Kremlin."[4]

Possession of the atomic bomb appeared to open up all sorts of previously unthinkable and extremely favourable perspectives for the protagonists of the hard-line policy. Thanks to the bomb, it would now be possible to force Stalin, in spite of earlier agreements, to withdraw the Red Army from Germany and to deny him a say in the post-war affairs of that country. It now also seemed a feasible proposition to install pro-Western and even anti-communist regimes in Poland and elsewhere in Eastern Europe, and to prevent Stalin from exerting any influence there. It even became thinkable that the Soviet Union itself might be opened up to American investment capital as well as American political and economic influence, and that this communist heretic might thus be returned to the bosom of the universal capitalist church. "There is evidence," writes the German historian Jost Dülffer, that Truman believed that the monopoly of the nuclear bomb would be "a passepartout for the implementation of the United States' ideas for a new world order."[5]

In comparison to Roosevelt's delicate and often difficult soft-line policy, the hard-line policy — that is, the policy of the all-powerful stick that the nuclear bomb promised to be — appeared to be simple, effective, and therefore extremely attractive. Had he remained alive, Roosevelt himself would probably have opted for this course. His successor, Truman, had no experience with the carrot-style approach. For this rather unsophisticated man from Missouri, the simplicity and the potential of the new hard line proved altogether irresistible. And so it came to atomic diplomacy, which has been elucidated in such enthralling fashion by the American revisionist historian Gar Alperovitz.

The monopoly of the atomic bomb was supposed to allow America to impose its will on the USSR. At the time of the German surrender in May 1945, however, the bomb was not yet ready, but Truman knew that he would not have to wait much longer. He therefore did not heed Churchill's advice to discuss the fate of Germany and Eastern Europe with Stalin as soon as possible, "before the armies of democracy melted," that is, before the American troops were to pull out of Europe. Eventually, Truman did agree to a summit meeting of the Big Three in Berlin, but not before the summer, when the bomb was supposed to be ready.

At the Potsdam Conference, which lasted from July 17 to August 2, 1945, Truman received the long-awaited message that the atomic bomb had been tested successfully on July 16 in Alamogordo, New Mexico. The American president now felt that the time had come to make his move. He no longer bothered to present proposals to Stalin, instead he made all sorts of demands; at the same time he rejected out of hand all proposals emanating from the Soviet side, for example proposals concerning the German reparation payments, including those based on earlier agreements such as Yalta. Stalin, however, failed to display the hoped-for willingness to capitulate, not even when Truman attempted to intimidate him by whispering into his ear that America had acquired an incredibly potent new weapon. The Soviet sphinx, who had certainly been informed already about the Manhattan Project by his spies, listened in stony silence. Truman concluded that only an actual demonstration of the atomic bomb could persuade the Soviets to give way. Consequently, no general agreement on important issues could be achieved at Potsdam.[6]

In the meantime, the Japanese battled on in the Far East, even though their situation was totally hopeless. They were in fact prepared to surrender, but not unconditionally, as the Americans demanded. To the Japanese mind, an unconditional capitulation conjured up the supreme humiliation, namely, that Emperor Hirohito might be forced to step down and possibly be accused of war crimes. American leaders were aware of this, and some of them, for example Secretary of the Navy James Forrestal, believed, as Alperovitz writes, "that a statement reassuring the Japanese that 'unconditional surrender' did not mean dethronement of the Emperor would probably bring an end to the war." It should indeed have been possible to bring about a Japanese capitulation in spite of their demand for immunity for Hirohito. There was the precedent of the German surrender at Reims three months earlier, which had not been entirely unconditional, as we have seen. Furthermore, Tokyo's condition was far from essential: later, after an unconditional surrender had been wrested from the Japanese, the Americans would never bother to lay any charges against Hirohito, and it was thanks to Washington that he was able to remain emperor for many more decades.[7]

Why did the Japanese think that they could still afford the luxury of attaching a condition to their offer to surrender? The reason was that in China the main force of their army remained intact. They thought that they could use this army to defend Japan itself and thus exact a high price from the Americans for their admittedly inevitable final victory. However, this scheme would only work if the Soviet Union did not get involved in the war in the Far East, thus pinning the Japanese forces down on the Chinese mainland. Soviet neutrality, in other words, allowed Tokyo a small measure of hope, not hope for a victory of course, but hope for negotiations with the United States and the possibility of somewhat more favourable conditions of capitulation. To a certain extent the war with Japan dragged on because the USSR was not yet involved in it. But already in Tehran in 1943, Stalin had promised to declare war on Japan within three months after the capitulation of Germany, and he had reiterated this commitment as recently as July 17, 1945, in Potsdam. Consequently, Washington counted on a Soviet attack on Japan by the middle of August. The Americans thus knew only too well that the situation of the Japanese was hopeless. "Fini Japs when that comes about," Truman wrote in his diary, referring to the expected Soviet intervention in the war in the Far East.[8] In addition, the American navy assured Washington that it was able to prevent the Japanese from transferring their army from China in order to defend the homeland against an American invasion. Finally, it was questionable whether an American invasion of Japan would be necessary at all, since the mighty US Navy could also simply blockade that island nation and thus confront it with a choice between capitulating or starving to death.

In order to finish the war against Japan without having to make more sacrifices, Truman thus had a number of very attractive options. He could accept the trivial Japanese condition with regard to immunity for their emperor; he could also wait until the Red Army attacked the Japanese in China, thus forcing Tokyo into accepting an unconditional surrender after all; and he could starve Japan to death by means of a naval blockade that would have coerced Tokyo to sue for peace sooner or later.[9] Truman and his advisors, however, chose none of these options. Instead, they decided to knock Japan out with the atomic bomb. This fateful decision, which was to cost the lives of hundreds of thousands of people, mostly civilians, offered the Americans considerable advantages. First, the bomb might still induce Tokyo to surrender before the Soviets got involved in the war in Asia. In this case it would not be necessary to allow Moscow a say in the coming decisions about postwar Japan, about the territories which had been occupied by Japan (such as Korea and Manchuria), and about the Far East and the Pacific region in general. The United States would then enjoy total hegemony over that part of the world, something that may be said to have been Washington's true, albeit unspoken, war aim in the conflict with Japan.

This point deserves closer examination. As far as the Americans were concerned, a Soviet intervention in the war in the Far East threatened to achieve for the Soviets the same advantage which their own relatively late intervention in the war in Europe had produced for the United States, namely, a place at the round table of the victors who would force their will on the defeated enemy, redraw borders, determine postwar socio-economic and political structures, and thereby derive for themselves enormous benefits and prestige. However, Washington absolutely did not want the Soviet Union to enjoy this kind of input. The Americans had eliminated their great imperialist rival in that part of the world. They did not relish the idea of being saddled with a new potential rival, a rival, moreover, whose detested communist ideology might become dangerously influential in many Asiatic countries.

American leaders believed that after the Japanese rape of China and the humiliation of traditional colonial powers such as Great Britain, France, and the Netherlands, and after their own victory over Japan, only the elimination of the USSR from the Far East — seemingly a mere formality — was required in order to realize their dream of absolute hegemony in that part of the world. Their disappointment and chagrin were all the greater when after the war the Soviets actually managed to maintain a measure of influence in North Korea, and when China was "lost" to Mao's Communists. To make things worse, in Vietnam, previously known as French Indochina, a popular independence movement under the leadership of Ho Chi Minh had plans that proved to be incompatible with the grand Asian ambitions of the United States. No wonder, then, that it would come to war in Korea and Vietnam, and almost to an armed conflict with "Red China."

But let us return to the summer of 1945 when, thanks to the atomic bomb, Washington could hope to go to work in the Far East on its own, that is, without its party being spoiled by unwanted Soviet gatecrashers. The atom bomb seemed to offer the American leaders an additional important advantage. Truman's experience in Potsdam had persuaded him that only an actual demonstration of this new weapon would make Stalin pliable. A nuclear explosion in Japan could therefore also serve as a new signal for the Kremlin, a signal that would make the one flashed at Dresden look like a mere wink of the eye.[10]

Truman did not have to use the atomic bomb in order to force Japan to its knees. As the post-war US Strategic-Bombing Survey was to acknowledge categorically, "certainly prior to 31 December 1945, Japan would have surrendered, even if the atomic bombs had not been dropped, even if Russia had not entered the war, and even if no invasion had been planned or contemplated."[11] However, Truman had reasons to want to use the bomb. The nuclear bomb enabled the Americans to force Tokyo to surrender unconditionally, to keep the Soviets out of the Far East and, last but not least, to terrorize the Soviet leaders and thus enable Washington to force its will on the Kremlin with respect to European affairs. Hiroshima and Nagasaki were pulverized for these reasons.[12] Many American historians realize this only too well. Sean Dennis Cashman writes:

> With the passing of time, many historians have concluded that the bomb was used as much for political reasons . . . Vannevar Bush [the head of the US Office of Scientific Research and Development] stated that the bomb "was also delivered on time, so that there was no necessity for any concessions to Russia at the end of the war." Secretary of State James F. Byrnes [Truman's Secretary of State] never denied a statement attributed to him that the bomb had been used to demonstrate American power to the Soviet Union in order to make [the Soviets] more manageable in Europe.[13]

Truman himself, however, hypocritically declared at the time that the purpose of the two nuclear bombardments had been "to bring the boys home," that is, to quickly finish the war without any further major loss of life on the American side. This explanation was uncritically broadcast in the American media and it developed into a myth eagerly propagated by the majority of American historians and still widely believed to this very day.[14]

The atomic bomb was ready just in time to be put to use before the USSR had a chance to become involved in the Far East. Even so, the nuclear obliteration of Hiroshima on August 6, 1945, came too late to prevent the Soviets from entering the war against Japan. This ruined Truman's delicate scenario, at least partly. Despite the terrible destruction wrought in Hiroshima, Tokyo had not yet surrendered when on August 8, 1945 — exactly three months after the German capitulation in Berlin — the USSR declared war on Japan. The next day the Red Army attacked the Japanese troops stationed in the northern Chinese region of Manchuria. It was not that long ago that Washington had wanted Soviet intervention in the war against Japan, but when in the summer of 1945 that intervention was about to materialize, Truman and his advisors were far from ecstatic about the fact that Stalin was keeping his word. It now became crucial to end the war as quickly as possible in order to limit the damage done by the USSR's intervention.

Tokyo did not immediately react to the bombing of Hiroshima with the hoped-for unconditional capitulation. Apparently, the Japanese government did not understand initially what had really happened in Hiroshima, because many conventional bombing raids had produced equally catastrophic results; an attack by thousands of bombers on the Japanese capital on March 9-10, 1945, for example, had exacted more victims than in Hiroshima. The Japanese authorities could not ascertain immediately that only one plane and one bomb had done the damage. That is why it took some time before the unconditional capitulation craved by the Americans was forthcoming. As a result of this delay the USSR did get involved in the war against Japan after all. This made Washington extremely impatient. Already one day after the Soviet declaration of war, on August 9, 1945, a second bomb was dropped, this time on the city of Nagasaki.[15] About this bombardment, in which many Japanese Catholics perished, a former American army chaplain later stated: "That's one of the reasons I think they dropped the second bomb. To hurry it up. To make them surrender before the Russians came."[16] (This chaplain was probably not aware that among the 75,000 human beings who were "instantaneously incinerated, carbonized, and evaporated" in Nagasaki there were numerous Japanese Catholics as well as an unknown number of Allied POWs, whose presence in the city had been communicated to the American air force command — in vain, as it turned out.[17] It nevertheless took another five days, until August 14, before the Japanese could bring themselves to capitulate. In the meantime the Red Army was able to make good progress, to the great chagrin of Truman and his advisors. And so it looked as if the Americans would be stuck with a Soviet partner in the Far East after all. However, Truman made sure that this was not the case. He acted as if the earlier cooperation of the three great powers in Europe had not set a precedent, by rejecting Stalin's request for a Soviet occupation zone in the defeated Land of the Rising Sun; this happened on August 15, 1945. (The Soviets had admittedly entered the war against Japan at a late stage, but had the United States not similarly entered the war against Germany at a late stage, namely well after the tide had turned in front of Moscow in early December 1941?) And when on September 2, 1945, General MacArthur officially accepted the Japanese surrender on the American battleship *Missouri* in the Bay of Tokyo, representatives of the Soviet Union, and of other allies in the Far East, including Great

Britain and the Netherlands, were allowed to be present only as insignificant extras. Japan was not carved up into occupation zones, like Germany. America's defeated rival was to be occupied in its entirety by the Americans only, and as American viceroy in Tokyo, General MacArthur would ensure that, regardless of contributions made to the common victory, no other power would have a say in the affairs of post-war Japan.[18]

The American conquerors recreated the Land of the Rising Sun according to their ideas and to their advantage. In September 1951, a satisfied Uncle Sam would sign a peace treaty with Japan. The USSR, however, whose interests had never been taken into account, did not co-sign this treaty.[19] The Soviets did pull out of China, but they refused to evacuate Japanese territories such as Sakhalin and the Kurils, which had been occupied by the Red Army during the last days of the war. They would be mercilessly criticized for this in the United States afterwards, as if the attitude of the American government itself had nothing to do with this issue. In the aftermath of the war, the Soviet declaration of war on Japan would also be presented as a cowardly attack on a defeated country, even though Washington had urged Moscow for years to take such a step.

America owed its monopoly of power in defeated Japan at least partly to the atomic bomb. In Europe, however, Truman's nuclear diplomacy was to have tragic consequences. Roosevelt's successor in the White House had hoped that the nuclear demonstration would force Stalin to give in to American demands with respect to Germany and Eastern Europe, but this hope was not to be fulfilled. Gar Alperovitz has described in great detail how, immediately after the bombings in Japan in early fall of 1945, the Soviet leader was apparently sufficiently intimidated to make concessions, particularly with respect to Balkan countries such as Hungary, Romania, and Bulgaria, where he allowed a political pluralism to blossom and free elections to be held. In the United States, the media noted these changes, applauded loudly, and did not hesitate to credit "Truman's firmness, backed by the atom bomb," as the *New York Herald Tribune* wrote on August 29, 1945. However, when the Truman administration kept making new demands, for example with respect to the makeup of governments in Sofia and Bucharest, and was clearly no longer interested in dialogue on the basis of the Yalta and Potsdam Agreements but determined to roll back Soviet influence in Eastern Europe, Stalin's attitude would harden and he would install exclusively Communist and unconditionally pro-Soviet regimes in all countries occupied by the Red Army.[20]

Stalin was undoubtedly willing to engage in a dialogue, that is, in a dialogue between equals, between co-victors in the war against Nazi Germany. Even much later he remained interested in such a dialogue, which was reflected in his reasonable approach to the post-war arrangements regarding Finland and Austria. The Red Army would in due course pull out of these countries without leaving behind any communist regimes. It was not Stalin, but Truman, then, who in 1945 (and afterwards) failed to display interest in a dialogue between equals. With the nuclear pistol on his hip, the American president did not feel that he had to treat "the boys in the Kremlin," who did not have such a super-weapon, as his equals. "The American leaders waxed self-righteous and excoriated Russia," writes Gabriel Kolko, "[and] they refused to negotiate in any serious way simply because as self-confident master of economic and military powers the United States felt it could ultimately define the world order."[21]

Viewed from the Soviet standpoint, America's nuclear diplomacy amounted to nothing less than nuclear blackmail. Although initially intimidated, Stalin ultimately refused to submit to this blackmail, so that Truman was never able to harvest the fruits of his nuclear policy. First, the Soviet leader soon learned that concessions in Eastern Europe merely led to an escalation of American demands, and that Washington would only be satisfied with a unilateral and unconditional Soviet withdrawal from countries such as Poland and Hungary, an unacceptable demand.

Contrary to conventional Cold-War-era wisdom, negotiated withdrawals of the Red Army from occupied countries, leaving capitalist socio-economic infrastructures very much intact, were in fact acceptable to Stalin. This was clearly demonstrated by the case of Finland. This country, which had fought against the USSR on the side of Nazi Germany, did not become a Soviet satellite because, as the Finnish scholar Jussi Hanhimaki has emphasized, a deal was negotiated whereby the Soviets achieved what they were after, namely, "security of their northwestern frontier and, in particular, [a] guarantee that the country would never again be used as a base for an attack against the USSR." As for the Americans, writes Hanhimaki, they "believed that if they became too aggressive in Finland they would only be inviting Finland's inclusion in the ranks of the people's democracies." The case of Finland demonstrates that it was not impossible to do business with Stalin. With respect to Poland and the rest of Eastern Europe, on the other hand, the Truman administration — overconfident with the nuclear pistol at its hip — did reveal itself too aggressive and denied the Soviets the security they sought; in doing so, they did indeed "invite the inclusion" of these countries in the ranks of the Soviet satellites.[22]

Second, after Soviet strategists had had the time to digest the lessons of Hiroshima and Nagasaki, they, like some Western military analysts, refused to believe that a war could be won solely from the air, even by means of atom bombs. Stalin and his generals concluded that the best defence against the nuclear threat consisted in having the Red Army cling as close as possible to the American lines in the liberated and/or occupied territories of Eastern and Central Europe. Under those conditions the American bombers would not only have to face a very long journey before they could drop their bombs on the USSR itself, but in case of an attack on the lines of the Red Army they would inevitably also endanger their own troops. This meant that the Red Army proceeded to entrench itself along the demarcation line between the occupation zones of the Western Allies and the Soviets themselves.

In 1944 and 1945, Stalin had initiated little or no social or political changes in the countries that had been liberated or occupied by the Red Army, including Hungary, Romania, and the Soviet occupation zone of Germany, and he had even countenanced certain anti-Soviet and anti-communist activities there. (In Romania in the summer of 1945, for example, anti-Soviet agitation by King Michael and other leaders had been tolerated by Moscow.) All that changed quickly under the pressure of American nuclear diplomacy. Communist and unconditionally pro-Soviet regimes were installed everywhere, and opposition was no longer tolerated. Only at that time, that is, in late 1945, did an "iron curtain" descend between Stettin on the Baltic Sea and Trieste on the Adriatic. This expression was first used by Churchill on March 5, 1946, during a speech in Fulton, a town in Truman's home state, Missouri. It was fitting in some way, because without Truman's atomic diplomacy, Europe may possibly never have been divided by an iron curtain.[23]

Chapter 19
A USEFUL NEW ENEMY

The Cold War, which was to last almost half a century and which forced the world to live in the shadow of a possible nuclear war, started when America's leaders believed that with the help of the nuclear bomb they could impose their will on the Soviets. Soon it would become obvious that Washington's atomic diplomacy would not bear the desired fruits. However, the concept of the Cold War revealed itself to be useful to the American power elite in other ways. It was hardly possible to explain to the American public, and to the Western Europeans, that the new conflict with the Soviets had been caused by Washington's policy. Far better to put the blame squarely on the back of the Kremlin, the place where all aggressive intentions allegedly originated. The Soviets had hitherto been portrayed as heroic allies in the crusade against Nazism. Now the time had come to transform the USSR into the great bogeyman of the free world, because the American power elite could expect considerable benefits from such a metamorphosis. A hostile Soviet Union was henceforth far more useful than an allied Soviet Union. First, it would thus be possible in America itself to discredit as "un-American traitors" not only the handful of communists but also — and this was far more important — the numerous Americans with more or less left-wing, radical convictions. Second, the existence of an allegedly hostile USSR could also justify the titanic "defence" expenditures that might serve to keep the country's economy humming at full speed also after the war. These two important points deserve our attention.

In spite of its many great deficiencies the USSR, or at least an idealized version of the USSR, had functioned before the war as source of inspiration and hope not only for America's relatively small number of communists, but also for union leaders and for radical and progressive US citizens, that is, for the not to be underestimated number of Americans who dreamed of some left-wing socio-economic alternative to their country's notoriously rugged capitalist system. In addition, the Bolshevik state had withstood the terrible test of the Nazi attack, and after Stalingrad the Soviets' industrial and military performance was outstanding. This achievement appeared to demonstrate the viability and merits of the Bolshevik experiment and enhanced the prestige and popularity of the Soviet Union among the American population. The Soviet image was also significantly promoted during the war by the American government, the media, and Hollywood, as we have seen earlier. In any event, the success of the Soviets served to stir the spirits of all sorts of left-wing radicals and unionists.

During the war, American workers developed a class-consciousness in the Marxist sense, as the renowned British historian Arthur Marwick — himself not a Marxist — has observed. This class-consciousness was expressed in words and deeds. American workers increasingly used words such as "workers" and "working class," and to the American establishment such discourse came across as the militant idiom of class struggle, as the perturbing linguistic vanguard of the kind of social revolution for which the Soviet Union had provided the inspiration and the model.[1] But there were other, more alarming symptoms of a militant class consciousness. During the war, American workers massively joined more or less radical labour unions, and primarily by means of strikes, including wildcat strikes, they revealed themselves all too capable of wresting higher wages from their employers. Many conservative Americans believed that behind this turn of events they could discern the hand of Moscow, even though America's own communists, who feared that strikes might jeopardize American aid for the USSR, unquestionably belonged to the more moderate elements in the union movement. In 1944-45, even before final victory in the war was achieved, a new wave of strikes appeared to indicate that labour was gearing up for a major post-war offensive on the social home front. Other than higher wages, America's workers now also demanded the kinds of social benefits that their counterparts in the Soviet "workers' paradise" had already enjoyed for quite some time, for example pensions, unemployment and health insurance, as well as paid holidays.[2] A *Fortune Magazine* survey taken during the war years and eventually published in September 1945 revealed clearly that the average American had a lot of admiration for Soviet achievements such as the "redistribution of wealth, equality, economic security, and . . . educational opportunities."[3]

Not only class-conscious workers, but all sorts of intellectuals, religious leaders, politicians, and even businessmen started to embrace and advocate "progressive" ideas during the war. These so-called liberals of the American middle class pursued a national system of social security, full employment, industrial democracy, and a more activist role for the state in social and economic life. They too were at least partly inspired by the romanticized model of the Soviet Union. The liberals may not have been communists or Reds, but in the eyes of at least some conservatives they were "fellow travellers" of Bolshevism and puppets of Moscow, "pinkos." As for intellectuals, America's leading economists, for example, had traditionally been devotees of free enterprise, but during the war some of them, including Alvin Hansen, a professor at Harvard known as the "American Keynes," changed their tune and started to advocate unorthodox policies such as the pursuit of full employment.[4]

After the gloom of the "dirty thirties" and the sacrifices made in the long dark night of war, a large segment of the population, not only in the United States but everywhere in the Western world, expected the rise of a new social dawn. In Great Britain, this hope for a social "new deal" was largely fulfilled, even though Conservative leaders like Churchill opposed it; it was for this reason that the British people exchanged his Conservative stewardship during the general election of the summer of 1945 for a government of the genuinely reformist Labour Party. Thus originated in the UK an extensive system of social security based on the blueprint of the famous Beveridge Plan, and soon to be known as the welfare state.[5]

In the post-war years the British model was to inspire similar social reforms in many countries of Western Europe as well as in Canada and in Australia, but not the United States. This was not due to the Americans' inborn individualism, as is often suggested. An American welfare state did not come about because the American power elite found a way to escape the pressure for social reforms, namely, the Cold War. Alarmed about what they perceived as "the trend toward socialism," the country's corporate leaders responded with a multi-faceted campaign to defend "the American economic system," characterized by free enterprise, as Robert Griffith writes.[6] Within this context, it made a great deal of sense to demonize the USSR, a country which until recently had been idealized. By declaring the Soviet Union the national enemy of America, it became possible to condemn as "un-American" all radical ideas, union demands, and most forms of social security vaguely associated with Bolshevism and the USSR.[7]

The demonization of the Soviet Union was also useful because the USSR was the virtual embodiment of central planning and state intervention in economic life. In the 1930s America had already experimented with statist planning and intervention in the form of Roosevelt's New Deal, and during the 1940s the country's gigantic military and industrial war effort had been successfully coordinated in this manner. The American liberals counted on an "activist" state to realize their hopes for the social and economic future of the country. America's power elite, however, feared not without reason that after the war the privileges of free enterprise, that is, the privileges of business-people and corporations, might be further eroded by state intervention and central planning, in other words by the growth of a "command economy." With the Soviet Union as enemy it also became possible to condemn all forms of economic statism as communist or at least un-American and, conversely, to defend "free enterprise" as the birthright of all American patriots, as "the American way of life," criticized only by traitors to the Stars and Stripes.[8]

And so an anti-communist and anti-Soviet campaign was launched in the United States even before the final shot of the war had been fired. This campaign has gone down in history as "McCarthyism" because Senator Joseph McCarthy played the role of Torquemada in this inquisition. The noble ideals of freedom of conscience and free expression, to which America is so devoted in theory, and the fine principles of the Atlantic Charter, for which America had presumably gone to war, were violated again and again during McCarthy's witch hunt, which was to last for many years. The thrust of McCarthyism was certainly not only directed against America's handful of communists, but against all left-wing, radical, progressive, socially committed or even slightly unorthodox elements in politics, in the labour

216

movement, even in intellectual and cultural life. (Albert Einstein, Charlie
Chaplin, and Bertolt Brecht had to leave the United States because of
McCarthyism.) It was only logical, furthermore, that the McCarthyist witch
hunt went hand in hand with a large-scale offensive against the unions.
A suffocating conformist atmosphere would thus reign until well into the
1960s in the land that considers itself the cradle of free expression and
individualism. Incidentally, the American example was to inspire similar
(though usually far less hysterical) anti-communist and anti-Soviet campaigns elsewhere in the so-called "free world."[9]

It was felt that not only the success and the prestige of the Soviet Union,
but even its mere existence, gave too much encouragement to the left-wing
forces in political and social life. However, the USSR would continue to
exist for half a century, so that in the Western world it would long remain
impossible to placate the workers with wages, working hours, holidays,
pensions, and so on, which were not at least equally favourable to those
enjoyed on the other side of the iron curtain. For the rich Federal Republic
of Germany and for the rich United States, for example, it would long
remain a source of embarrassment that while workers in the much poorer
German Democratic Republic did make less money than their counterparts
in the West, they actually enjoyed social services that were in many ways
superior to those offered in West Germany.[10]

With either higher wages (as in the United States) or with a more or less
comprehensive system of social security (as in Great Britain, Canada, and
most Western European countries) it proved possible to secure the loyalty
of the majority of the population vis-à-vis the existing socio-economic system.[11] After the demise of the Soviet Union, therefore, we can understand
why employees, as well as the unemployed, women, and so on, almost
everywhere in the Western world have had to put up with the clawing
back of all sorts of social benefits they had come to take for granted during
the Cold War era. Because the existing capitalist socio-economic order no
longer faces any competition, it no longer needs to go through the effort
of securing the loyalty of the population by means of high wages or a high
level of social services.[12] It was "the pressure of being in competition with
an alternative economic system," writes Michael Parenti, which in the days
when the Soviet Union still existed "set limits on how thoroughly Western

politico-economic leaders dared to mistreat their working populations." When the Soviets were no longer there, adds Parenti, these same leaders felt that the time had come

> to cast off all restraint and sock it to the employee class. The competition for their hearts and minds was over. There was no alternative system, no place else for them to think of going. Big Capital scored a total victory and now would be able to write its own ticket at home and abroad . . . There would be no more accommodation . . . [13]

During the war the Soviet Union had been useful to America as an ally. After the war the Soviets soon became useful to America, or rather, to the American power elite, as an enemy. If after the Second World War there had been no USSR, the Americans would have had to invent this "evil empire," since as an enemy of the United States the Soviet Union was also extremely useful for a second reason. Only when the United States was threatened by a powerful and dangerous enemy would it be possible to justify the enormous sums that would be spent on defence, that is, on a continuing armament program. The more the new Red Peril was exaggerated, the easier it became to persuade Congress to dispense all sorts of funds for the benefit of the Pentagon, which would use the money to order ever-improved bombs, planes, and tanks.[14] This scheme has been given names such as Military Keynesianism, the Pentagon System, the War Economy, or, in contrast to the welfare state, the warfare state. Thanks to this system it could be ensured that after the war American industry would not slide back into a crisis. The primary beneficiaries of the Pentagon System were of course the large corporations that had always exerted great influence in Washington; during the war they had learned to engage in highly profitable business deals with the Pentagon, and thanks to the Cold War they would achieve even greater riches. The Pentagon System amounted, and continues to amount, to a "public subsidy, private profit" scheme, that is, a system whereby taxes paid by the general public allow individuals and private firms to pocket huge earnings. Already during the war, armament, soon euphemized as defence, had become the dynamo of the American economy. After the war this economy would continue to degenerate into a war economy, in other words, it would become even more dependent on the drug of Pentagon orders.[15] Consequently, in the United States power was to be concentrated increasingly in the hands of the generals, bureaucrats, and corporate leaders who collectively form the military-industrial complex against which President Eisenhower was to issue a noble warning — unfortunately only after he had proved himself an eager devotee of its cause during eight years in the White House.[16]

More than half a century after the end of the Second World War, and decades after the end of the Cold War, the Pentagon System has continued to run on all cylinders, if necessary with the help of new enemies such as Saddam Hussein, and crises such as the Gulf War in 1991, the conflict over Kosovo in 1999, and more recently the terrorist attacks of September 11, 2001. America's military budget already amounted to 265 billion dollars in 1996 and 350 billion dollars in 2002, in 2007 it reached 450 billion dollars, and in 2010 the Pentagon was allocated the mindboggling sum of 680 billion dollars. And when the unofficial military expenditures are included, such as the interest on the government bonds that financed the military expenditures of the past, care for veterans, as well as the costs of the wars in Iraq and Afghanistan, which are actually financed via "supplementary spending bills outside the federal budget, not included in the military budget figures," the costs of the warfare state amount to trillions of dollars; for example, an estimated 1 to 1.3 trillion dollars for the year 2010.[17]

Just as during the Second World War and during the Cold War, today military expenditures constitute a source of incredibly high profits for the large corporations and thus serve to fill the pocketbooks of their wealthy managers and shareholders. Furthermore, the costs of these expenditures continue to be financed predominantly through loans, and the interest on these loans is paid out primarily to the American individuals and firms who can afford to purchase the bonds.[18] Therefore, the American public debt, which had already risen enormously during the Second World War, has continued to increase after 1945 and after the end of the Cold War in 1990.[19] In the media and in scholarly studies, however, that development is usually not blamed on the catastrophic Pentagon System but on the allegedly unaffordable state expenditures for social services. In any event, it is primarily the average American citizens, who all "own" their share of the public debt whether they like it or not, who must foot the bill for the public debt with their taxes.

Economists such as the aforementioned Paul Samuelson, author of textbooks perused by millions of university students, argue that defence is one of the public goods whose costs must inevitably be borne by all citizens who benefit from it. However, they never point out that while the profits of the Pentagon System are conveniently *privatized* to the great advantage of corporations and wealthy Americans, the costs are mercilessly *socialized* to the detriment of ordinary Americans.[20]

The Cold War was a very complex historical phenomenon, caused by a plethora of factors, of which some can be traced back to the Russian Revolution of 1917. In this sense, the Cold War had already started toward the end of the First World War and may be defined as an international reaction to the Russian Revolution, a contra-revolutionary project that ended only with the destruction of the Soviet Union. However, once it had made its appearance on the scene of history, the Cold War revealed itself useful for a variety of purposes. For example, although it had obviously not been deliberately planned with this particular function in mind, the Cold War made it possible for America's industrial engine to continue to run at full speed after the ending of hostilities with Germany and Japan to the great advantage of corporate America. Furthermore, the new conflict performed yet another service for the American power elite. It forced the Soviet Union, which had never disposed of the kind of wealth accumulated in the United States, and which had been virtually ruined by the war, to invest the lion's share of its national wealth into armament for an indefinite period of time in what amounted to a desperate attempt to keep up with the Americans in the constantly accelerating arms race. (Incidentally, the expression "arms race" falsely creates the impression that it involved a voluntary and fair competition between two evenly matched competitors.) It thus became less and less likely that the Soviets might successfully build up a socialist society; instead, the chances were greatly increased that this task would end in a fiasco, which is precisely what was to happen in the end, even though the American power elite had to wait almost fifty years before their moment of triumph would come.[21]

Chapter 20
CORPORATE COLLABORATION
AND THE SO-CALLED
"DE-NAZIFICATION"
OF GERMANY (1)

Starting in the spring of 1945, the Americans had the opportunity of set-tling accounts with Nazism in Germany, and with fascism in general. As far as Germany is concerned, this episode has gone down in history under the label of "de-Nazification." However, it would be a big mistake to believe that de-Nazification involved a determined and consistent effort to eradi-cate all vestiges of Nazism.

It was not in the interest of the American power elite to reveal the true nature of Nazism, and of fascism in general. Fascism was a socially and politically reactionary phenomenon, whose advent to power in Italy and Germany had been made possible by the policies and the intrigues of conservative elements such as bankers, industrialists, large landowners, the army, and — not only in Italy but also in Germany — the leadership of the Catholic Church. In other countries, these same conservative elements had sympathized with foreign as well as domestic fascists. Germany's Nazis and the fascists of other countries defended the existing socio-economic order, were deadly enemies of labour unions, socialists, and communists; and, as American businessmen used to point out, they were "good for business." Like the European elites, the US power elite was mostly "philofascist," that is, it sympathized with fascism and appreciated the advantages it could reap from collaborating with fascist movements and regimes.

The United States had definitely not gone to war as a result of anti-fascist sentiment in general and of anti-Nazi sentiment in particular. If

Washington did eventually become involved in the war against Nazi Germany (and against fascist Italy), this was made possible by the fact that support for Germany's enemy, Great Britain, had opened up prospects for profitable business deals with Great Britain, the enemy of Nazi Germany, without jeopardizing the lucrative German connection, which continued to function thanks to the presence of US branch plants in the Reich. Even so, it took a Japanese attack on Pearl Harbor, and Hitler's own declaration of war, to cause the United States to "back into" the war against Nazi Germany.

This unexpected turn of events required a major effort to convince the American people that the enemy was henceforth Hitler's Germany and not the hitherto vilified USSR. The Nazis and fascists were now demonized as criminal monsters, from whom their formerly philofascist conservative associates urgently needed to distance themselves. This required diverting attention from the true nature of fascism. It was for this reason that in the United States the so-called "gangster theory of National Socialism" was developed and propagated. Hitler and Mussolini were henceforth portrayed, caricaturelike, as power-thirsty scoundrels who had arrived on the scene from nowhere and who operated entirely on their own account, within a kind of socio-economic vacuum, so to speak. The fascists were portrayed as sadistic gangsters, bloodthirsty adventurers whose advent to power in Germany happened to be a tragic but mysterious quirk of history. Seen from this perspective, the task of de-Nazification was simple; it consisted in dragging the culprits before a court and meting out a punishment likely to deter potential imitators, thus hopefully bringing the German nightmare to an end.[1]

It came to a series of trials of war criminals, exemplified most spectacularly by the notorious Nuremberg trials, which resulted in prominent (as well as some less prominent) Nazis receiving severe punishment, including the death penalty. However, conservative "enablers" and collaborators of the Nazis came away, to the chagrin of many, with minor penalties and even acquittals. Hitler's banker, Schacht, was thus acquitted, and so was the slippery politician von Papen, who had helped to pave the way for Hitler. The limits of de-Nazification were particularly evident when it came to punishing the German banks and corporations whose principals — owners, top managers, major shareholders — had supported the Nazis sometimes long before 1933, and who had profited handsomely from Hitler's rearmament program and from his war of conquest. In many cases they had also known how to profit from a close collaboration with the Nazi Party and with Himmler's sinister SS. For example, leading German firms had established factories and laboratories near concentration and extermination camps, including Auschwitz; in return for a modest financial contribution to the SS, they were allowed to use inmates as slaves, and in some cases even as human guinea pigs in vivisections. After the war, these firms were hardly bothered by the American occupation authorities; in fact, they were often energetically defended by the Americans against all those — German anti-fascists, survivors of the camps, Jewish organizations, the Soviets, and so on — who considered these businessmen to be war criminals of the same stature as the Nazis themselves.

In a series of post-Nuremberg trials, deliberately organized by the Americans alone and later to be disrespectfully described by the American prosecutor as "symbolic measures," German industrialists and bankers with Nazi connections were treated with kid gloves and frequently acquitted. All those who did receive (generally light) sentences were to benefit within three years after the verdict from an amnesty, compliments of the American occupation authorities.[2] In reality, then, the German business elite, which had supported Hitler and profited from his dictatorship, received from Uncle Sam a kind of "de facto amnesty," as the American historian Christopher Simpson has called it.[3]

Today, many German firms that collaborated eagerly with the Nazis and with the SS continue to do wonderful business thanks to the Americans, not only in Germany but in all of Europe and all over the globe. A good example is IG Farben, a huge German enterprise that had supported Hitler with great devotion, profited handsomely from the abundant use of slave labour made available by the SS, and collected considerable sums from the SS paymasters for the Zyklon-B poison gas delivered by its branch plant, Degesch, to the gas chambers of Auschwitz. IG Farben was in fact taken to court by the US authorities, but the firm's principals got away with penalties that were "light enough to please a chicken thief," as American prosecutor Josiah DuBois put it.[4] The huge cartel was then broken up into a number of successor firms, but in such a superficial way that property

223

relations and corporate power were preserved in spite of popular demands for drastic reforms. IG Farben's own managers were conveniently allowed to work out this presumably purely businesslike "de-cartelization" with the help of bankers and economists such as Josef Abs and Ludwig Erhard, who had earlier done useful work for the Nazi regime. The foremost among these allegedly "new" enterprises — Bayer, Hoechst, and BASF — continue to this very day to make money on behalf of anonymous shareholders who used to pocket the dividends of IG Farben.[5] Other German firms that collaborated keenly with the SS include AEG, Siemens, Daimler-Benz, and BMW, in other words, the *crème de la crème* of German industry today.[6] It was not without reason that some Germans complained that the kind of de-Nazification practised by the Americans permitted "the big fish" to slip all too easily through the net.[7]

The remarkable and successful movie *Schindler's List* may be based on true facts, but it nevertheless violates the historical truth in some way, in that it creates the impression that the collaboration between German businessmen and the SS was not only something extraordinary — the initiative of an individual — but also that it served to save lives. In reality, the SS collaborated systematically with countless German firms big and small, and this collaboration cost the lives of many thousands of people who served as slaves or guinea pigs. It is unlikely that Hollywood will ever make a film about the true relationship between the SS and Germany's leading enterprises, which include former partners and branch plants of American corporations.

The scientific and technical advances achieved by many German firms during the war by means of their sinister collaboration with the SS, but of course also by means of conventional research, were appropriated by and large by the United States after the war, although the Soviets also acquired a share of the booty. Starting in the spring of 1945, the Americans confiscated patents, plans, blueprints, and all sorts of know-how, not only in their own occupation zone, in order to make them available to their leading corporations. This amounted to a veritable "intellectual plunder" or, as an official from the US Commerce Department's Office of Technical Services, John C. Green, preferred to call it, "intellectual reparations."[8] Furthermore, a large number of concentration camp doctors who had been involved in experiments on human guinea pigs as well as other scientists and experts were transferred as quickly as possible to the United States. This operation was carried out under the code names Overcast and, later, Paperclip. A blind eye was turned to the Nazi past of these people; they were handed the necessary immigration papers, and many of them even received American citizenship. In return for this they went to work for the Pentagon and for other public or private American institutions and firms. For example, Washington took a keen interest in German rocket technology, a discipline that happened to be the specialty of a former SS-man, Wernher von Braun, as well as in the production of poison gas and all kinds of other chemical and bacteriological weapons. Many Nazis with horrible crimes on their conscience were thus allowed to live long and happy lives in the land that had presumably gone to war out of revulsion against Nazism.[9]

The American authorities had a great deal of understanding for the fact that during the era of the Third Reich, Germany's industrial elite had been guided by the motto "business as usual." After all, in the United States the large corporations had likewise known how to profit from the war. In addition, American leaders viewed the great German firms as indispensable partners in constructing a new Germany in which private property and free enterprise would be as sacrosanct as in the United States. The Nazi past of the principals of these firms was swept under the rug, because the arduous task of rebuilding Germany could presumably not be accomplished without the help of these "experts." All those who were clamouring for the heads of Hitler's financiers, the principals of IG Farben, arms producer Krupp, et al. were denounced as enemies of free enterprise, as "commies."[10]

Last but certainly not least, the magnanimity of the Americans also resulted from the intimate and highly profitable links that influential American enterprises maintained with many German firms. In the 1920s American corporations had founded branch plants, taken over enterprises, or entered into strategic partnerships with firms in Germany, and in the dark years of the Great Depression they had done lucrative business there. After the outbreak of the war, and even after Pearl Harbor, these German connections were preserved in one way or another.[11]

Coca-Cola's plant in Essen, for example, prospered from the war; its sales and bottling operations expanded considerably as the German subsidiary followed the victorious Wehrmacht into occupied countries such as France and Belgium. When it was prevented from importing Coke's syrup from the United States after Pearl Harbor, it continued to do business with a new soft drink, Fanta, of which nearly 3 million cases were sold in 1943 alone. Coca-Cola's wartime conduct in the land of the Nazi enemy was hardly compatible with its image at home, writes Mark Pendergrast, where the soft drink from Atlanta "symbolize[d] . . . American freedom [and] all the good things . . . the GI was fighting for." However, Coke's connection with the swastika is a pretty harmless example of the wartime activities of US corporations in Nazi Germany — at least in comparison to the German ventures of firms such as IBM, ITT, Ford, and General Motors.[12]

According to Edwin Black, IBM's know-how enabled the Nazis and their war machine to "achieve scale, velocity, efficiency." Black claims not only that IBM "put the blitz into the *Blitzkrieg*" via its German subsidiary, Dehomag, but that its punch card technology, precursor to the computer, also enabled the Nazis to "automate persecution." IBM allegedly put "the fantastical numbers in the Holocaust," Black continues, because it supplied the Hitler regime with the Hollerith calculating machines and other tools that were used to "generate lists of Jews and other victims, who were then targeted for deportation," and to "register inmates [of concentration camps] and track slave labor." (There was an IBM office, called *Hollerith Abteilung*, in every concentration and extermination camp, including Auschwitz.) It is very likely true that the Nazis could have achieved this deadly efficiency without IBM technology, as is claimed by certain critics of Black's study. However, the case of IBM shows how large American companies placed their most modern technology at the disposal of the Nazis, and showed little concern for the use Hitler and his cronies were to make of it. In any event, Black claims that IBM managed to continue to do business in Nazi Germany after Pearl Harbor, "using its European subsidiaries as a facade," and that the corporation made millions of dollars in the process.[13]

ITT, managed by the pro-fascist Sosthenes Behn, had acquired a quarter of the shares of airplane manufacturer Focke-Wulf in the 1930s, and was thus involved during the war, at least indirectly, in the construction of fighter planes that shot down hundreds of Allied aircraft. (An important ingredient in the fuel needed by ITT's Focke-Wulfs as well as other German fighter planes was synthetic tetraethyl; it was produced by an enterprise named Ethyl GmbH, which happened to be a daughter firm of a trio formed by Standard Oil, Standard's German partner IG Farben, and General Motors. In German documents recovered after the war, American military personnel were able to read that "without tetra-ethyl, we could never have dreamed of our form of [lightning] warfare.")[14] Until the very end of the war, ITT's production facilities in Germany as well as in neutral countries such as Sweden, Switzerland, and Spain were to provide the German armed forces not only with planes but also with many other martial toys.[15] Charles Higham offers specifics:

> After Pearl Harbor the German army, navy, and air force contracted with ITT for the manufacture of switchboards, telephones, alarm gongs, buoys, air-raid warning devices, radar equipment, and thirty thousand fuses per month for artillery shells . . . This was to increase to fifty thousand per month by 1944. In addition, ITT supplied ingredients for the rocket bombs that fell on London, selenium cells for dry rectifiers, high-frequency radio equipment, and fortification and field communication sets. Without this supply of crucial materials it would have been impossible for the German air force to kill American and British troops, for the German army to fight the Allies, for England to have been bombed, or for Allied ships to have been attacked at sea.

Without sophisticated communications equipment provided by ITT, Germany in the early stages of the war would not have been able to inflict on its enemies the deadly form of warfare known as the blitzkrieg, which postulated highly synchronized attacks by air and by land. After Pearl Harbor, ITT supplied Germany with even more advanced communication systems, to the detriment also of the Americans, whose diplomatic code was broken by the Nazis with the help of such equipment.[16]

The gigantic car manufacturer GM provides what is perhaps the most spectacular example of the illicit activities of American big business in the land of the Nazi enemy, but its competitor, Ford, also made a considerable contribution to the Nazi war effort. During the war, Ford built not only countless trucks but also engines and all sorts of spare parts for the Wehrmacht; Ford did so not only in its Ford-Werke factory in Cologne, but also in its branch plants in occupied France, Belgium, the Netherlands, and Denmark, as well as in Finland, Italy, and other countries allied with Nazi Germany.[17] The German branch plants of General Motors were converted entirely to war production after a meeting of Hitler and Göring, not only the Luftwaffe boss but also Germany's economic czar at the time, with GM executive Mooney in Berlin on September 19–20, 1939. The result was that the Opel factory in Brandenburg, founded in 1935, switched to the production of "Blitz" trucks for the Wehrmacht, while Opel in Rüsselsheim henceforth produced primarily for the Luftwaffe, assembling planes such as the JU-88, the workhorse of Germany's fleet of bombers. At one point, General Motors and Ford together reportedly accounted for no less than half of Germany's entire production of tanks. Incidentally, the German tanks were generally of better quality than those produced in the United States itself, such as the Sherman, which the GIs cynically nicknamed the Ronson because with their bazookas the Germans could generally "light it up at the first attempt"; a similar claim was made for the Ronson lighter in a contemporary commercial.[18]

Experts believe that GM's and Ford's best wartime technological innovations primarily benefitted their branch plants in Nazi Germany rather than their factories in the United States or Great Britain, which produced for the Allied war effort. As examples they cite all-wheel-drive Opel trucks, which proved eminently useful to the Germans in the mud of the Eastern Front and in the desert of North Africa, as well as the engines for the brand new Me 262, the first jet fighter, also assembled by Opel in Rüsselsheim. As for the Ford-Werke in Cologne, in 1939 this firm had created a "cloak company," Arendt GmbH, for the purpose of producing war equipment other than vehicles, and toward the end of the war this factory was involved in the top-secret development of turbines for the infamous V-2 rockets that wreaked devastation on London and Antwerp. It was not without reason, then, that the German subsidiaries of American enterprises were regarded as "pioneers of technological development" by the planners in the Reich Economics Ministry and other Nazi authorities involved in the war.[19]

Only very few people know that GM, Ford, ITT, and other giants of corporate America functioned during the war in Germany as a kind of "arsenal of Nazism." These enterprises themselves have naturally always kept mum about this delicate subject.[20] Moreover, even the rare cognoscenti tend to assume that these German branch plants were ruthlessly confiscated by the Nazis after Pearl Harbor and only returned to the control of the corporate owners and managers in the United States after the war. This was not the case. A German expert, Hans Helms, writes categorically that "not even once during their terror regime did the Nazis undertake the slightest attempt to change the ownership status of Ford or Opel."[21] Even during the war, Ford retained its 52 per cent of the shares of the Ford-Werke in Cologne, and General Motors remained Opel's sole proprietor. (Incidentally, a large block of the remaining Ford-Werke shares were controlled by IG Farben.) The American owners and managers maintained a sometimes considerable measure of control over their branch plants in Germany also after the German declaration of war on the United States. There is evidence that the corporate headquarters in the United States and the branch plants in Germany stayed in contact with each other, either indirectly, via subsidiaries in neutral Switzerland, or directly by means of modern worldwide systems of communications. The latter were supplied by ITT in collaboration with Transradio (a joint venture of ITT itself), RCA (another American corporation), and the German firms Siemens and Telefunken. Edsel Ford, Henry Ford's son, was thus able to continue to intervene personally in the management of the Ford-Werke in Cologne and the Ford plants in occupied France.[22] As for IBM, Edwin Black writes that during the war its general manager for Europe, Dutchman Jurriaan W. Schotte, was actually stationed in the corporate headquarters in New York, whence he "continued to regularly maintain communication with IBM subsidiaries in Nazi territory, such as his native Holland and Belgium." IBM, Black continues, could also "monitor events and exercise authority in Europe through neutral country subsidiaries," and especially through its Swiss branch in Geneva, whose director, a Swiss national, "freely travelled to and from Germany, occupied territories, and neutral countries." Finally, like many other large US corporations, IBM could also rely on American diplomats stationed in occupied and neutral countries to forward messages via diplomatic pouches.

Black concludes that "despite the illusion of non-involvement, IBM [in] NY continued to play a central role in the day-to-day operations of its subsidiaries [in Germany and elsewhere in Europe] . . . It was business as usual throughout the war."[23] The Nazis graciously allowed the American owners to retain possession of their subsidiaries in Germany, and they even permitted them a certain amount of control over their administration. Furthermore, the Nazis' own intervention in the management of, say, Opel and the Ford-Werke, remained minimal. After the German declaration of war against the United States, the American staff members did admittedly disappear from the scene, but the existing German managers — confidants of the bosses in the US — generally retained their positions of authority and continued to run the businesses, thereby keeping in mind the interests of the corporate headquarters and the shareholders in America. In the case of Opel, GM's headquarters in the United States retained virtually total control over the managers in Rüsselsheim. At least this is the opinion of the American historian Bradford Snell, who already devoted attention to this theme in the 1970s, but whose findings were contested by GM. However, a recent study by the German researcher Anita Kugler confirms the accuracy of Snell's allegations while providing a more detailed and more nuanced picture. After the German declaration of war on the United States, she writes, the Nazis initially did not bother the management of Opel at all. It was only on November 25, 1942, almost one year after Pearl Harbor, that Berlin appointed an "enemy-assets custodian," but the significance of this move turned out to be merely symbolic. The Nazis simply wanted to create a German image for an enterprise that was owned 100 per cent by General Motors, and which was to remain so for the duration of the war. Kugler supplies details:

In contrast to the legend promoted by Opel and General Motors, the trusteeship did not amount to a dictatorial repression by anti-American Nazis . . . The custodian was no autocratic outsider, but someone who had been selected in 1935 by the Americans themselves as member of the board of directors and appointed by them to a leading managerial position . . . Furthermore, de facto as well as de jure he was

230

*subordinated to the decisions of the board of directors . . . He
did not even have the rank of general manager.*[24]

In the Ford-Werke a certain Robert Schmidt, an ardent Nazi, served as
general manager during the war, and his performance greatly satisfied both
the authorities in Berlin and the Ford managers in America. Messages of
approval and even congratulations — signed by Edsel Ford — were regularly forthcoming from Ford's corporate headquarters in Dearborn, Michigan.
The Nazis, too, were extremely happy with Schmidt's work; in due course
they were to award him the pompous but prestigious title of "leader in the
field of the military economy." Even when, months after Pearl Harbor, a
custodian was appointed to oversee the Ford plant in Cologne, Schmidt
retained his prerogatives and his freedom of action. After the war Schmidt
chose to disappear from the scene for a while because of his devotion to
National Socialism and his eager collaboration with the SS, but from 1950
on he was back in a position of authority in the Ford-Werke and he was to
remain there until his death in 1962.[25]

The prospect of having an enemy-assets custodian overseeing their
subsidiaries was not really all that abhorrent to parent corporations in
the United States. The American owners had every reason to expect that
enemy property would be treated in Germany as it had been during the
First World War, and as German investments were in fact being treated in
the United States during the Second World War.[26] As Edwin Black emphasizes, investors on both sides could expect their property in enemy territory
"to be safeguarded, managed properly and then returned intact when the
conflict ended," with the temporarily blocked profits to be released at the
end of the hostilities. Like the Americans, the Nazis subscribed to the written and unwritten rules of international capitalism, and it was as good as
certain that, as Black writes, "the Nazi receiver would diligently manage
[the enemy] subsidiaries" and that "their money [i.e., profits] would be
waiting when the war was over." Moreover, as Black points out, having a
custodian actually involved a considerable advantage, namely, "plausible
deniability": the presence of an enemy-assets custodian made it possible for
the stateside owners and managers to make money through collaboration
with the enemy while retaining the ability to deny any responsibility for

whatever was being perpetrated in the money-making process.[27]

As far as IBM was concerned, its wartime experience with enemy-assets custodians in Germany (as well as France, Belgium, and other occupied countries) was far from traumatic. According to Black, "they zealously protected the assets, extended productivity, and increased profits"; moreover, "existing IBM managers were kept in place as day-to-day managers and, in some cases, even appointed deputy enemy custodians." Of the Dehomag custodian, Hermann B. Fellinger, Black writes that he "functioned with as much commercial zeal and dedication to the IBM enterprise as any senior executive Watson could have personally selected." In view of this, it is not surprising that Fellinger was to be retained in a leading managerial position at Dehomag after Germany's capitulation.[28]

The Nazis were far less interested in the nationality of the owners or the identity of the managers than in production, because after the failure of their blitzkrieg strategy in the Soviet Union they experienced an ever-growing need for airplanes and trucks mass-produced by the Ford-Werke, for example. Ever since Henry Ford had pioneered the use of the assembly line and other such "Fordist" techniques, American firms had been the leaders in the field of industrial mass production, and the American branch plants in Germany, including GM's Opel subsidiary, were no exception to this general rule. Nazi planners like Göring and Speer knew this, and they understood only too well that radical changes in Opel's management might hinder production in Brandenburg and Rüsselsheim. In order to maintain Opel's output at high levels, the managers in charge were allowed to carry on, because they were familiar with the particularly efficient American methods of production. This was the main reason why in the Opel plants things continued according to the motto "business as usual," even after Pearl Harbor. Berlin's production quotas were even regularly exceeded, so that the Nazi authorities awarded the GM subsidiary the honorary title of "model war enterprise." Opel's managers were so successful in the field of production that the Nazis allowed them more and more "entrepreneurial freedom." The German researcher Anita Kugler arrives at the conclusion that GM's branch plant Opel "made its entire production and research available to the Nazis and thus — objectively speaking — contributed to enhance their long-term capability to wage war."[29]

For the American managers and owners of GM and Ford, it was unimportant who happened to serve as managers in their German branch plants and which products came off the assembly lines there, and it bothered them little or not at all that the activities of their German subsidiaries possibly served to lengthen the war. What counted for themselves and for the shareholders, in the final analysis, were only the profits. Too few people know that branch plants of American corporations in Germany achieved considerable earnings during the war, and that this money was not pocketed by the Nazis. For the Ford-Werke precise figures are available. The profits of Dearborn's German subsidiary rose from 1.2 million RM in 1939 to 1.7 million in 1940, 1.8 million in 1941, and 2.1 million in 1943.[30] The Ford subsidiaries in occupied France, Holland, and Belgium, where the American corporate giant also made an industrial contribution to the Nazi war effort, were likewise extraordinarily successful. Ford-France, for example — not a flourishing firm before the war — became very profitable after 1940 thanks to its unconditional collaboration with the Germans; in 1941 it registered earnings of 58 million francs, an achievement for which it was warmly congratulated by Edsel Ford.[31]

No details of the profits registered by Opel are available, but it is known that the German branch plant of GM also did very well. According to Anita Kugler, few other German enterprises could match Opel's cash flows during the war, and the GM subsidiary accumulated more and more liquid assets each month. Opel's profits skyrocketed to the point where the Nazi Ministry of Economics banned their publication; this was done in order to avoid bad blood on the part of the German population, which was increasingly being asked to tighten its collective belt, and which probably realized that the profits of this American branch plant did not accrue to Volksgenossen, that is, to Teutonic "racial comrades."[32]

As for IBM, Edwin Black writes that the earnings of its German branch plant "boomed" during the war. Dehomag already registered record profit increases in 1939, and as the war progressed its riches "mushroomed even more rapidly . . . especially as a result of the Nazi takeovers of Belgium, Poland, and France," so that the value of IBM's subsidiary in the Third Reich "was catapulting daily." As in the case of Ford, the profits of IBM in occupied France soared primarily because of business generated through eager collaboration with the German occupation authorities, and it was soon necessary to build new factories. Above all, however, if we are to believe Black, IBM prospered in

> Germany and in the occupied countries because it sold
> the Nazis the technological tools required for identifying,
> deporting, ghettoizing, enslaving, and ultimately exterminating
> millions of European Jews, in other words, for organizing the
> Holocaust.[33]

The Nazis themselves had nothing against the fact that American invest-ment capital made considerable profits in Germany during the war. This comes as no surprise, considering that it was precisely because of their respect for the rules of the capitalist game that long before the war the fascists had been admired and supported by the industrialists of Germany, and of America. These rules, which the Nazis themselves condensed in the motto "to each his own," would indeed be observed by Hitler and his cron-ies until the bitter end. The Nazis were no communists, and in the Third Reich the proceeds of an enterprise did not accrue to the state, as things were often wrongly presented in the American media, or the workers, but to the owners or shareholders. This was and remained true also in the case of the American branch plants, even though the profits were not directly transferred to the corporate headquarters in the United States.

It is far from clear what happened to the profits made in Germany by American subsidiaries during the war, but some tantalizing tidbits of infor-mation have nevertheless reached the light of day. Already before the war, in the 1930s, American corporations had developed a number of strategies to circumvent the Nazis' embargo on profit repatriation. IBM's head office in New York, for example, had made it a habit of regularly billing Dehomag for royalties due to the parent firm, for repayment of contrived loans, and for other fees and expenses; this practice and other byzantine inter-com-pany transactions also minimized profits in Germany and thus simultan-eously functioned as an effective tax-avoidance scheme. It is unlikely that IBM was the only stateside corporate parent to develop such "accountancy transmogrifications," as Black calls them, such "complicated, untaxable intercompany shunts," essentially the predecessors of transfer pricing and other tricks used widely by multinationals in today's global village in order to avoid taxes and maximize profits.[34]

We have seen earlier that there were other ways of handling the embargo on profit repatriation, such as reinvestment within Germany, but after 1939 this option was no longer permitted — at least not in theory. Nevertheless, many American subsidiaries did manage to increase their assets that way. In 1942 Opel thus took over a foundry in Leipzig that had been supplying it with engine blocks for quite some time. And of course it remained possible to use earnings in order to improve and modernize the branch plant's own infrastructure. That, too, happened in the case of Opel.[35] As for the Ford-Werke, their total assets increased between 1939 and 1945 from 60.4 to 68.8 million RM and the firm's value reportedly more than doubled during the war.[36] There also existed opportunities for expansion in the occupied countries of Europe. Ford's subsidiary in France used its profits in 1941 to build a tank factory in Oran in Algeria; this plant allegedly provided Rommel's Africa Corps with the hardware needed to advance all the way to El Alamein. Since the Ford-Werke in Cologne maintained close contacts with Ford-France, it is not impossible that the Algerian venture was partly financed with profits made by Ford in Nazi Germany.[37]

It would appear that at least a small portion of the lucre accumulated in the Third Reich was transferred back to the United States by way of Switzerland. According to Edwin Black, that neutral country functioned "like a kind of switchboard for commercial intrigue at the time of the Nazis." Many US corporations maintained offices there that served as go-betweens between stateside headquarters and their subsidiaries in enemy or occupied countries. These offices were allegedly involved in "profit funnelling," as Edwin Black writes in connection with the Swiss branch of IBM.[38] Swiss banks, and international banks based in Switzerland, proved helpful in this respect, for example the Bank for International Settlements (BIS), conveniently based in the city of Basel, a Swiss city on the German border. This international bank had been founded in 1930 within the framework of the Young Plan for the purpose of facilitating German reparation payments after the First World War. American and German bankers (such as Schacht) dominated the BIS from the start, collaborated cozily in this financial venture, and continued to do so during the war — even after Pearl Harbor. A German, Paul Hechler, a member of the Nazi party, was the director, and an American, Thomas H. McKittrick, served as president.

Throughout the war, the BIS functioned as a kind of private club in which German and American bankers and businessmen could hold friendly and mutually beneficial meetings while, as the German weekly *Der Spiegel* wrote in 1997, "far from the neutral and idyllic country in which they found themselves, soldiers of their respective countries were busy killing each other mercilessly on all fronts."[39] (As Paul Valéry expressed it at the end of the First World War, "War [is] a massacre of people who do not know each other, for the benefit of people who know each other but do not kill each other.") The BIS was a kind of beehive buzzing with American bankers, industrialists, and lawyers as well as their German counterparts. The latter even included a number of high-ranking Nazis, including bigwigs of the SS, who came to Switzerland with gold looted from murdered Jews in order to pay for the purchase of all kinds of imported goods, such as iron ore from Sweden or tungsten from Portugal, needed to continue the war for as long as possible.[40] Prominent among the Americans who hovered around the BIS was Allen Dulles, the OSS agent in Switzerland since 1942, who was a friend of McKittrick. His brother, John Foster Dulles, meanwhile, served as the BIS lawyer in New York. Is it unreasonable to suspect that the BIS may have been involved in the repatriation of profits made by German branch plants of US corporations, in other words, money hoarded by folks such as the clients and associates of the ubiquitous Dulles brothers? Not surprisingly, the corporations and banks that participated in those transactions have always observed the greatest discretion. But some information has nevertheless come to light. It is known, for example, that the BIS was kind enough to forward to the oil magnate William Rhodes Davis, via Lisbon and Buenos Aires, a part of the profit made by his German subsidiary, Eurotank Handelsgesellschaft, based in Hamburg.[41]

Chapter 21
CORPORATE COLLABORATION AND THE SO-CALLED "DE-NAZIFICATION" OF GERMANY (2)

The contemporary phenomenon known as downsizing, which requires a constantly decreasing number of employees to work harder and harder in order to guarantee higher and higher profits for the employers (and the foreign or domestic investors), demonstrates clearly that profits depend not only on high prices and cheap raw materials but also to a large extent on low wages.[1] The lower the price of labour, the higher the profits achieved by capital. In this respect the practitioners of downsizing might learn something from the experience of the American branch plants in Germany during the Second World War. Already before the war, most if not all German corporations had eagerly taken advantage of the big favour done for them by the Nazis, namely, the elimination of the labour unions. This arbitrary measure had emasculated the German working class and transformed it into a powerless "mass of followers" *(Gefolgschaft)*, to use Nazi terminology, that — in accordance with the authoritarian top-down "leadership principle" *(Führerprinzip)* thereafter prevailing in private as well as in public life — was unconditionally put at the disposal of their employers. Not surprisingly, in Nazi Germany real wages declined rapidly while profits increased correspondingly.

During the war, Germany's workers were called up to serve as cannon fodder. This was supposed to amount to a temporary inconvenience only, as the blitzkrieg concept called for a short war followed by total victory, but the failure of lightning warfare in the Soviet Union prevented the return of millions of men to the labour force. They were stuck on the Eastern Front, and untold numbers of them would never make it back to Germany. As a result of the ensuing labour shortage, the law of supply and demand would normally have caused wage costs to escalate, and profits to decline. However, this disagreeable prospect was prevented by the resourceful Nazis, who promulgated a moratorium on wage and price increases as early as September 4, 1939. In practice, prices continued to rise, while wages were gradually eroded and working hours were increased. This was also the experience of the labour force of the American subsidiaries. Starting in May 1940, for example, the workers at Opel had to work sixty hours per week for lower wages, which led to protests against this "wage theft," as some Opel workers called it. Even so, in Rüsselsheim the work week would gradually become even longer, so that by the end of 1942 employees had to put in sixty-six hours per week.[2]

In order to combat the labour shortages in the factories, the Nazis relied increasingly on foreign labourers who were put to work in Germany under frequently inhuman conditions. Together with hundreds of thousands of Soviet and other POWs as well as inmates of concentration camps, these *Fremdarbeiter* formed a gigantic pool of forced labour that could be exploited at will by any firm that opted to use them, in return for a modest remuneration paid to the SS. The SS, moreover, also maintained the required discipline and order with an iron hand. Wage costs thus sank to a level of which today's downsizers can only dream, and the corporate profits augmented correspondingly. The German branch plants of American corporations also made eager use of slave labour supplied by the Nazis, not only in the form of *Fremdarbeiter* but also in the form of POWs and even concentration camp inmates. For example, the Yale & Towne Manufacturing Company based in Velbert in the Rhineland reportedly relied on "the aid of labourers from Eastern Europe" to make "considerable profits," as Stephan H. Lindner writes, and Coca-Cola is said to have benefitted from the use of foreign workers as well as prisoners of war in its Fanta plants. Kodak was another American corporation whose German branch plants, based in Stuttgart and in Berlin-Köpenick, made use of forced labour.[3] However, the most spectacular examples of the use of forced labour by American subsidiaries appear to have been provided by Ford and General Motors. Of the

Ford-Werke it is alleged that starting in 1942 this firm "zealously, aggressively, and successfully" pursued the use of foreign workers and POWs
from the Soviet Union, France, Belgium, and other occupied countries, and
apparently with the knowledge of the corporate headquarters in the United
States. Karola Fings, a German researcher who has carefully studied the
wartime activities of the Ford-Werke, writes:

> [Ford] did wonderful business with the Nazis. Because the
> acceleration of production during the war opened up total-
> ly new opportunities to keep the level of wage costs low. A
> general freeze on wage increases was in effect in the Ford-
> Werke from 1941 on. However, the biggest profit margins
> could be achieved by means of the use of so-called Ostarbeiter
> [forced workers from Eastern Europe].[4]

The thousands of foreign forced labourers put to work in the Ford-Werke
were forced to slave away every day except Sunday for twelve hours, and
for this they received no wage whatsoever. Presumably even worse was the
treatment reserved for the relatively small number of inmates from the
Buchenwald concentration camp, who were made available to the Ford-
Werke in the summer of 1944. In contrast to the Ford-Werke, Opel never
used concentration camp inmates, at least not in the firm's main plants in
Rüsselsheim and Brandenburg. However, the German subsidiary of GM
did have an insatiable appetite for other types of forced labour, such as
prisoners of war. Already in the summer of 1940 the first POWs were put to
work in the factory in Rüsselsheim, and this first POW work detail involved
Frenchmen. They were to be joined later by large numbers of Soviets, who
received particularly bad treatment. Deported civilian workers from mostly
Eastern but also Western Europe were likewise put to work at Opel. Typical
of the use of slave labour in the Opel factories, particularly when it involved
Russians, writes historian Anita Kugler, were "maximum exploitation, the
worst possible treatment, and . . . capital punishment even in the case of
minor offences." The Gestapo was in charge of supervising the foreign
labourers.[5] ·

During the war, then, America's big corporations had a knack for making money through business with enemies as well as with allies. However, it is doubtful if the famous business schools of the United States, where ambitious (and moneyed) young foreigners as well as Americans are acquainted with the ways of American entrepreneurship, ever pay attention to this particularly interesting and instructive success story. And the more or less official chronicles of these corporations, as well as the biographies of Henry Ford and similar corporate giants generally shed little or no light on this theme. As far as the North American media are concerned, they tend to focus their muckraking activities on the Swiss banks that purloined the gold the Nazis had robbed from their Jewish victims, and on German firms, such as Volkswagen, which took advantage of slave labour during the war; but they hardly ever utter a word about the connections between American corporations and the Nazis. In the US, and also in Canada, where Ford and GM own important subsidiaries, the universally praised freedom of the press (and of speech in general) seems to reach its limits whenever newspapers, magazines, and TV channels risk losing advertising revenue by offending big-spending firms such as Ford and Coca-Cola by delving into their corporate pasts. (Just as some TV programs are said to be "made possible" by a high-profile corporation, many programs are made *impossible* as a result of corporate sponsorship.)

A similar self-censorship can also be observed at the universities, where academic freedom reigns supreme — but only in theory. An American expert on the history of the Third Reich and the Second World War, who shall remain unnamed, thus succeeded not so long ago in writing a book of more than 1,000 pages about the war without mentioning the Ford-Werke or Ford in general, or General Motors and its Opel subsidiary, even once. This is quite understandable in light of the fact that he has made a career in Michigan — at one of the universities whose financial well-being depends largely on the patronage of that state's automobile manufacturers.

Back home in the United States, the parent corporations of German subsidiaries hardly experienced any problems at all over their activities in the land of the Nazi enemy. Quite naturally, these corporations maintained the greatest possible discretion and even secrecy about that aspect of their business, so that most Americans had no idea of what was concocted during the war by American capital in Cologne, Rüsselsheim, and elsewhere in

Germany. Moreover, by means of pompous words and grandiose gestures these firms tried very hard to convince stateside public opinion of their patriotism. Consequently, no ordinary American could ever have imagined that GM, for example, a firm that financed anti-German posters at home, was involved on the distant banks of the Rhine in activities that really amounted to a kind of treason.[6]

Washington was far better informed than John Doe, but the American government observed the unwritten rule stipulating that "what is good for General Motors is good for America," and turned a blind eye to the fact that American corporations accumulated riches through their investments in, or trade with, the Third Reich. Incidentally, the Roosevelt administration just happened to feature a number of former GM executives in high positions, such as William S. Knudsen, a friend of Göring in the 1930s and until 1940 the president of General Motors. Barely one week after the Japanese attack on Pearl Harbor, on December 13, 1941, President Roosevelt himself discreetly issued an edict allowing American corporations to do business with enemy countries — or with neutral countries that were friendly with enemies — by means of a special authorization. This order clearly contravened the supposedly strict laws against all forms of "trading with the enemy," and stands in great contrast to the way in which analogous laws are enforced with regard to Cuba even today: American citizens are not even allowed to bring Havana cigars bought in Canada back to the United States.[7]

Washington also counted on the active collaboration of the country's big corporations in order to bring the war to a successful end. As Charles Higham has written, Roosevelt's administration "had to get into bed with the oil companies in order to win the war." Consequently, government officials could not afford to ask difficult questions, and so a blind eye was turned to the unpatriotic conduct of American investment capital abroad and especially in Germany. "In order to satisfy public opinion," says Higham, token legal action actually had to be taken in 1942 against the best-known violator of the "Trading with the Enemy" legislation, Standard Oil. But Standard pointed out that it "was fueling a high percentage of the Army, Navy, and Air Force, [thus] making it possible for America to win the war." The Rockefeller enterprise eventually agreed to pay a minor fine "for having betrayed America" but was allowed to continue its profitable commerce with the enemies of the United States.[8] A tentative investigation into IBM's arguably treasonous activities in the land of the Nazi enemy was similarly aborted because the United States needed IBM technology as much as the Nazis did. Edwin Black writes:

> IBM was in some ways bigger than the war. Both sides could not afford to proceed without the company's all-important technology. Hitler needed IBM. So did the Allies.[9]

Uncle Sam briefly wagged a finger at Standard Oil and IBM, but the majority of the owners and managers of corporations who did business with Hitler were never bothered at all. The connections of ITT's Sosthenes Behn with Nazi Germany, for example, were a public secret in Washington, but he never experienced any difficulties as a result of them. Charles Higham explains:

> Despite the fact that all branches of American Intelligence were monitoring Behn at every turn . . . and in general knew exactly what he was up to, nothing whatsoever was done to stop him. As the war neared its end, whatever mild internal criticisms were voiced within the American government were quickly silenced by the prospects of Germany's capitulation and the expectation of a coming confrontation with the Soviet Union.

Behn cultivated intimate contacts with America's military leadership, and he even received the highest civilian award, the Medal for Merit, for his presumably invaluable services to the American army. Behn's final resting place may be found in Washington's Arlington Cemetery, not far from the tomb of John F. Kennedy and close to the graves of thousands of American soldiers who lost their lives in the war against his Nazi friends.[10]

Stateside, then, the big American corporations did not experience any serious difficulties as a result of the services they rendered to the enemy. Furthermore, it would appear that the headquarters of the Western Allies were keen to go as easy as possible on the American-owned enterprises in Germany. Thus, while Cologne's historical city centre was flattened in repeated bombing raids, the large Ford factory on the outskirts of the city enjoyed the reputation of being the safest place in town during air attacks. The locals who tell this story exaggerate perhaps somewhat, but it is a fact that during Allied bombing raids surprisingly little property of the Ford-Werke was destroyed, and that the infrastructure of the enterprise remained intact, so that Ford's subsidiary in Cologne would be able to resume operations virtually immediately after the end of the hostilities. The first post-war truck was actually produced on May 8, 1945, the day of the German surrender. According to German expert Hans G. Helms, Bernard Baruch, a high-level advisor to President Roosevelt, had given the order not to bomb certain factories in Germany, or to bomb them only lightly. It is hardly surprising that the branch plants of American corporations fell into this category. About the Ford-Werke, Helms writes categorically that "they could not be bombed, and consequently they were not bombed," except in "simulated attacks." On October 15 and 18, 1944, a neighbouring terrain with workers' barracks was thus the target of an Allied air attack. Another enterprise spared was Bayer in Leverkusen, affiliated with Standard Oil via IG Farben. Helms claims that this plant produced certain types of medication against tropical diseases, needed by the American army in the Pacific and duly supplied by the Germans via Switzerland and Portugal.[11] The Opel factory in Rüsselsheim, on the other hand, was actually bombed, but only towards the end of the war, on July 20 and on August 25 and 26, 1944, causing the destruction of half of the buildings. By that time, however, the most important machinery and productive facilities had already been transferred into the countryside in an operation known as a "dispersement" (Auslagerung). Production could thus continue until March 25, 1945, when the GIs arrived in Rüsselsheim.[12]

IBM's German branch plants also emerged from the vicissitudes of war with remarkably little damage. Among the very first GIs to enter the Dehomag facility in Sindelfingen near Stuttgart, writes Edwin Black, happened to be some former "IBM soldiers," that is, IBM employees temporarily released for army service. They found everything "100% intact" and "in very good condition," with "every tool, every machine well-preserved [and] ready to start work at a moment's notice." They excitedly reported to Thomas Watson himself that "the entire factory [was] intact, spared for some unknown reason by our airmen." Watson, who enjoyed privileged access to all of Washington's nerve centers, including the White House, undoubtedly knew the reason. The IBM factory in Berlin, however, had been destroyed during the many Allied bombing raids on the German capital, but not, *dixit* Black, before "most of the departments had been transferred to different places in southern Germany" in a dispersal operation similar to the one that saved most of GM's plant in Rüsselsheim.[13]

After the war, GM and the other American corporations that had done business in Germany were not only not punished, but were even compensated for damages suffered by their German subsidiaries as a result of Anglo-American air raids. GM thus received 33 million dollars and ITT 27 million from the American government as indemnification, partly in the form of tax credits. The Ford-Werke had suffered relatively little damage during the war, and had actually received more than $100,000 in compensation from the Nazi regime itself. Ford's branch plant in France, meanwhile, had managed to wrest an indemnification of 38 million francs from the Vichy regime. Ford nevertheless applied in Washington for 7 million dollars worth of damages, but ended up receiving only slightly more than $500,000. These compensations, no matter how high or low, constituted a particularly striking example of the largesse of the US Treasury Department, especially when one is aware that these corporations had already been given tax breaks during the war to make up for their presumably lost assets in Germany. GM, for example, had written off its entire investment in Opel on its 1941 federal tax return, resulting in a tax reduction of approximately $22.7 million. Theoretically, this meant that the US government was entitled to confiscate Opel's holdings, but after the war, in 1948, GM was graciously permitted to repossess its German subsidiary by means of a tax payment of $1.8 million, which was almost $21 million less than the tax break the company had enjoyed on its 1941 return. Ford managed to achieve a similar stunt, writing off the Ford-Werke in 1943 as a loss of approximately $8 million, and officially recuperating its German subsidiary in 1954 at a "fair value" of $557,000. Incidentally, the judicial fiction that their German assets were lost had also enabled the owners and managers of American firms to deny all responsibility for the activities of their German subsidiaries.[14]

If after the war the American authorities had caused difficulties for the German enterprises that had collaborated so intimately with the Nazis, certain unpleasant facts might have come to light. The public might then have understood that American industry had worked closely together with the Nazis, that corporations such as Ford and GM had done fantastic business not only by supplying arms to the American forces but also to the Wehrmacht, and that by trading with the enemy these same firms had not only behaved most unpatriotically, but even committed a form of treason. An American expert on US policy with regard to Germany at the end of the Second World War, Carolyn Woods Eisenberg, writes that one of the many reasons why the American occupation authorities in Germany hesitated to delve into the Nazi connections of the big German firms was that "the conduct of the German cartels could not easily be separated from the dubious activities of certain American corporations." A consistent judicial prosecution of German firms such as IG Farben might have led to confiscations and nationalizations, as happened in France to the collaborator car manufacturer Renault, and in this case the American parent or partner firms might have suffered serious losses.[15] As "Hitler's banker," Schacht, told an American officer during an interrogation when he was a defendant at Nuremberg: "If you want to put on trial the [German] industrialists who helped [Hitler] you must put on trial your own industrialists."[16]

The big American corporations with German connections belonged to the corporate elite that had learned during the war to multiply its wealth, influence, and power. After the war this elite had an inordinate amount of influence on the way in which the American authorities treated defeated Germany. The American occupation authorities in Germany itself featured many influential representatives of firms such as GM and ITT. According to Carolyn Woods Eisenberg, many of these men

[had been appointed] on account of their personal experience in relations with German firms, or also because their own firms had already done business in Germany before the war. So it involved people . . . from General Motors . . . and [ITT-affiliate] ATT. The director [William Draper, a friend

of IBM's Thomas Watson] . . . came from Dillon, Read &
Company, a big financial institution which had made con-
siderable investments in Germany as early as the 1920s . . .
Many of these people had a personal connection with some big
German firm or other . . .

The American corporations thus prevented not only the revelation of their own dubious wartime activities in Germany, but also any serious difficulties for their German subsidiaries or partners. A small number of Nazis such as Sauckel, the slave driver who supplied German industry during the war with masses of foreign labourers, ended on the gallows — deservedly so. However, the principals of German firms and American branch plants that had used forced labour were hardly inconvenienced at all.[17]

In Japan, the Americans proceeded in similar fashion after the war. A number of war criminals did receive their deserved punishment, but too many of the militarist "big fish" were all too leniently dealt with, above all Emperor Hirohito. The reason for this was that US leaders and their occupation authorities in Japan had more sympathy for that country's conservative political and business elites, even though they were responsible for war crimes, than for the anti-fascist and democratic elements that resurfaced after the war with progressive plans for a new Japan. The former were viewed by the Americans as respectable and serious businessmen with whom they could work — to mutual advantage — on entrenching a solid capitalist system in Japan, and as reliable statesmen with immaculate anti-communist credentials. The latter, on the other hand, loomed as dangerous left-wing revolutionaries and potential Moscow sympathizers. Consequently, under the auspices of the American proconsul in occupied Japan, General MacArthur, the purges were quickly brought to a conclusion and the country's traditional authoritarian structures were soon restored, albeit covered up with a thin layer of democratic varnish. The labour unions were neutralized and Japan's democrats and anti-fascists were given no input whatsoever into the post-war reconstruction of their country.

Symbolic of this policy was the treatment of Emperor Hirohito. The Japanese head of state, the so-called Mikado, who could be considered a war criminal, was not only not charged by the Americans, but not even

246

required to appear as a witness in the trials in which some of his closest collaborators stood accused of war crimes. By whitewashing the Japanese monarch, writes Noam Chomsky, Washington made it clear that in the Land of the Rising Sun the United States would not allow any new democratic experiments, but was determined to restore the traditional conservative order.[18]

Chapter 22
THE UNITED STATES, THE SOVIETS, AND THE POST-WAR FATE OF GERMANY

In European as well as American newspaper articles, films, and history books, we are usually presented with a rather simplistic picture of the situation in Europe at the end of the Second World War. The Americans, it is suggested, wanted nothing more than to pull quietly out of the liberated old continent in order to withdraw to the other side of the Atlantic Ocean, just like in old Westerns, where the hero, high in the saddle and impervious to the admiring glances of the locals, would ride slowly out of the village he had just rid of all sorts of malefactors. It is implied that this attractive scenario could not become reality through the fault of the nasty Soviets, who would presumably have taken advantage immediately of the withdrawal of the Americans to mercilessly subjugate the entire Occident. This story is a fairy-tale, typical for the Cold War era. The historical truth, however, is very different.

The intriguing theme of the role of the Soviets and the Americans in Europe after May 1945 is really beyond the scope of a study of the Second World War. However, we need to focus for a moment on the issue of post-war Germany, because after the end of the hostilities, accounts needed to be settled with the country that had started the war, and this revealed itself to be a difficult and complex task. The important events that took place between the Rhine and the Oder in the months and years after May 1945, events in which the Americans and the Soviets were so intimately involved, thus merit — and indeed demand — being sketched and interpreted briefly within the framework of this study. Let us start by examining Moscow's point of view.

The post-war policy of the Soviets aimed at (re)creating a single German state, for the simple reason that they could expect many more benefits from such an arrangement than from the division of Germany. From the defeated German enemy Moscow as co-victor expected two very important concessions, concessions which were not at all unreasonable and had been approved at least in principle by their American and British partners at the Yalta Conference: first, considerable reparation payments, and second, security vis-à-vis a potentially revanchist post-war German state.

Reparations and security were crucially important to the USSR in order to reconstruct the country and, in particular, to erect a socialist society on Soviet soil without outside interference. The construction of "socialism in one country" was a task that Stalin had always considered far more import-ant than the fomenting of Red revolutions elsewhere in the world, an alternative communist strategy whose great protagonist had been Stalin's rival and enemy, Trotsky. The realization of these Soviet plans depended to a large extent on the existence of a single German state, prosperous enough to afford the huge reparation payments.[1] Such a German state, moreover, would inevitably also be rather powerful, so that it would have to be coerced into carrying out its obligations by a concert of all Allied victors. It mattered relatively little to the Soviets what this post-war German state would look like. They definitely did not expect that it would be a com-munist country, because they realized only too well that pushing for such an option was a sure recipe for conflict with the Americans and the British. (Stalin once tried to reassure his Western partners in this respect with the sarcastic remark that "communism fits on Germany the way a saddle fits on a sow!") The Soviets actually counted on a new version of the Weimar Republic, that is, a Western-style parliamentary democracy that would be acceptable to Washington and London. Moscow fervently wanted to con-tinue to collaborate for a long time with the Americans and the British, since only such an inter-Allied collaboration could ensure that the new Germany would pay reparations and not constitute a threat to the Soviet Union. *The Soviets, then, had a united and democratic post-war Germany in mind because that was the most advantageous option for them.* This is the reason why the Soviet Union consistently opposed the division of Germany from the start, and continued to oppose it until well into the 1950s.[2]

The Soviet plans with regard to Germany were far from unreasonable, and most components of these plans had already been approved by the Western Allies in Yalta and elsewhere. However, the Americans refused to accept them because after the defeat of Germany they viewed the situation through entirely new spectacles. From the creation of a single post-war German state, the United States could only expect an advantage if they themselves would dominate this Germany politically and economically. When it became obvious that this goal could not be reached, not even by means of Truman's aggressive atomic diplomacy, Washington realized that it was more profitable to preserve the existing division of Germany into supposedly temporary occupation zones.[3]

America's policy regarding Germany was determined above all by economic factors. In order to avoid a new economic crisis at home, Washington sought to open the world's markets to the export products of American industry. The principle of the open door therefore needed to be adopted, preferably all over the globe, but at the very least in those countries that as a result of the war found themselves in the American sphere of influence. The leaders of the United States were determined that Germany, in particular, would be available as a market for American industrial products, the more so since the coming reconstruction of that country promised to become a real gold rush. Incidentally, after the war America's industrial leaders were not only scouring the globe for new markets for their products, but also for new opportunities to invest the huge profits made during the war. For American investment capital, too, Germany at the time looked like a promised land, a Teutonic El Dorado abounding with opportunities for accumulation.[4]

What was urgently required, then, was to integrate Germany into the new "Hullian" economic world order rooted in free trade. However, such a scheme was hard to reconcile with the plans of the Soviets who, banking on the agreements concluded at Yalta, expected that the economic potential of the new Germany would primarily serve their own interests in the form of reparation payments, since their country had contributed so much to the final victory and had suffered so much from the Nazis' aggression. It is hardly surprising, however, that President Truman revealed himself to be much more sensitive to the wishes of American industry than to the needs of the USSR, no matter how legitimate. If Germany were made to disgorge reparation payments for the benefit of the USSR for an unlimited period of time, then it would hardly be possible for American exporters and investors to engage in the kind of profitable business deals their eager minds associated with the coming reconstruction of Germany; worse, they might even partially or totally lose the usufruct of their own assets in Germany. These assets had already been huge before the war, and during the war they had grown considerably while suffering relatively little damage. Most German subsidiaries of the American corporations had survived the war virtually intact and were able to continue production at the end of hostilities or resume it shortly after.[5] In 1945, American corporations held bigger assets in Germany than ever before, and they looked forward to earning big, and possibly unprecedented, profits in that country's coming reconstruction. (They were right: already by the end of 1946, IBM Germany, for example, would be valued at over RM 56 million, while reporting a profit of RM 7.5 million.)[6] However, based on the agreed-upon program of reparation payments, this lucre might well have to contribute to paying off Germany's enormous war debt vis-à-vis the Soviet Union. In Rüsselsheim, for example, the Opel management feared for a long time after the German capitulation that their firm might be required to contribute to the reparation payments.[7] And IBM, which under Nazi rule had profited immensely from the fiction that Dehomag was a German firm, was now extremely worried that its German subsidiary might be considered enemy property and therefore be made available for reparation purposes. "IBM very much wanted to be excluded [from reparations]," writes Edwin Black, so the corporation went to work to have its branch plant "carved out of the sphere of culpability" instead of "becom[ing] a candidate for reparations."[8]

Not surprisingly, lobbyists for the big American corporations went to work in Washington to prevent American branch plants in Germany from being included in any reparation schemes. Now that the Soviet Union was no longer needed as an ally, moreover, the anti-communists started to regain influence in the US capital, and they found it abominable that the wealth of post-war Germany might be skimmed off for an unlimited period of time for the benefit of communism in the USSR. They abhorred the thought that capital amassed by American "free enterprise" in Germany might serve for an indefinite period of time to finance the construction of communism in the land of the Soviets, instead of producing dividends destined for the pocketbooks of American shareholders.

The Soviet plans with respect to Germany, no matter how legitimate and moderate, were thus totally unacceptable to Uncle Sam. Washington wanted the Soviets to simply disappear from Germany in order to leave the delicate task of reconstructing that country (and Europe in general) to American know-how. If the Soviets were not prepared to do this voluntarily, then the Americans, enjoying the advantage of the atomic bomb, were quite prepared to force them. As we have already seen, President Truman's atomic diplomacy purported to coerce Stalin to unilaterally withdraw the Red Army from all of Germany and Eastern Europe. However, this strategy proved to be counterproductive: it was precisely in order to defend against the atomic bomb that Moscow kept its troops as far west as possible, including eastern Germany. The Soviets entrenched themselves in their own German occupation zone, but on a diplomatic level they continued to push for an undivided Germany, their favourite solution to the German problem.[9] But Washington preferred the status quo, that is, the division of Germany along the inter-zonal demarcation line fixed at Yalta. This division, after all, gave the Americans (together with their British and French allies) control over the most important part of Germany, which included the great North Sea ports, the highly industrialized Ruhr and Saar regions, the prosperous Rhineland, and the German Texas, Bavaria. Incidentally, most (though not all) branch plants of American corporations were located in that part of Germany, later to constitute the Federal Republic of Germany (FRG).[10]

The privilege of dominating the German heartland and of being able to do business there, and conversely, to deny all this to the USSR, was worth the small price the United States had to pay in allowing the Soviets, at least temporarily, to do as they pleased in their occupation zone, which included recouping reparations there for their war damages. This price was reasonable indeed, because the Soviet zone — the later German Democratic Republic (GDR) — had not only suffered more from the war, but also happened to be far smaller, less densely populated, and economically far weaker than the Western zone. (A considerable share of what had been the German East before the war — the area east of the rivers Oder and Neisse — was ceded as agreed to Poland in order to compensate that country for territories east of the Curzon Line that were recuperated by the Soviet Union.)[11]

In this context it should be pointed out that during the last weeks of the hostilities the Americans themselves had occupied a considerable part of the Soviet zone, namely, Thuringia and much of Saxony, including the aforementioned city of Leipzig. When they pulled out at the end of June, 1945, they brought back to the West more than 10,000 railway cars full of the newest and best equipment, patents, blueprints, and so on from the firm Carl Zeiss in Jena and the local plants of other top enterprises such as Siemens, Telefunken, BMW, Krupp, Junkers, and IG Farben. This East German war booty included plunder from the Nazi V-2 factory in Nordhausen: not only the rockets, but also technical documents with an estimated value of 400 to 500 million dollars, as well as approximately 1,200 captured German experts in rocket technology, one of whom being the notorious Wernher von Braun.[12] Finally, the Americans also brought back with them a sizable amount of gold — a relatively small yet important part of the so-called *Totengold der Juden,* gold robbed from the Jews that the SS had been unable to transfer to Switzerland at the end of the war. This treasure was discovered by American soldiers in a salt mine in the Thuringian town of Merkers and in the Buchenwald concentration camp. It is clear that this transfusion of gold, technology, and all sorts of capital greatly increased the already considerable asymmetry between the Eastern and Western occupation zones of Germany.[13]

We may assume that the Americans also made sure that nothing was left in the bank accounts and safes of these Saxon and Thuringian enterprises. But even more economically damaging was probably the fact that the Americans simply kidnapped thousands of managers, engineers, and all sorts of experts, as well as the best scientists — the brains of Germany's East — from their factories, universities, and homes in Saxony and Thuringia in order to put them to work to the advantage of the Americans in the Western zones — or simply to have them waste away there. The German historian of this operation, in which only very few deportees did not have to be coerced, does not mince words. He describes the American bloodletting of the Soviet zone as a "forced deportation" and as a "kidnapping"; he even compares this action, undoubtedly somewhat unfairly, with the Gestapo's infamous "Night-and-Fog" deportations of opponents of the Nazi regime to concentration camps. In any event, it can hardly be denied that this transfusion of capital and human resources was extremely advantageous to the Americans and to the FRG or "West Germany," but extremely disadvantageous to the GDR or "East Germany."[14]

By abandoning the smaller and poorer eastern part of Germany to the Soviets, the Americans could do as they pleased in the bigger and wealthier western part of that country. There were still other reasons why a divided Germany was more advantageous to Washington. Nazism, like fascism in general, had been an extreme-right phenomenon that had not only shown respect for the existing capitalist socio-economic order, but that had also performed major services for capital in that it had eliminated the labour unions as well as the socialist, communist, and all other left-wing parties. It was for that reason that Germany's huge enterprises such as IG Farben, Thyssen, Krupp, and so on, had provided generous financial support for the Nazis during their march to power, had associated themselves with them after having arranged to bring them to power, and had cooperated in, and profited from, the typically fascist state initiatives such as the persecution of the regime's opponents, the expropriation of the Jewish population, rearmament, and international aggression.[15] Max Horkheimer once pithily stated that those who want to talk about fascism cannot remain silent about capitalism, because in the final analysis fascism was a form of capitalism, a manifestation of capitalism.[16] In Germany and the rest of Europe in 1945, just about everybody was keenly aware of the intimate connection between fascism and capitalism, of the place of fascism within the capitalist system. Or, as Edwin Black puts it in his study of IBM's role in the Holocaust, "the world understood that corporate collusion [had been] the keystone to Hitler's terror."[17]

This essential insight was squandered only later, when fascism started to be presented — in the American style — as though it had emerged in a socio-economic vacuum, the handiwork of thoroughly evil, criminal, dictatorial individuals like Hitler, who had appeared seemingly out of nowhere on the historical scene. The famous Hitler biography by Alan Bullock, first published in 1952 and destined to be imitated by many other psycho-biographies and psycho-histories, made a major contribution to this "displacement" process, a shift away from a genuine understanding of the social-economic phenomenon of fascism in favour of the "gangster theory" of fascism, and of Nazism in particular. Subsequently, even when studies of Nazism made an attempt to provide a historical background to Hitler's rise to power, the influence of German business interests was conveniently overlooked in favour of factors such as the supposedly peculiar quirks of German history, the unfair terms of the Treaty of Versailles, and of course the alleged grassroots support provided by the German people.

After the demise of German Nazism and of European fascism in general, the general mood was (and would remain for a few short years) decidedly anti-fascist and simultaneously more or less anti-capitalist. Almost everywhere in Europe radical grassroots associations, such as the German anti-fascist groups or *Antifas*, sprang up spontaneously and became rather influential. Labour unions and left-wing political parties also experienced successful comebacks, especially in Germany, and this was clearly reflected in the results of regional elections, for example in the British occupation zone and in the central German region of Hessen.[18] Left-wing parties and unions enjoyed wide popular support when they denounced Germany's bankers and industrialists for their support of the Nazis and their collaboration with the Hitler regime, and when they proposed more or less radical anti-capitalist reforms such as the socialization or nationalization of certain firms and industry sectors. Even the conservative CDU (*Christlich-Demokratische Union*), which was to transform later into Germany's great champion of American-style free enterprise, was forced to adjust to the anti-capitalist mood. In its so-called Ahlen Program of early 1947 it sharply criticized the capitalist system and proposed an economic and social new order. However, such reform plans violated American dogmas regarding the inviolability of private property and free enterprise.[19]

The Americans were also far from happy with the emergence of democratically elected works' councils that demanded input into the affairs of firms. To make matters worse, the workers frequently elected communists to these councils. This actually happened in the most important American branch plants, namely, in the Ford-Werke and in the Opel plant. The communists would play an important role in Opel's works' council until 1948, when General Motors officially resumed Opel's management and promptly dissolved the institution. These councils clearly constituted a form of industrial democracy for which the American owners and managers had very little enthusiasm. Moreover, the works' councils reminded many of the committees ("soviets") of soldiers and workers of the Bolshevik revolution of 1917 and of the workers' councils of Germany's own failed Red revolution at the end of the First World War.[20] The American authorities were keenly aware of these historical precedents. Louis A. Wiesner, a labour specialist in the State Department, for example, warned his superiors that "works' councils in Germany (as in Russia) were after the last war [i.e., the First World War] the organ of attempted revolutionary change," and he suggested that these councils functioned as "a gratuitous invitation to German workers to recall their revolutionary traditions."[21] The works' councils, then, clearly disquieted all those who feared that the Second World War might give birth to a social revolution, exactly as the Franco-Prussian War of 1870–71 and the First World War had led, respectively, to the Paris Commune and the October Revolution.[2]

To the annoyance of American leaders, the radical socialization and council projects not only met with the sympathy and support of the Soviet occupation authorities, but they also enjoyed, at least temporarily, a modest measure of understanding on the part of the British, whose policies were fashioned since the general elections of July 1945 by the moderately left-wing Labour Party led by Prime Minister Clement Attlee. The British Labour government had nothing in principle against social and economic reforms and was actually poised to introduce in Britain itself not only the social reforms of the welfare state, but also a far-flung program of nationalizations. Within their own occupation zone in northwest Germany, which included the important industrial area of the Ruhr, the British were ready to undertake a major nationalization program in cooperation with the local Antifas, the labour unions, Labour's Social-Democratic German sister-party (SPD), and other left-wing forces.[23] This meant that the United States would have found it difficult if not impossible to prevent the Left from setting the tone in an undivided German state and from introducing possibly far-reaching reforms with the support of the (Red) Soviets and the (pink) British; in this case even the German subsidiaries of American corporations could have become victims of nationalizations.[24]

Consider the advantages associated with the alternative option, the continued division of Germany. This option offered the United States the opportunity to enforce its own will in the Western occupation zones, not only vis-à-vis the British partner — no match for Uncle Sam in a bilateral situation — but also vis-à-vis the left-wing, anti-fascist, and therefore in certain respects anti-capitalist Germans. The Americans could count on the collaboration of conservative, right-wing Germans — if necessary also ex-Nazis — to nullify all those irksome reform plans. The American authorities did indeed systematically oppose the anti-fascists and sabotage their schemes for social and economic reform. They did so at all levels of public administration as well as in private business.[25] In the Opel plant in Rüsselsheim, for example, the American authorities collaborated only reluctantly with the anti-fascists; they did everything in their power to prevent the establishment of new labour unions and to deny the works' councils any say in the firm's management.[26] At the Ford-Werke in Cologne, anti-fascist pressure forced the Americans to dismiss the Nazi general manager, Robert Schmidt, but thanks to Dearborn and the American occupation authorities he and many other Nazi managers were soon firmly back in the saddle.[27]

Instead of allowing the planned democratic "bottom-up" reforms to blossom, the Americans proceeded to restore authoritarian "top-down" structures wherever it was in their power to do so. They pushed the anti-fascists aside in favour of conservative, authoritarian, right-wing personalities, including many former Nazis, whom they could count on to help maintain the traditional power relations in the western part of Germany. It was a familiar policy, already consistently practised by the United States in liberated countries such as Italy. This policy saw its debut in Germany in the fall of 1944 in the first city to fall into American hands, Aachen.[28] According to a disillusioned American war veteran, the same thing was to happen afterwards in Germany again and again:

In Germany, there were anti-fascist groups functioning. The crime of it all is that we would take a little town, arrest the

257

mayor and the other big shots, and put the anti-fascist in charge of the town. We'd double back to that town three days later, the Americans had freed all the officials and put 'em back in power. And they threw this other guy aside. Invariably, it happened. You see, after you came in, the military government took over.[29]

And so it happened that "many outright Nazis, Nazi sympathizers, or other nondemocratic elements...found their way...into the good graces of the U.S. military government," writes a German-American historian, Michaela Hoenicke.[30]

Two key conservative figures within this American policy were Konrad Adenauer and Ludwig Erhard. Erhard, allegedly the architect of Germany's post-war "economic miracle," had already been an eager defender of the interests of free enterprise against state interventionism in the Third Reich, and was known as an opponent of social experiments and a champion of the continuity of the economic order; he has already been mentioned as the godfather of the spurious decartelization of IG Farben. Adenauer, known in Germany as the "old fox," had been imprisoned by the Nazis, but that does not mean that he was a committed democrat. Instead, he was a typical representative of the old, authoritarian Germany, and has been described by the historian T. H. Tetens as a "conservative nationalist," a "symbol for extreme political toryism" and even as a "reactionary autocrat." As chancellor of the FRG, Adenauer would also reveal himself to be a shameless protector of the German industrialists and bankers who had enabled Hitler to come to power, and as a protector of all sorts of former Nazis — including notorious war criminals.[31]

American leaders were not fond of anti-fascism. Not surprisingly, they entrusted the stewardship of the FRG, which was founded under their auspices, to men such as Adenauer, who were equally averse to anti-fascism. In the West German state anti-fascism was frowned upon because it was equated, not without reason, with anti-capitalism. For the same reason, anti-fascism would be energetically cultivated in the GDR. However, since the reunification of the two German states or, more accurately, the annexation of the GDR by the FRG, anti-fascism has been systematically pounced upon in Germany's east as well, for example by means of the renaming of streets and squares, the destruction of monuments, and the closure or "reorientation" of museums and memorials. It is shameful how in Germany in general the names of the country's own heroic anti-fascist resistance fighters have been erased from public view and from official memory, while prominent friends of fascism such as the sinister John Foster Dulles, who would serve as secretary of state in the Eisenhower administration while his brother Allen became head of the CIA, have had major thoroughfares named after them in Berlin.[32] In West Germany, the campaign against anti-fascism had already been allowed to score a triumph on the home front much earlier, namely, when President Ronald Reagan, accompanied by Chancellor Helmut Kohl, deposited a wreath on the graves of SS men in Bitburg in 1984. It may well be that the vicious campaign against anti-fascism in post-reunification Germany has served in some ways to rehabilitate fascism itself, and has made a major contribution to the fact that neo-Nazism has reared its ugly head throughout the country.

For the purpose of countering anti-fascism, the American authorities discovered a particularly enthusiastic and useful partner in the Vatican. It was with papal cooperation that in all countries where left-wing anti-fascism was making too much headway for their taste, the Americans were to recruit and endorse conservative, Catholic politicians of the Adenauer type, and to fabricate Catholic or, better still, Catholic-dominated Christian political parties such as Germany's CDU and Italy's corrupt Democrazia Cristiana, whose electoral campaigns they also financed. In cooperation with the Vatican, the Americans tried by all means at their disposal to combat and discredit the Left, as was the case in the notorious Italian electoral campaign of 1948, which threatened to be won by the Communists and Socialists. Thankful for the valuable services rendered by the Vatican to their international campaign against anti-fascism, the American elites were to remember their friends in Rome when in 1949 a West German state would be established under their auspices. The Vatican must have been gratified indeed that the Basic Law of the FRG — a constitution all but in name — preserved many of the privileges acquired by the Catholic Church at the time of the 1933 Concordat with Hitler, including a church tax, which continues to be collected by the state to the annoyance of many Germans;

this quasi-medieval "tithe" has turned Germany into the Vatican's greatest financial benefactor after the United States. As a small but touching gesture of appreciation, papal automobiles have been purchased since the 1930s from a German car manufacturer — not Volkswagen, but Mercedes.[33]

Finally, the division of Germany was also advantageous to the United States militarily. An undivided Germany would have had to be impartial vis-à-vis all its victors, and therefore neutral. Such a Germany, moreover, might actually have sympathized with the USSR if, as was not unlikely, it ended up choosing a left-wing government — an unattractive scenario for Washington, certainly compared to the opportunities offered by a divided Germany.[34] A division gave the United States hegemony over Western Germany, even by itself the most powerful and militarily strongest country on the European continent. As a result of its strength and strategic location, such a state loomed as the potential keystone of the kind of anti-communist and anti-Soviet coalition Washington had in mind for Europe, later to become reality in the guise of NATO. In other words, a division offered the possibility of using Germany, or at least the biggest and most important part of the country, as a bulwark against Bolshevism, as an anti-Soviet bastion. Such a dream had mesmerized the elites of the Western world, most spectacularly exemplified by Chamberlain, before the war, and was revived with the war's end. The dream of Germany's integration into an anti-Soviet scheme under Western auspices was to become a formal reality when Adenauer inducted a remilitarized West Germany into NATO in 1954.[35] A specialist in US-German relations has described this development as "the retooling of West Germany [by the US] into a junior partner against the former ally, the Soviet Union."[36]

Under these circumstances, then, it is not surprising that Washington, not Moscow, was responsible for all the important initiatives that caused Germany to remain divided for half a century. As for the issue that was foremost on the minds of the Soviets, the reparation payments, Truman already tried to make it clear to Stalin in the summer of 1945 in Potsdam that he could not count on American cooperation, that he could best try to help himself to reparations in the Soviets' own occupation zone. To the great chagrin of the Americans, the Soviets actually did receive some dismantled industrial equipment from the Ruhr region for a while, albeit largely in return for foodstuff from the agricultural eastern part of Germany.[37] Finally, on May 3, 1946, General Lucius Clay, the American military governor in Germany, unilaterally and definitively denied the Soviets the right to seek reparations in the Western occupation zones for the wartime destruction wrought in the Soviet Union in the name of all of Germany. Still in that same year, the Americans arranged for the amalgamation of their own occupation zone with that of the British; the French zone was to join later, in April 1949. It was a step that would irrevocably lead to the official establishment of the FRG on May 8, 1949.[38]

Another important milestone on the road to the creation of a separate state in the western regions of Germany was taken by Washington in the summer of 1947, with the introduction of the famous Marshall Plan. This plan is usually described somewhat ambiguously as a large-scale project of financial "aid" for Europe. Just as in the case of Lend-Lease, it is assumed by many that this involved purely altruistic aid, in other words, a gift from the princely Uncle Sam. However, this was not the case at all. The famous plan did not amount to a free gift; it was not a generous present amounting to billions of dollars, but a complex combination of credits and loans. Very similar kinds of credits and loans are offered today by financial institutions and all sorts of firms — often in the form of credit cards — to creditworthy customers. This practice reflects an understanding of an important principle of modern marketing, namely, the potential of extending credit for the purpose of winning customers and of tying customers to the supplier. The Marshall Plan served not exclusively, but certainly primarily, as a kind of collective credit card, made available in order to win Western Europe as a customer for American industry and to tie that part of the world to the United States, not only economically but also politically. (Most "development assistance" plans similarly aim to win or keep Third World countries as customers or vassals.) Carolyn Woods Eisenberg has rightly written about the Marshall Plan that "America's political and economic self-interest" required that Europe was reconstructed in this manner after the war.[39]

From an economic point of view, the Marshall Plan functioned to keep the engine of American industry firing on all cylinders, to make the western part of Germany and Europe in general more dependent on the United States, and to integrate that part of the world more closely into the new

"Hullian" world economy. It could be said that the much-praised Marshall Plan inaugurated in Europe the process of "Americanization" or, as it is sometimes cynically said of the Third World, the "Coca-Colonization." Politically, the Marshall Plan's goal was the political integration of Western Europe into an anti-Soviet block led by America. With respect to Germany, the plan represented a step toward the creation of a pro-American and anti-Soviet state in the West of Germany, and thus also a milestone on the road to the long-term division of the country.[40]

Marshall Plan credits were also offered to the Soviet Union, but under conditions which, as the Americans knew very well, were totally unacceptable. Indeed, these conditions amounted to a demand that the Soviets abjure their communist heresy and return to the bosom of the true capitalist faith. Today, credits are awarded very similarly by the IMF and the World Bank only to countries of the Third World and of Eastern Europe that disavow all forms of communism or socialism and promise to respect the rules of the game of international capitalism — rules which, not surprisingly, end up favouring the creditors, not the debtors.[41]

The Soviets abhorred the prospect of a divided Germany, so they specifically ordered the German communists to focus not on the construction of socialism in Germany but on the preservation of German unity. It was not the Soviets, but the Americans who proved guilty of the kind of diplomatic obstruction that led to Germany's division. Frustrated by the lack of cooperation from the American side, the Soviets would even temporarily blockade Berlin, but they did so ineffectively, for example by allowing US planes with supplies to overfly the Soviet zone on their way to Berlin during the famous airlift. The blockade even turned out to be counterproductive, since the Americans managed to derive enormous public relations advantages from it. Afterwards the USSR would long continue to plead for a single German state. In their own occupation zone they would only establish a socialist state in the form of the GDR after the creation of the FRG, and they did so reluctantly. As late as 1953 they would offer to dissolve this GDR in return for a single, neutral German state. But the Americans preferred to wait for an opportunity to wrest the eastern part of the country from the Soviets, and this opportunity would finally present itself in 1989. In the meantime they stuck to the German formula that was most advantageous to themselves: a division between a big and wealthy West Germany on the one side, with whom profitable business deals could be concluded, and a small and poor East Germany, to whose meager resources the hungry Soviets were allowed to treat themselves, on the other side.[42]

Seen from a Soviet perspective, the GDR was indeed, as the German historian Wilfried Loth has written, an "unloved child," that is, a child whom the Soviets, obsessed by the need for German reparations, would gladly have exchanged for an ideologically less kindred but more affluent Germany. With respect to East Germany, Moscow did in fact behave like a wicked stepmother; this remained the case even after the Soviets had brought a communist regime to power there. Since Germany's wealthy west lay out of their reach, the Soviets would haul away from Germany's paltry eastern cupboard — already looted, in fact, by the Americans — everything that might serve to indemnify them for their war damages. They even dismantled the East German railways that would have been vital for their own troop transports in case of a war with the West.[43] Under these circumstances, it actually amounted to a genuine "economic miracle" that the GDR eventually managed to achieve a relatively high standard of living — one that was admittedly far lower than that of West Germany, but higher than that of the USSR itself and that of millions of inhabitants of the American ghettos, of countless poor white Americans, and of the population of most Third World countries that have been integrated willy-nilly with the international capitalist world system.

The case of the GDR does not permit the seemingly logical — and for some particularly gratifying — conclusion that communism necessarily breeds poverty. The (relative) poverty of East Germany was unquestionably due primarily to the incontestible fact that the less numerous and poorer Germans of the east, the Ossis, have had to pay the bill for the barbarities perpetrated by the Nazis, while thanks to their American patrons the far more numerous and wealthy Germans of the West, the Wessis, never had to pay their fair share. The FRG has paid a total of 600 million dollars in reparations to the USSR in the form of dismantled industrial equipment, for example from the Ruhr. The American historian John H. Backer deems this sum so low that he concludes that thanks to the Americans, the FRG was exempted from a "meaningful reparations burden."[44] The opposite applied to the much smaller and poorer GDR, whose reparation payments to the USSR have been described by a West German expert, Jörg Fisch, as "extraordinarily high in relative as well as absolute terms." Fisch states that "according to conservative estimates" the GDR had to cough up no less than 4.5 billion dollars, or seven times the amount paid by the FRG, and this after the German East had already been administered a bloodletting by the Americans. The result, he writes, was a "considerable de-industrialization."[45] A hypothetical capitalist East Germany would likewise have been ruined by such an unfair course of events and would have also had to build a wall in order to prevent its population from seeking salvation in another, more prosperous Germany. Incidentally, people have fled, and continue to flee, to richer countries also from poor capitalist countries. However, the numerous black refugees from extremely poor Haiti, for example, have never enjoyed the same kind of sympathy in the United States and elsewhere in the world that was bestowed so generously on refugees from the GDR during the Cold War. And should the Mexican government decide to build a "Berlin Wall" along the Rio Grande in order to prevent their people from escaping to El Norte, Washington would certainly not condemn such an initiative the way it used to condemn the infamous East Berlin construction project.

Thus, the uncheerful saga of the GDR does not lead to any logical conclusions concerning the (in)efficiency of communism. But it does cast an interesting light on the internal problems of American capitalism and of Soviet communism. It can be said that the Americans forced the Soviets to present their justified bill to poverty-stricken East Germany, while they themselves carried off the riches of Germany's wealthy West. In doing so, they provided America's capitalist system with an antidote against a new depression; and they simultaneously prevented the Soviets — after the endless problems of revolution, civil war between Reds and Whites, foreign intervention, Stalinist purges, and Hitler's murderous aggression — from taking advantage of the huge capital represented by reparation payments from Germany in its entirety in order to continue their communist experiment, and possibly to do so successfully.

Even from the two German states combined, the USSR never received more than 5.1 billion dollars in reparations, which is barely more than half of the relatively modest sum of 10 billion dollars agreed upon in Yalta. This did not even amount to one twentieth of the sum arrived at in a later and more realistic estimate of total war damages in the USSR, namely 128 billion dollars. This figure may sound astronomical, but it hardly conveys the magnitude of the damage caused in the USSR during the war. There are more vivid ways to describe that devastation. For example, American experts estimate that the Soviet Union lost all the wealth it had accumulated during the speedy (and painful) industrialization of the thirties; that the Soviet economy shrank 20 per cent between 1941 and 1945; and that the damage caused by the war had still not been made good by the early sixties. According to the British historian Clive Ponting, the war damage suffered by the Soviets amounted to the Gross National Product of no less than twenty-five years.[46]

The Soviets have thus undoubtedly received far less in German reparation payments than they were entitled to, and certainly far less than they required to reconstruct their country. (Even so, the USSR emerged from the ordeal of World War II as the second most powerful coutnry on earth, a fact that appears to falsify the theory of the intrinsic inefficiency of communism.) The Americans, on the other hand, who made no claim to reparations, did in fact receive considerable reparation payments from Germany, as we have already seen, in the form of technology and know-how carried off from the leading enterprises of their defeated German enemy — not only in their own occupation zone but also in the Soviet zone. "The popular and enduring myth that the United States took few, if any, reparations from Germany after the Second World War . . . obviously needs to be dispelled," writes an American expert, John Gimbel. He points out that this "intellectual plunder" relied on "vacuum cleaner methods to acquire all the scientific information the Germans [had]," and involved

> virtually every aspect of German industry and technology, including wind tunnels, tape recorders, synthetic fuels and rubber, diesel motors, color film processing, textiles and textile equipment, machine tools, acetylene chemistry, ceramics, optics and optical glass, heavy presses, the cold extrusion of steel, heavy machinery, electric condensers, electron microscopes, die-casting equipment, and a long list of other things.

Gimbel concludes that American science and industry thus appropriated "the most valuable [intellectual] capital of defeated Germany," of which the total worth was higher than all the already obsolete machinery the Soviets were allowed to cart off.[47]

In summary, we can say that the division of Germany made it possible for American capitalism, which had profited from the war but was threatened by the economic implications of peace, to be enriched and rejuvenated, while the Soviet communists, who hoped to profit from the peace after their country had suffered so much in the war, were left empty-handed.

Chapter 23
AFTER 1945: FROM THE GOOD WAR TO PERMANENT WAR

In the United States the Second World War is often referred to as "the good war." Just a few years ago, the American historian Michael C. C. Adams even called his book about this war *The Best War Ever*. And Howard Zinn has used an almost identical term, the "best of wars," albeit with a touch of irony. In many ways, the Second World War was truly a "good" war for the United States, and it may well have been the very best war in the country's history. First, the world conflict of 1939–1945 really does look like a good war when we compare it with the bad wars of American history, exemplified by the many "Indian Wars" against the Cherokees and other indigenous North Americans. These Indian Wars actually amounted to a series of bloodbaths and deportations; they added up to a form of genocide that aroused Hitler's admiration and inspired his attempt to conquer "living space" in Eastern Europe, a kind of European equivalent of America's Wild West, a vast "frontier" predestined to be colonized by Germans at the expense of the presumably inferior natives.[1] The hall of infamy of America's bad wars naturally also houses the brutal Vietnam War, condemned by countless Americans — to their great credit — as an imperialist and immoral enterprise. Furthermore, the Second World War was also a good war in the sense that it was fought against "an enemy of unspeakable evil," as Howard Zinn has put it.[2] That enemy was fascism in general and its German version, Nazism, in particular — an ideology and a system which will forever remain associated with oppression at home, with aggression abroad, with horrible war crimes, and with genocide, a Moloch to which millions of people fell victim in relatively few years. A war against such an evil was necessarily a good war, even though the victors — the Americans, the British, and the Soviets — certainly did not emerge with clean hands from this "crusade" against fascism, as the names Dresden, Katyn, Hiroshima, and Nagasaki remind us. In any event, it is a good thing that not the fascists, but rather their opponents, were victorious in this Armageddon. This victory was not an easy one; it required enormous efforts on the part of all allies, and the Americans certainly deserve our respect and gratitude for the contribution they made.

But in what respects was the Second World War a good war for the United States itself? For whom was this a good war, and for what? For the power elite of America, and above all for the country's big corporations and banks, the Second World War was undoubtedly a very good war for a number of reasons. First, by rekindling economic demand, the war ended the Great Depression. In other words, the war offered a solution to the great crisis of the capitalist economic system, at least as far as the USA itself was concerned. "The war," observes the American writer Lawrence Wittner succinctly, "rejuvenated American capitalism."[3] It was far from certain whether that remedy amounted to more than temporary relief, brought about by the war and therefore predestined to end with the return of peace, but that mattered far less than the fact that this kind of solution to the crisis of capitalism was a non-revolutionary solution, that is, one that did not jeopardize the survival of the system itself. Second, the war was good for the American power elite because it revealed itself as a cornucopia of profits. Third, the war brought business leaders enhanced prestige and, more importantly, an even more privileged place behind the levers of power in Washington. For the American power elite, then, the Second World Was not simply good, it was truly wonderful. Furthermore, when the great Armageddon of the twentieth century came to its conclusion, America was the great victor, and the entire world appeared to wait with open doors for US export products and investments. The coming *pax americana* promised to bring the kind of worldwide free trade that US leaders believed to be the *sine qua non* of permanent postwar corporate profitability and general prosperity.

For the working and middle classes of the United States — ordinary as opposed to upper-crust Americans, employees as opposed to employers, labour as opposed to capital — the Second World War was also a good war. The war itself, not Roosevelt's New Deal, terminated the Great Depression and its misery, particularly the curse of unemployment. Suddenly there was work for everyone, and thanks to collective bargaining — and, if necessary, strikes — wages climbed to unprecedented heights. As their living standard improved significantly, workers and liberal representatives of the middle class began to dream of an even more glorious tomorrow, which would bring them social services such as health insurance, paid holidays, and other benefits. To ordinary Americans, the war brought a taste of a better future, the prospect of a new social dawn; for them too, the Second World War was a good war, but when it came to an end, many of the expectations it had raised remained unfulfilled.

For the American power elite the war had been good, even wonderful, but not perfect. It could have been so, but was not, because of the advantages realized simultaneously by the employees; in other words, because the war had brought about a modest redistribution of the wealth. Without concessions in the form of higher wages, the corporations could have pocketed even greater riches. (Was this fact of economic life not clearly demonstrated by the case of the American branch plants in Germany, where the use of unpaid slave labour had helped to produce unprecedented earnings?) The wartime gains of America's employees, then, in some way represented losses for America's corporations. Moreover, corporate America was also deeply worried about the post-war plans of workers and liberal members of the middle class, plans that included all sorts of social services, for which the employers would have to foot at least part of the bill, and about the envisaged dirigist state intervention in the economy, which threatened to undermine the traditional privileges of free enterprise. Economists, moreover, warned that the postwar reconversion of the economy might be accompanied by a serious crisis and possibly a thirties-style depression. Foreign trade might provide a remedy, but it was far from certain that the entire world would open its doors to US exports and investments. To correct these imperfections, which were the legacy of the good war, it turned out that a new war was needed, an even better war than the Second World War, a perfect war. That war was the Cold War.

From the perspective of the American power elite, the Cold War was perfect, first of all, because it was fought against the perfect enemy. The Second World War had been "the war against the wrong enemy," as some West Point generals had put it. Indeed, German Nazism — and fascism in general — had not been the natural enemy of the political and socio-economic leaders of the USA, because they had instinctively recognized fascism for what it was, namely a manifestation of capitalism, which functioned in favour of business. The American power elite had therefore been reluctant to embark on a crusade against fascism. It had only stumbled into the war against Hitler, and had continued to do business with the fascists even after Pearl Harbor; when the war was over, it had no interest in the genuine eradication of Nazism and fascism. "We ought to be fighting the commies," the West Point generals also said, and that comment reflected the reality that from the perspective of the American power elite, which had become obsessed with the threat of the Red Peril long before the Second World War, the natural enemy was and remained communism and its Soviet motherland, even while that state was such a useful temporary ally from 1941 to 1945. In fact, at the end of the Second World War, the Soviet Union and its communist ideology loomed as an even greater nuisance than in the thirties. The existence of a socialist "counter model" to capitalism, a source of inspiration and guidance to radicals and revolutionaries even stateside, had always been strongly resented. And in 1945 the Soviets revealed themselves determined to resume work on the construction of a socialist society instead of returning to the bosom of the universal church of capitalism. Moreover, the USSR was not prepared to grant an unconditional open door to American export products and investment capital in the homeland of communism and in Eastern Europe. The Soviet Union was thus also perceived as an obstacle to the planned worldwide expansion of US trade and investment, and as a nefarious example to other countries that were expected to open their doors. In fact, in 1945 the USSR symbolized just about everything the American power elite loathed and feared: closed economies instead of free trade, statism instead of free enterprise, welfarism instead of rugged individualism, socialism instead of capitalism. (The dichotomy dictatorship versus democracy need not be invoked here, mainly because the American power elite, while professing total devotion to the theoretical ideal of democracy, has demonstrated time and again that is has nothing against dictatorships — as long as they maintain the capitalist socio-economic order and offer America the open doors it wants.) As the Second World War came to an end, then, the Soviet Union appeared from the perspective of America's rich and powerful as the cause of all remaining imperfections and the major obstacle to the realization of their dreams for the postwar era.

The US power elite had profited gloriously from the Second World War. About the two major enemies against whom that conflict was fought, however, it can only be argued that the US power elite had wanted, expected, and even provoked war against Japan; against Germany, war was neither wanted, nor planned, nor expected — even though it was arguably unavoidable. In any event, it required an irrational decision by Hitler to bring the US into the war in Europe. The Cold War against the Soviet Union, on the other hand, was very much wanted and orchestrated by the American establishment. As the Second World War ground to an end, the power elite — exemplified by the aforementioned anonymous West Point generals and, even more so, by that illustrious colleague of theirs, Patton — was eager for a faceoff with the detested Soviet Union. A hot war, preferably side-by-side with the remains of the Nazi host, appears to have been the preferred option, but domestic and international public opinion would not allow such a venture. So Patton could not be given the green light for a march to Moscow. However, the Americans now had the atom bomb, and felt that they could use that "hammer," as Truman called it, to force "the boys in the Kremlin" to cave in to all US demands, starting with those with respect to Eastern Europe. When Moscow refused to submit, the Cold War was on.

From the perspective of the American power elite the Cold War achieved, or at least approached, perfection not only because it focused from the start on the perfect enemy. The Cold War turned out to be wonderful regardless of the identity or nature of the enemy, simply because it was a war, and not peace. With the defeat of Germany and Japan, a new conflict — any new conflict against anybody — was a godsend because it made it possible to maintain military expenditures at high levels, thus sustaining the wartime boom. Thanks to the new conflict, armament could continue also after 1945 to function as the Keynesian dynamo of the American economy. The

271

outbreak of the Cold War, then, sheltered the American economy from the risks of reconversion to peacetime conditions, including the possibility of a new depression. Moreover, the key feature of the Cold War, the ever-escalating arms race, would provide a wellspring of profits for the big corporations that had learned during the Second World War to help themselves to the trough of military expenditures. So in 1945 any new conflict against any new enemy would have been welcomed by the American power elite. However, precisely because the new enemy happened to be, unlike the earlier fascist foe, the true ideological enemy — the Soviet Union, the motherland of communism — the Cold War offered yet another advantage. With such an enemy, not only American commies but all domestic advocates of radical change could be discredited as un-American subversives, as agents of the Soviet Union. The Cold War, mostly obviously during the years of McCarthyism, served to silence dissent.

During the Cold War, the USSR was the perfect enemy. But to the USSR the Cold War was the fatal war, a far less bloody, but in some ways a much more terrible, experience than the terrible Second World War had been. The Soviet Union had performed gloriously during the ordeal of fire of Hitler's blitzkrieg, and had emerged victoriously from it, but would perish ingloriously as a result of America's long, slow, and cold version version of Operation Barbarossa. During the Second World War, the Soviet Union had suffered a setback of decades in terms of economic development. In 1945, Moscow hoped to kickstart its reconstruction with the help of a hefty postwar capital influx in the form of German reparations, but that prospect was nullified by a de facto veto from the Americans, who controlled the bulk of Germany's wealth and planned to use it for their own benefit. Furthermore, as the American economic historian James R. Millar has observed, the Soviets were unable to devote their own resources fully to the reconstruction — along socialist lines — of their country, because the onset of the Cold War forced them into a large-scale armament program in order to keep pace with the Americans in the arms race.[4] So the Cold War also amounted to a form of sabotage of the postwar reconstruction of the USSR. One result of this — certainly also of other factors, namely intrinsic problems — was that the USSR could never achieve a high level of prosperity, even though the Soviet people were in fact better off materially than many Americans, the majority of the population of Latin America and the rest of the so-called Third World, as well as the majority of the people in the capitalist Russia of today. Another nefarious byproduct of the Cold War, as far as the Soviet Union was concerned, was that the external threat produced internal oppression, as it had already done during the Civil War, during the thirties and, of course, during the Second World War. In this respect Michael Parenti has observed that the Soviet system was necessarily a form of "siege socialism," a beleaguered and therefore unattractive and grim kind of socialism.[5]

The need to simultaneously keep pace with the Americans militarily and to keep its own population as well as that of its "satellite states" under control required an inordinate effort, which the USSR was unable to maintain in the long run. The homeland of communism had to throw in the towel toward the end of the 1980s, thus putting an end to a Bolshevik project that had filled the world with either hope or horror for more than seventy years. While in this demise other factors undoubtedly played a role, factors such as the inefficiency of the Soviet bureaucracy, it is essentially true, as the German author Jürgen Bruhn has written, that the Cold War amounted to the deliberate "arms-racing to death" (Totrüstung) of the Soviet Union.[6]

The Soviet defeat in the Cold War has been presented in the Western world as evidence that communism is intrinsically inefficient. However, such a view gives no consideration to the undeniable fact that the communist experiment launched in Russia in 1917 was systematically disturbed and sabotaged from start to finish by external pressure, and above all by monumental armed intervention, whereby the ultimate aim was always the total destruction of the Soviet state. The most spectacular initiative of this kind was of course Barbarossa, Hitler's invasion in 1941. Patton was another St. George who dreamed of slaying the communist dragon in its Soviet lair, and his march to Moscow might have have been even more dramatic than the blitzkrieg, but it never happened. In the end, it was a far less sensational war, but a long and cold one, that finished the Soviet experiment. For such an achievement, Hitler would have loved to claim credit, but those who actually did make it possible — and their domestic and foreign paladins and PR people — prefer that we believe the Soviet Union collapsed unassisted.

Could the Cold war have been avoided? Historians generally do not consider it very useful to think about alternatives to historical development, in other words, to consider what might have been. In this case, however, it is worthwhile to indulge for a moment in such speculation. Things could have been different. At the end of the war, America's leaders could have engaged in a dialogue with the Soviets, and they could have collaborated with them. Stalin was admittedly not an easy interlocutor (neither were de Gaulle or Churchill), but there is overwhelming evidence that he preferred dialogue and cooperation, rather than confrontation, with the most powerful country in the world. Long after the Americans made it clear that they did not intend to permit the USSR to harvest the fruits of its war efforts, the Soviet leader remained ready to collaborate. This produced positive results with regard to Finland and also Austria, a country whose division into occupation zones was eventually brought to an end, and from which the Red Army duly withdrew in return for a constitutionally anchored neutrality, leaving the existing capitalist system entirely intact. With respect to Germany, a Soviet withdrawal would, of course, have depended primarily on a fair solution to the reparations issue. In other words, an undivided Germany would have had to pay for the enormous damages caused by the Nazis in the Soviet Union. Germany's post-war economy would undoubtedly have been sufficiently robust to make the payments associated with the hefty reparations mortgage. After all, after 1945 an economically weaker Great Britain spent many years paying for the war but was still able to reattain a high level of prosperity. Things might have gone better for the Soviet Union too after the war, at least if it had come to a fair peace treaty with Germany, one that would have provided for reparations as well as a lasting good relationship between the wartime allies instead of a Cold War. Had the Soviet Union not already experienced an extremely rapid economic development before the Second World War, even during the Great Depression of the 1930s? With the help of the considerable capital of reparation payments and without the enormous financial burdens of the arms race, the Soviet economy might well have "taken off" in the fifties and sixties, and this might have paid dividends for the Soviet people in the form of a higher standard of living and possibly a greater amount of individual freedom.

From a fair solution to the German problem, then, both the Soviet people and the Soviet system might have been able to profit. But this was not the case for the United States, or at least not for the American power elite, because an undivided (and neutral) Germany would probably not have been quite as open to an American economic penetration as West Germany. For example, committed to pay considerable reparations to the Soviets, an undivided Germany could not have been as good a customer of US export products as the FRG actually turned out to be. And in a single neutral German state with financial obligations vis-à-vis the USSR, the profits generated by the German subsidiaries of the big American corporations might not have served to enrich their shareholders. Without an economically privileged place in Germany, the United States would perhaps have slid back into an economic depression, but not necessarily so. With a non-hostile Soviet Union, which would have experienced not only economic but also political and social improvement, the United States would definitely have been able to engage in profitable business deals, much as is the case with China today. On the other hand — and this was undoubtedly a crucially important consideration in the minds of the leaders of the United States — a thriving Soviet Union would have served as an even more dangerous source of inspiration for America's own unionists, liberals, socialists, other radicals, and (admittedly rare) revolutionaries. America's power elite decided not to run the risks associated with a fair solution to the German problem, and decided instead to opt for the path that loomed as safer and more advantageous, namely the division of Germany and Europe, and the Cold War. In a speech in Texas in March of 1947, Truman admitted that he himself and many other American leaders had worried about the prospect of a possible post-war economic revival of the Soviet Union. In the case of such a revival, he explained, the model of a socialist planned economy might well have served as "the example for the next century" — an example that might eventually have been replicated all over the world, even in the United States. In order to forestall such a scenario and thus save the American system of free enterprise, Truman added, there was only one solution: that the American system be put into practice all over the globe, and for the Soviet model to be wiped from the face of the earth.[7]

The Cold War ultimately achieved the objectives for which it had been unleashed, and which Truman had formulated so clearly. The Soviet Union was indeed wiped from the face of the earth, thus making it possible for the capitalist American system to march into the eastern part of Germany, Eastern Europe and all the lands of the defunct Soviet state, and thus finally to triumph all over the world. In this sense, the twentieth century became the American Century during its very last decade. Even more important was the fact that the demise of the socialist "counter model" released capitalism — in the United States and elsewhere — from the need to worry about the loyalty of its own workers and other subjects and secure that loyalty by offering (only where necessary) relatively high salaries and/or extensive social services. Immediately after the Second World War, when radical and even revolutionary change had been in the air, it had been deemed prudent to institute a system of relatively high wages and/or generous social services in the Western world. These concessions, symbolized by the welfare state, had been made reluctantly, so it was only a matter of time before an attempt would be made to undo them. In the eighties, a vicious assault on the welfare state was duly launched under the auspices of Margaret Thatcher in the United Kingdom and Ronald Reagan in the United States. However, it was the disappearance of the Soviet Union that made it possible to dismantle the welfare state with virtual impunity, to claw back social benefits, and to terrorize workers and other employees with what has become known as "downsizing." The end of the Cold War, then, permitted capitalism to again become the brutally exploitative system that it had already been in its 19th-century incarnation and that it has always remained in the Third World. Capitalism had temporarily been "capitalism with a human face," writes Michael Parenti, but since the fall of the Soviet Union has revealed itself increasingly as "capitalism-in-your-face."[8]

Of the First World War, propagandists such as President Wilson had said that it was "the war to end all wars," or, "the war to make the world safe for democracy." Of the Cold War, one could similarly say that it was "the war to end all alternatives to capitalism," or "the war to make the world safe for capitalism." With the fall of the Soviet Union, all alternatives to capitalism apparently ceased to exist. "There is no alternative," crowed Margaret Thatcher. The world henceforth belonged to capitalism, more specifically, to the rugged kind of capitalism bred in the United States. For the American power elite, the end of the Cold War constituted such a happy ending that, with perfection seemingly achieved, they wanted to stop the clock of time at that blissful moment. This task was accomplished by an academic mercenary, Francis Fukuyama, who proclaimed "the end of history" in *The End of History and the Last Man*, a book that was predestined to be celebrated in the corporate-dominated media.[9]

Since then, however, history has marched on relentlessly and has revealed the considerable remaining problems. For one thing, while the Second World War had been a very good war indeed for the wealthy and powerful Americans, it had also been a good war for ordinary Americans. The Cold War, on the other hand, while truly wonderful for the former, was far from kind for the latter, and the main reason is that the American people were saddled with the huge costs of this long conflict. The Cold War represented the triumph of the Pentagon System, but this military kind of Keynesianism caused the public debt to skyrocket to dizzying heights. In 1945, when the Second World War ended and the Cold War started, the public debt amounted to nearly 260 billion dollars; in 1990, when the Cold War ended, the debt stood at approximately 3,200 billions of dollars. It has continued to grow spectacularly since then, even with a Nobel Peace Prize winner in the White House. In 2009 the debt reached approximately 10,000 billion dollars, in 2010 approximately 13,500 billion, and in 2013 it came close to 17,000 billion.[10]

According to Keynesian theory, Washington could have balanced its books by levying taxes on the profits of the big firms that benefitted from the Pentagon System, but there was never any question of such a thing. Corporations in general accounted for 50 per cent of all tax revenue in the United States in 1945; during the Cold War era, that percentage dropped consistently, and stands at less than ten per cent today. This was possible because after the Second World War, America's big enterprises became multinationals (or transnationals) — "at home everywhere and nowhere," as an American author has written in connection with ITT.[11] The multinationals have used "transfer pricing" and all sorts of other accounting tricks — some of them apparently pioneered by their subsidiaries in Nazi Germany — in order to demonstrate year after year to the revenue department of any host country that the local subsidiary incurred high expenses, while the profits were made by branch plants elsewhere. Multinationals have thus been able to avoid paying considerable taxes, also in the case in the United States, the country where they really have their home, and where the business generated by the Cold War was always most profitable. In 1991, 37 per cent of all American multinationals — and more than 70 per cent of all foreign multinationals — did not pay a single dollar in taxes in the United States, while the other multinationals paid less than 1 per cent.[12] The breathtakingly high costs of the military expenditures of the Cold War, then, were not borne by those who profited from the Pentagon System and pocketed the interest payments on the national debt, but by ordinary Americans of the working class and the middle class. During the Cold War, the Pentagon System degenerated into a gigantic swindle, a perverse redistribution of America's wealth to the advantage of the very rich and to the disadvantage of the rest. While the elite became wealthier and wealthier, the prosperity that ordinary Americans had achieved during the Second World War was slowly eroded and their standard of living gradually declined. As for the meagre social services that had been introduced after 1945, they were declared unaffordable and slashed, if not entirely terminated. By the time the Cold War came to an end, in 1989, more than 13 per cent of the American people — approximately 31 million people — had incomes that were ranked below the official poverty line. (By 2013, the percentage of officially poor Americans had risen to 14.9.)[13] The United States may well be the richest country on earth, but its wealth is distributed extremely unevenly, and while the rich get richer, the poor become poorer.

The enormous cost of the Cold War, then, did not constitute a problem for the American power elite; it was a problem for ordinary Americans. When the Cold War ended, these ordinary Americans were relieved; they hoped that the immense resources of their country would cease to be used, or rather abused, for the purpose of waging wars cold and hot, and they looked forward to reaping a so-called "peace dividend." That was precisely the problem for the power elite. With the end of the Cold War — the perfect war — the American power elite was orphaned of its perfect enemy, the one whose existence had justified the military expenditures of the profitable Pentagon System during half a century. As in 1945, a new enemy, or new enemies, were urgently required. A genuine demilitarization of the

American economy would not only have smothered the main fountain-head of profits; it would also have confronted the country with the capital-ist system's key economic problem, insufficient economic demand. This problem had revealed itself dramatically in the Great Depresssion, and it had not been genuinely solved by the remedy of military Keynesianism that had been administered during the Second World War and the Cold War. A confrontation with this systemic problem might have stimulated grassroots interest in radical and even revolutionary changes, as had happened during the "Red thirties," and this was clearly not in the interest of the power elite.

The problem of the lack of enemies was quickly compensated by the deus ex machina-like arrival on the scene of "new Hitlers," such as Saddam Hussein. Nowhere in this book is it stated that Hitler was a decent human being, and neither is it being alleged here that Hussein and his ilk are any-thing but brutal dictators. However, Washington has a history of counten-ancing brutal dictators, exemplified by Pinochet and Suharto, and earlier in his career the dictatorial Saddam himself used to be perceived by Uncle Sam as a good friend. Is it a coincidence that when the Cold War was barely defunct he suddenly metamorphosed into a major menace, requir-ing massive military intervention even though a negotiated settlement was not out of the question? With the alleged Soviet threat gone, and the irritating demand for a "peace dividend" growing stronger, new menaces urgently needed to be fabricated, and the danger represented by Hussein was unquestionably grossly overstated in order to justify war and keep America armed to the teeth. It is not impossible that at the end of the Gulf War Saddam Hussein was allowed to remain in power in Bagdad so that Washington could continue to invoke to its own advantage the huge threat he was supposed to represent.

Another convenient "new Hitler" soon appeared on the scene in the person of the Serbian leader Milosevic, and the military action shifted to the Balkans. Then George W. Bush became president, and China was temporarily cast in the role of America's bogeyman. But none of these villains loomed as sufficiently scary to justify maintaining, let alone increasing, America's colossal arsenal. On September 11, 2001, however, a terrible crime was perpetrated in New York, and full advantage was taken of this opportunity. This unprecedented act of terrorism was immediately compared to the Japanese attack on Pearl Harbor, and comparisons with the Second World War, the "good war," were invoked ad nauseam by the president and the media as Washington prepared to fight a major "war against terrorism." For many reasons, such a comparison does not make sense. The people and even the government of Afghanistan, who were the victims of the *furor americanicus*, had not been responsible for the terrorist outrages of September 11. Furthermore, can war be waged against an abstract and vague concept like "terrorism"? A war against such a foe cannot possibly lead to a clear victory or a satisfactory conclusion of any kind. On the contrary, such a "war" could be expected to yield more and potentially even greater terrorist atrocities. But from the perspective of the American power elite, personified by George W. Bush, who was president at the time, such a war did make sense, because it provided a solution to the problem caused by the end of the Cold War. A war against an ill-defined enemy, a war without geographic limits, a war that will go on for as long as the President tells us it must go on, a war that requires unconditional support from all who do not want to be perceived as being on the side of terrorism, is in fact the ultimate panacea, since it ensures that the Pentagon System may carry on indefinitely to the great satisfaction of those who profit from it. Even the 2008 exit of Bush, generally perceived to be a warmonger, and his replacement by a supposedly peace-loving president, Barack Obama, did not change this reality in the least. And there is no reason to believe that things will change with whomever will be elected president in a few years. Welcome to the brave new era of permanent war!

The "war against terrorism" has recently flared up in countries such as Libya, Syria, and Iraq, and is now being complemented by a new Cold War against Russia. If it depends on the American power elite, new "good wars" may sooner or later also have to be fought against Iran, North Korea, and maybe even China. Preventing such wars will not be easy, but is certainly possible. Even with the eager assistance of the majority of our media, Bush and Blair found it difficult to "sell" their war against Iraq. If the United States would ever be forced to stop waging wars, the moment of truth would arrive for the American economy. Could US capitalism survive such an "outbreak" of peace? Subjected to a permanent state of siege, Soviet socialism could not survive. Could American capitalism survive without being under siege, that is, without enemies, without being threatened, without being able to fight wars, "good" wars or other wars?

ENDNOTES

FOREWORD

1 *Dirty Truths* is the title of a book, published in 1996, by Michael Parenti.

2 Ambrose (1998), p. 66.

3 Among the "classics" of American revisionism are the books by Williams (1962) and Kolko (1968).

4 See e.g., the studies of Henke, Loth (1994).

5 See the studies of Chomsky, Dieterich.

6 Parenti (1999), pp. xv-xvi.

CHAPTER 1

1 Adams, pp. 4 ff., 11–14, 17.

2 Eisenhower and Roosevelt as quoted in Fussell, p. 167.

3 Quotation of Isaiah Berlin from Fussell, ibid.

4 Fussell, pp. 79 ff., 179.

5 Adams, pp. 81, 147; Lichtblau, p. 22.

6 Hynes, pp. 114–15; Doenecke and Wilz, pp. 6–7.

7 Fussell, pp. 129 ff., 141, 179. See also Blum, pp. 67–68; Sherry (1995), pp. 90–91; Mazzeno; Kolko (1994), pp. 210–11; Hoenicke (2010), p. 116.

8 See the comments on *Saving Private Ryan* in Zinn (2001), pp. 102, 104.

9 Blum, p. 46; Ponting, p. 175; Cashman, p. 230.

10 For a critique of the "great men of history" theory, see Edelman, pp. 37–65; also Whitelam, p. 9.

11 See the critical remarks about American pluralism in Mills, p. 242 ff.; Parenti (1978), p. 27 ff.

CHAPTER 2

1 Schmitz (1999); Vidal, p. 928; Lens, p. 96.

2 Diggins, pp. 335–39; Schmitz (1985), pp. 117–38; Deschner (1990), p. 59; Lacroix-Riz (1996), pp. 168–70, 253 ff.

3 See Pauwels (2013), Part One.

4 Higham (1983), *passim;* Kolko (1962), pp. 713–28; Doares; Knapp, Link, Schröder, Schwabe, pp. 86–92; Grosser, p. 8; Jonas, p. 222; Simpson (1993), pp. 11, 46 ff.; Offner (1969), p. 7, n. 23; Wilkins, pp. 187–88; Schäfer, p. 207; Bettelheim, p. 94; Cray, p. 315n; Zilg, pp. 213, 304–08, 313–14; Pendergrast, p. 218 ff.

5   Pendergrast, p. 221; Jones and Ritzmann, pp. 10–12; Reymond, pp. 302–05.

6   H. A. Turner , p. 12.

7   H. A.Turner , p. 10. Commentary on Turner in Black (2009), pp. 123–124.

8   Billstein, p. 24; Lindner, p. 121; Reich (1990), pp. 109, 117, 247; Silverstein, *passim*; Kolko (1962), p. 725; Dobbs (1998a and 1998b); Jersak; Matthias, pp. 134–35; Black (2009), pp. 101–102; Gassert, pp. 347–348.

9   Black (2001), pp. 76–77, 86–87, 98, 119, 120–21, 164, 198, 222. The Reichsmark exchange rate is from Billstein et al., p. 17.

10 Black (2001), pp. 60, 99, 116, 122–23.

11 Higham (1983), introduction, p. xvi.

12 Higham (1983), p. xviii.

13 "All in the Family: The Apple Does Not Fall Far from the BUSH"; Aris and Campbell; Buchanan and Stacey; Mikhah and Kofoet.

14 Black (2009), p. 9; Losurdo (2006), pp. 219–220, 224–225, and (2007), p. 114 ff.; Zilg, pp. 294, 304–08, 314; Higham (1983), pp. 162, 165; Sampson (1973), p. 27 ff.; Sampson (1975), pp. 81–82; Doares; Warburg, pp. 34–35; Deschner (1992), pp. 219–26.

15 Jersak.

16 Billstein et al., p. 25; H. A. Turner, p. 23.

17 Overesch (1993), p. 64.

18 Higham (1983), p. 163; also Berghahn (2004), p. 142 ff.

19 Higham (1983), p.165.

20 Watkins, pp. 222–24, 247–48, 323; O'Reilly, pp. 122, 165 ff.; David Brinkley, p. 17; Blum, p. 182 ff.; Adams, pp. 12, 145; Roeder, pp. 45, 84; Zinn (1980), p. 406; Terkel, p. 564; Kühl, p. 38.

21 Ambrose (1998), p. 146.

22 Hoenicke (2010), p. 152.

23 Hoenicke (2010), p. 72 ff.

24 Adams, p. 146. Ford's and Du Pont's anti-Semitism: Losurdo (2007), p.114 ff.; Silverstein, p. 12; Dobbs (1998a and 1998b); Higham (1983), pp. 161–62; Hoenicke (2010), p. 73; Amblard, p. 49 ff.; Baldwin, p. 279.

25 Dodd and Dodd, p. 107.

26 Adams, p. 146; Watkins, p. 320; Morse, *passim*.

27 Morse, pp. 270–88.

28 Hilliard, *passim*, and document on pp. 216–17; see also the comments in Terkel, pp. 572–73, and Zezima, p. 68.

29 Zunes.

30 Cray, p. 315; Dobbs (1998a and 1998b); Sampson (1975), p. 82; Higham

(1983), p. 97; Cashman, pp. 70–72; Black (2001), pp. 132–34.

31 Jersak; Martin (1976), p. 82; Dobbs (1998b); Black (2001), p. 208.

CHAPTER 3

1 Parenti (1989), pp. 136–38; Chomsky, pp. 66–67; Aronson, p. 26 ff.; Leibovitz and Finkel, p. 35 ff.

2 Filene, pp. 35–42; Foner, p. 42 ff.

3 Murray; Foner, p. 20 ff.

4 Williams (1967); Aronson, pp. 29–30; Loewen, p. 12 ff.

5 Paterson, Clifford, and Hagan, pp. 289–93.

6 Vidal, p. 926; Barson, pp. 5–8.

7 W. Turner, p. 177.

8 Russo.

9 Zieger, p. 71.

10 Backer, p. 162.

11 Thurston, p. 221; Losurdo (2008), pp 138–143; Heale, p. 99; Watkins, pp. 76–107; Greiner, p. 62 ff.; Kutulas, pp. 46–51.

12 Cowley as quoted in Watkins, p. 338.

13 Millar (1985), p. 288.

14 Quotation from a commentary of the *Times Literary Supplement*, reprinted on the dustcover of Diggins.

15 For the case of France, see the studies of Lacroix-Riz (2006 and 2008).

16 Mayer, p. 30 ff.; Dülffer, p. 84; Overy (1997), pp. 34–35.

17 Martin (1974), pp. 313–14.

18 Schmitz (1985), *passim*; Schmitz (1999), p. 87 ff.; Leibovitz and Finkel, p. 35; Parenti (1989), p. 141; Kühnl (1989), pp. 34–35; Engelmann, pp. 272–74; Chomsky, p. 68.

19 Hoenicke (2010), p. 61.

20 Hitchens, p. 25; Adams, p. 34; Sobel, pp. 87–88; Schäfer, p. 207.

21 Kershaw, pp. 143–44; van der Pijl, p. 86; Parenti (1989), pp. 142–43; Harbutt, pp. xi–xii; Higham (1983), pp. 5, 182; Davies, pp. 16, 19; Kühnl (1989), p. 37; Soete, pp. 102–08.

22 Quoted in Higham (1988), p. 241.

23 For details of the appeasement policy in Europe, see the study by Leibovitz and Finkel, also Soete.

24 Horn; Knapp, Link, Schröder, and Schwabe, p. 109.

25 Schmitz (1999), pp. 88–89; Simpson (1993), p. 52; Maddux (1977), *passim*.

26   Meyer, p. 32; Offner (1983).

27   Schmitz (1999), p. 87 ff.; Farnham,pp. 76–77; Hass, p. 81; Offner (1969), pp. 146, 234; Offner (1971), pp. 54–76; Ambrose (1998), p. 73.

28   Kolko (1976), p. 220.

29   Leibovitz and Finkel, p. 235 ff.; Soete, pp. 249–52; Knightley, pp. 225–26.

30   Offner (1983), pp. 215–16; Paterson, Clifford, and Hagan, p. 329; Hass, pp. 89, 109, 153 ff.; Barson, pp. 19–22; Billstein et al., pp. 37–44; Völklein, pp. 81–88; H. A. Turner, p. 104 ff. The Catholic and Protestant periodicals are cited in Hoenicke (2010), pp. 66, 71; Mooney quotation from Hillgruber (1967), p. 85.

31   Heale, pp. 122–25; Cashman, pp. 269–71; Soete, pp. 275–83.

CHAPTER 4

1   Viorst, pp. 37–40; Aglion, pp. 118–27, 136; David Brinkley, p. 32.

2   Du Boff, p. 72; Oppelland, pp. 16–17.

3   Doenecke and Wilz, p. 63; Schäfer, p. 207.

4   For details, see Pauwels (2014), p. 457 ff.

5   Ambrose (1993), p. 3; Hass, p. 70; Fussell, pp. 147–48; *Historical Statistics*, p. 903.

6   MacDonald, pp. 400–01, 409; Williams (1962), p. 233; Barber, p. 154; Doenecke and Wilz, pp. 104–05.

7   Maddox (1992), p. 76; Blum, pp. 309–10; A. J. P. Taylor (1965), pp. 513, 533.

8   Puth, p. 522; Cashman, p. 214; Blum, p. 230; Reynolds, Kimball, and Chubarian, p. 181.

9   Cashman, p. 214.

10   Harbutt, p. 62; Keegan, pp. 97–98.

11   Crombois, p. 291 ff.

12   Carroll and Noble, p. 345.

13   Schäfer, pp. 207–08; Berghahn (1993), pp. 85–86; Hoenicke (2010), pp. 65–66; Hearden, pp. 109–10, 126–27; Knapp, Link, Schröder, and Schwabe, pp. 119–25, 145–50; Schäfer, p. 207; Hass, pp. 37–38.

14   Pommerin (1977), pp. 23–27; Junker (1975), pp. 97–102; Knapp, Link, Schröder, Schwabe, pp. 137–46; Gatzke, pp. 122–23; Hass, p. 39 ff.; Carroll and Noble, p. 346.

15   Hearden, p. 110.

16   Quotation from Hallgarten and Radkau, pp. 337–38.

17   Lewis, pp. 222, 270.

18 Black (2001), p. 212.

19 Cashman, p. 56; Carroll and Noble, p. 347.

20 Cashman, pp. 67–68.

21 Ambrose (1998), p. 66.

CHAPTER 5

1   See the study by Rolf-Dieter Müller, *Der Feind steht im Osten*, published in 2011.

2   Cited in Müller, p. 152.

3   Soete, pp. 289–290, including p. 289, n. 1.

4   See, e.g., Ueberschär (2011b), p. 39.

5   Müller, p. 169.

6   Ueberschär (2011a), p. 95.

7   Müller, pp. 209, 225.

8   Ueberschär (2011b), p. 15.

9   Pauwels, op. cit., p. 62; Ueberschär (2011a), pp. 95–96; Domenico Losurdo, *Stalin: Storia e critica di una leggenda nera*, Rome, 2008, p. 29.

10 Müller, p. 243.

11 Overy (1997), p. 87; Ueberschär (2011a), pp. 97–98.

12 Ueberschär (2011a), p. 97.

13 Overy (1997), pp. 64–65.

14 Furr, p. 343: Losurdo (2008), p. 31; Soete, p. 297.

15 Losurdo (2008), pp. 31–32; Wegner, p. 653; Ueberschär (2011a), p. 100.

16 Müller, p. 233.

17 Ueberschär (2011a), pp. 99–102, 106–107.

18 Ueberschär (2011a), p. 106.

19 Ueberschär (2011a), pp. 107-111; Roberts, p. 111.

20 Hillgruber (1989, p. 81.

21 Ueberschär (2011a), p. 120.

22 Lacroix-Riz (1996), p. 417.

23 Bourgeois, pp. 123, 127.

24 Ueberschär (2011a), pp. 107–108.

25 Gatzke, p. 137.

26 Wegner, pp. 654–656.

27 Ueberschär (2011a), p. 116.

28 Ponting, p. 130; Ambrose (1998), p. 72.

CHAPTER 6

1   Overy (1995), p. 254; Overy (1997), pp. 194–197; Martin (1974), pp. 459, 475; Ambrose (1998), pp. 76–77; Hass, pp. 233–234; Hillgruber (1989), p. 78; Sivachev and Yakovlev, p. 165; Dülffer, pp. 138–141; Keyssar and Pozner, pp. 151–152. Steinhardt is quoted in Mayers, p.131.

2   Levering, p. 156; Hillgruber (1989), pp. 80–81; Fohlen, pp. 147–48; Gaddis, pp. 22–23.

3   David Brinkley, p. 152 ff.

4   Levering, p. 46; Cole, pp. 433–434; Parenti (1969), p. 126; Levering, p. 46–47; Douglas, p. 86; Koppes and Black, p. 189; Adler and Paterson, p. 1051.

5   Ponting, p. 106; Overy (1997), pp. 194–197; Martin (1974), p. 459; Deutscher, p. 512, n. 1; Hillgruber (1989), p. 81; Hass, p. 234; Sivachev and Yakovlev, p. 165; Adams, p. 71.

6   Statistics from Jersak, who used "top secret" documents produced by the Werhmacht Reichsstelle für Mineralöl, available in the military section of the Bundesarchiv, Germany's federal archives, file RW 19/2694; also Snell, p. 16; Higham (1983), pp. 59–61.

7   See, e.g., Zhilin, pp. 55–56.

8   See, e.g., Zinn, p. 305 ff.

9   Hearden, p. 105.

10 See the article "Anti-Japanese Sentiment."

11 Rudmin, op. cit.

12 Knox quotation from the article by Buchanan.

13 Under the terms of the Tripartite Treaty concluded by Japan, Germany, and Italy in Berlin on September 27, 1940, the three countries undertook to assist each other when one of the three contracting powers was attacked by another country, but not when one of them attacked another country.

14 Hillgruber (1989), pp. 75, 82–83, Iriye, pp. 149–150, 181–182.

15 Stinnett, op. cit., pp. 5–6, 9–10, 17–19, 39–43, 60 ff.; Buchanan.

16 The American public had similarly been made to rally behind the flag before, namely at the start of the Spanish-American War, when the US battleship *Maine* had mysteriously blown up in Havana harbour, an act that was immediately blamed on the Spanish. After World War II, Americans would again be conditioned to approve of wars, wanted and planned by their government, by means of contrived provocations such as the 1964 Gulf of Tonkin Incident.

17 Stinnett, pp. 152–154.

18 Zinn (1980), p. 401.

CHAPTER 7

1 Data from *Historical Statistics*, p. 126; Adams, pp. 115–16; Du Boff, p. 91.

2 Terkel, p. 9.

3 Brandes, pp. 253–59, 263; Adams, p. 118; Zinn (1980), p. 416; Cashman, pp. 202–08.

4 Stimson as quoted in Sherry (1995), p. 72; Overy (1995), p. 198.

5 Black (2001), p. 345.

6 Farber, p. 223.

7 Brandes, pp. 259–62; Cashman, pp. 202–03; Sherry (1995), p. 73; Mills, pp. 100–01; statistics from David Brinkley, p. 53; Truman quotation from Brandes, p. 262.

8 David Brinkley, pp. 53–54.

9 Vatter, p. 149; also Sherry (1995), p. 72.

10 Adams, p. 117; Weiher, pp. 98–99; Reynolds, Kimball, and Chubarian, pp. 181–82; Cashman, p. 213; Roeder, p. 65.

11 Mills, pp. 100–01.

12 Zieger, p. 62 ff.; Brecher, p. 221 ff.; Marwick, pp. 246–47; Cashman, pp. 245–47; Cardozier, pp. 150–152; Fohlen, pp. 213–16; Sivachyov and Yazkov, pp. 183–87; Levine et al., pp. 459–63. Zinn quotation: Zinn (1980), pp. 408–09. The inflation rate between 1939 to 1945 was calculated via the "The Inflation Calculator," www.westegg.com/inflation.

13 See the remarks on collective action in Parenti (1996), pp. 123–24; Chapter 3 of Olson's book deals with this issue.

14 Keen, pp. 27, 33, 89.

15 Hoenicke (2010), p. 157 ff.; Steele, especially pp. 233–34.

16 Dick, p. 196; Shull and Wilt, pp. 36, 94–95; Maddox (1992), pp. 186–87; Howell, p. 806; Hoenicke (2010), pp. 236–240.

17 Small (1974); Parenti (1969), p. 125; Koppes and Black (2001), pp. 185 ff., 210, 219; Roeder, pp. 128–29; Barson, pp. 23–32; Adams, p. 139; Levering, p. 73; Adler and Paterson, p. 1051.

18 Levering, pp. 111–12; Parenti (1969), p. 125; Deutscher, pp. 474–75, 477; Hillgruber (1989), p. 124; Small (1974), p. 472.

19 Reynolds, Kimball, and Chubarian, pp. 193–94.

CHAPTER 8

1 Reynolds, p. xxiii.

2 Deutscher, p. 499; Bagguley, p. 95; Davies, p. 52.

3 Desquesnes, pp. 262, 265.

4 Overy (1995), p. 34.

5   Levering, p. 78; Gaddis, pp. 66–67; Deutscher, pp. 92 and 479, n. 2; Harbutt, p. 39; Lynd, p. 568; Loth (1988), p. 60; Stoler, *passim*.

6   Sainsbury, p. 37; Maddox (1992), pp. 134–36; Harbutt, p. 46; Gaddis, p. 70; Ambrose (1993), p. 17.

7   Chomsky, pp. 68–69; Ponting, p. 80; Sivachev and Yakovlev, pp. 174, 180–81; Levering, p. 46; Cole, pp. 433–34.

8   Ross, pp. 28–29.

9   Deutscher, p. 499; Bagguley, p. 95; Desquesnes, pp. 262, 265.

10   See the book by David O'Keefe, *One Day in August: The Untold Story Behind Canada's Tragedy at Dieppe*.

11   Knightley, pp. 319–20.

12   Carroll and Noble, p. 354.

13   Adams, pp. 53-54, 108–110; Overy (1995), pp. 101–33; Murray and Millet (1996), pp. 106–08, 122–27, 140; Kolko (1994), pp. 185, 206; Maddox (1992), pp. 259–65; Roeder, p. 84; O'Neill, pp. 314–15.

14   Bagguley, p. 92; Ponting, pp. 130–31.

CHAPTER 9

1   Overy (1995), pp. 63–100; Ebert, p. 53; Davies, p. 58.

2   Harbutt, pp. 36–37, 50; Gaddis, p. 74.

3   Stoler, pp. 136–37.

4   Ponting, p. 130; Ambrose (1998), p. 72.

5   Kimball, pp. 19–20.

6   Blasius, pp. 166–73; Hillgruber (1989), pp. 85–86, 101, 104; Gaddis, p. 73; Maddox (1988), p. 4; Maddox (1992), p. 141; Ambrose (1993), pp. 23–24; Sainsbury, pp. 142–43.

7   Blasius, pp. 164–67.

8   Mayers, p. 138.

9   Gaddis, p. 15.

10   Gaddis, p. 75; Junker (1989), pp. 67–68; Ponting, p. 130.

11   Williams (1962), p. 210 ff.; Lynd, p. 571; Harper, p. 81; Harbutt, pp. 43, 54 ff.; Loth (1988), p. 30.

12   Maddox (1988), pp. 6–7; Harbutt, p. 55.

CHAPTER 10

1   Quoted in Stoler, p. 137.

2   For the role of Badoglio in Ethiopia, see Del Boca, *passim*.

3   Kolko (1968), pp. 56–57; Lacroix-Riz (1996), pp. 430–33; Feldbauer, pp.

132–147; Gaja, pp.151–60.

4   Caretto and Marolo, pp. 39 ff.; Zezima, pp. 148–51; p. 133, n. 6; Kruger, p. 14.

5   Ambrose (1993), p. 25; Lynd, p. 572; Ponting, p. 247; Kolko (1968), p. 52; Kimball, p. 20.

6   Deutscher, p. 518; Harbutt, p. 68. Kolko quotation: Kolko (1968), pp. 50–51.

7   Loth (1994), p. 20; Harper, p. 122.

8   Carroll and Noble, p. 354.

9   Stoler, p. 138.

10 Kolko (1968), p. 29; Ross, p. 81; Stoler, pp. 137–38.

CHAPTER 11

1   Kimball, p. 19; Overy (1997), pp. 240–44.

2   Kolko (1968), p. 144 ff.

3   On Greece, see, e.g., Gaja, pp. 145–150.

4   "1944: Charte du Conseil National de la Résistance," www.ldh-france.org/1944-CHARTE-DU-CONSEIL-NATIONAL-DE.

5   Thomson, pp. 233–34; Davies, pp. 56–57; Kolko (1968), pp. 72–73, 77.

6   Harbutt, pp. 76–77; Hoge.

7   Grosser, p. 24; Viorst, pp. 115–33, 220; Kolko (1968), p. 64 ff.; Aglion, p. 195.

8   Rossi; Hoge; Loewenheim, Langley, and Jonas, pp. 344–45; Kolko (1968), pp. 82–83.

9   Stimson quotation from Rossi, p. 61.

10 Rossi, p. 64; Kolko (1968), p. 77.

11 Viorst, pp. 210–11.

12 Overy (1997), pp. 244–49.

13 A. J. P. Taylor (1967), p. 299.

14 Kolko (1976), p. 228; Harbutt, p. 78.

15 Kolko (1968), pp. 96–98.

CHAPTER 12

1   Leibovitz and Finkel, p. 206; Losurdo (2008), pp. 179–180. See also Harper, p. 104, for a relevant remark by Roosevelt.

2   Knightley, pp. 324–25; Keyssar and Pozner, p. 153.

3   Overy (1997), pp. 256–60; Kolko (1968), pp. 350–52; Maddox (1992), pp. 250–51; Keyssar and Pozner, p. 154.

4   MacArthur's opinion is cited in Schwinge, pp. 10–11.

5   Bennett, p. 156.

6   Steininger, pp. 20–22; Kolko (1968), pp. 353–55, quotation from p. 355.

7   Harbutt, p. 82; Horowitz (1965), p. 35.

8   Stettinius quotation from Parenti (1969), p. 131.

9   Eisenberg (1996), p. 61.

10 Steininger, p. 28; Loth (1994), p. 15.

11 Loewenheim, Langley, and Jonas, p. 656.

12 Harbutt, p. 72; Loth (1994), p. 18; Hoenicke (2010), p. 293 ff.; Krieger, pp. 36, 40–41; Paterson, Clifford, and Hagan, p. 409; Kolko (1968), pp. 331, 348–49; Link, pp. 107–08; Gardner, pp. 250–51.

13 Fisch, p. 48.

14 Eisenberg (1982), p. 26; Gromyko's comment is from Hoenicke (2010), p. 302.

15 Parenti (1969), p. 135; Cochran, p. 42.

16 Parenti (1969), p. 137.

17 Weinberg, p. 809; Düllfer, p. 29.

18 Parenti (1969), p. 139.

19 Gaddis, p. 88; Deutscher, pp. 473–74; Simpson (1993), pp. 118–19; Maddox (1992), p. 251; Paterson, Clifford, and Hagan, p. 413; Loth (1994), p. 16; Parenti (1969), p. 131.

CHAPTER 13

1   Knightley, p. 313.

2   F. Taylor, pp. 354, 443–448; Bergander, chapter 12, and especially pp. 210 ff., 218–219, 229; "Luftangriffe auf Dresden", p. 9; Irving, pp. 224–27.

3   Sherry (1987), p. 260; a similar view is expressed in Irving, p. 231.

4   See, e.g., the comments made by General Spaatz cited in Hansen, p. 243.

5   Overy (1995), pp. 127–33.

6   F. Taylor, p. 416.

7   F. Taylor, pp. 321–322.

8   Groehler, p. 414; Hansen, p. 245; "Luftangriffe auf Dresden"; F. Taylor, pp. 152–154, 358–359.

9   Spoo, pp. 367–70.

10 F. Taylor, p. 190; Groehler, pp. 400–401. Citing a study about Yalta, the British author of the latest study of Allied bombing during World War II notes that the Soviets "clearly preferred to keep the RAF and the USAAF away from territory they might soon be occupying." See Grayling, p. 176.

11 McKee, pp. 264–265; Groehler, pp. 400–402.

12 Davis, p. 96.

13 F. Taylor, pp. 185–186, 376; Grayling, p. 71; Irving. pp. 96–99.

14 Hansen, p. 241.

15 Harris. p. 242.

16 McKee, p. 46, 105.

17 Groehler, p. 404.

18 Groehler, p. 404.

19 The Americans preferred "precision bombing" in theory, if not always in practice.

20 F. Taylor, p. 318; Irving, p. 147.

21 Cited in F. Taylor, p. 319.

22 Irving, p. 148.

23 Quotation from Groehler, p. 404. See also Grayling, p. 260.

24 Cited in Broadfoot, p. 269.

25 F. Taylor, pp. 361, 363–65.

26 See, e.g., Dahms, p. 187.

27 Cited in Schaffer, p. 330.

28 Parenti (1989), pp. 146–47; Simpson (1988), pp. 55–56; Loth (1994), p. 14; Millar (1985), p. 284; Horowitz (1965), pp. 51–52, n. 3; Leffner (1992), p. 5.

29 Simpson (1988), pp. 55–56; Leffner (1992), pp. 5–6; Williams (1962), pp. 230–31; Dieterich, pp. 122–24. The JCS-report is quoted in Poole, p. 12.

CHAPTER 14

1 Henke, pp. 669–72.

2 Knightley, p. 327.

3 Eisenberg (1996), p. 72; Sivachev and Yakovlev, pp. 195–96.

4 Maddox (1992), p. 255; Shtemenko, pp. 388, 390; Henke, p. 673.

5 Henke, p. 714 ff.; Harbutt, p. 102; Gaddis, pp. 208–10.

6 Offner (1991), pp. 49–60; McCullough, p. 355.

CHAPTER 15

1 Bruhn, pp. 17–18.

2 Higham (1983), p. 98; Liebig.

3 Bruhn, pp. 17–19; Lacroix-Riz (1996), p. 438; McCormick, p. 37; Heideking and Mauch, pp. 12 ff., 28 ff.; Engelmann, pp. 268–70; see also Carl Goerdeler's "Geheime Denkschrift" of March 26, 1943, reproduced in Kühnl

(1980), pp. 446–48; Higham (1983), p. 98; Liebig.

4   Schwinge, p. 4.

5   Smith (1974); Smith (1977), p. 54 ff.; Harbutt, pp. 102–3; Kolko (1968), p. 505; Hillgruber (1989), p. 147; Bacque, pp. 139–40; Pommerin (1995), p. 17; "No Canadian Scandal"; Loth (1988), p. 89; Altmann, p. 24; Kraus, p. 16; Zhilin., p. 95.

6   Yeldell, pp. 23–25; Simpson (1988); Zezima, pp. 155–5; Grose, pp. 22–25; Adams, p. 147; Ponting, pp. 288–93; Terkel, pp. 465–69; Lacroix-Riz (1996), pp. 438–40, 453–55; Lee; Milano and Brogan; Lichtblau, pp. 33–34.

7   Bruhn, p. 19; Leibovitz and Finkel, p. 41; Aronson, pp. 33–35; Terkel, pp. 124, 127, 477; Smith (1974), p. 20; Roeder, p. 174, n. 21; Gaja, p. 99.

8   Matthias, p. 113; also Drechsler, pp. 119–20.

9   Quotation of war veteran: Terkel, pp. 44–45; similar comments in Terkel, pp. 303, 478.

10   Gaja, pp. 77–89; Waters, p. 280 ff.; Matthias, pp. 345–46; Heartfield, pp. 152, 397.

11   Ambrose (1998), pp. 122, 172; Blumenson, pp. 269–70; Gaja, p. 106.

12   Patton quotation: Buhite and Hamel, p. 372.

13   Buhite and Hamel, p. 372.

14   Smith (1977), p. 49; Gaja, pp. 161–165; Lacroix-Riz (1996), p. 438; Simpson (1988), pp. 92–93; Simpson (1993), p. 199 ff., 236 ff.; Alperovitz (1985), pp. 25–33; Heideking and Mauch, p. 142 ff.; Kolko (1968), p. 375 ff.; Parenti (1969), p. 132, n.; Badia, pp. 215–16; Shtemenko, pp. 283–84; Lichtblau, pp. 14–21, 24–29.

15   Henke, pp. 677–87; Gellermann.

16   Gellermann, pp. 112, 119.

CHAPTER 16

1   *Germany Surrenders* 1945, pp. 2–3.

2   Kraus, pp. 4–5, 12; *Germany Surrenders* 1945, p. 6; Henke, pp. 687, 965–67; Keyssar and Pozner, p. 233.

3   Henke, pp. 967–68.

4   Kolko (1968), p. 387; *Germany Surrenders* 1945, p. 8.

5   *Germany Surrenders* 1945, pp. 8–9.

6   Kolko (1968), p. 388.

7   Albrecht.

CHAPTER 17

1   Du Boff, p. 153.

2   Leffner (1992), p. 2; McCormick, p. 48; Adams, p. 6; Levering, p. 96.

3   Lapham quotation: Terkel, p. 6.

4   Puth, p. 521; Adams, p. 6; Paterson, Clifford, and Hagan, p. 421.

5   Du Boff, p. 91.

6   Feagin and Riddell, p. 53; David Brinkley, p. 54.

7   Martel, p. 98; Adams, p. 132; Gaddis, pp. 21, 189; Williams (1962), p. 232 ff.; Loth (1988), p. 23; Dieterich, pp. 120–21.

8   Kolko (1976), p. 235.

9   Garraty, pp. 231–32.

10   Mills, pp. 100–01, 212–13.

11   Acheson as quoted in Williams (1962), pp. 202–03.

12   Carroll and Noble, pp. 354–55.

13   Adams, p. 30; Gaddis, p. 20.

14   Chomsky, pp. 10, 34; Kolko (1976), pp. 221–25; Zinn (1980), pp. 404–05.

15   Davies, p. 81; Loth (1988), pp. 24–25; Gaddis, pp. 22–23.

16   Zinn (1980), p. 404.

17   Davies, pp. 81–82; McCormick, pp. 52–53; Barber, pp. 156–57; Blum, pp. 307–08; Dippel, pp. 101–02; George and Sabelli, p. 21 ff.; Williams (1962), p. 203 ff.; Dieterich, pp. 89–90.

18   See, e.g., Gaja, pp. 30–33.

19   Delanty, p. 121.

20   Irons, p. 75; Levering, pp. 156–59; Gaddis, pp. 185, 187–88; Loth, (1988), pp. 26, 64.

21   Adler and Paterson, pp. 1050–52; Gaddis, pp. 52–53; Parenti (1969), p. 126; Doenecke, *passim*; Heale, pp. 119, 124; Gaja, pp. 47–48.

22   Vidal, pp. 929, 1097; Hitler and "Rosenfeld": Hoenicke (1997), p. 78; Matthias, pp. 133–34; Zezima, pp. 35–38.

23   Isenberg.

24   Terkel, p. 570.

25   Gaja, p. 18.

CHAPTER 18

1   Deutscher, p. 519; Parenti (1969), pp. 136–38.

2   Horowitz (1965), p. 278; Christopher Lasch in introduction to Alperovitz (1985), pp. 19–20.

3   McCullough, pp. 376–377; Williams (1962), p. 250; also McCormick, p. 45.

4   Truman quotation: Bernstein, p. 32; Parenti (1969), p. 126.

5 Düllfer, p. 155.

6 Alperovitz (1985), p. 223; Gaja, pp. 38–39.

7 Alperovitz (1985), pp. 28, 156.

8 Truman quote: Alperovitz (1985), p. 24.

9 See, e.g., the article by Fraser.

10 Zezima, p. 127.

11 Quoted in Horowitz (1967), p. 53, n.

12 Levine et al., p. 469; Slusser, p. 121.

13 Cashman, p. 369.

14 About Hollywood's participation in this mythmaking process, see the article by Mitchell; see also the article by Elder about the presentation of Hiroshima and Nagasaki in American schools.

15 Alperovitz (1985), pp. 26–27; McCormick, p. 46.

16 Quoted in Terkel, p. 535.

17 Kohls.

18 Ambrose (1993), p. 49; Paterson, Clifford, and Hagan, p. 457; Slusser, p. 121; Sherry (1987), p. 339. See also Gaja, p. 45: "The real reason for the bombing of Hiroshima and Nagasaki was to ensure that Japan surrendered exclusively to MacArthur…"

19 Paterson, Clifford, and Hagan, p. 458.

20 Alperovitz (1985), pp. 248–64; Alperovitz (1970), p. 14; Horowitz (1967), p. 56 ff.; Gaja, pp 109, 114. *New York Herald Tribune* quoted in Alperovitz (1985), p. 252, n.

21 Kolko (1976), p. 355.

22 Hanhimaki, pp. 354–55.

23 Gaja, pp. 107–109; Horowitz (1965), pp. 95, 255, 270–71; Holloway, p. 147; Alperovitz (1985), pp. 266–68.

CHAPTER 19

1 Marwick, pp. 247–48.

2 Eiler, pp. 436–37; Irons, pp. 77–78; Levine et al., pp. 470–77; Fones-Wolf, pp. 15, 20; Oshinsky, pp. 124–27; Zieger, pp. 87, 92, 97–99.

3 Filene, p. 164.

4 Alan Brinkley, *passim*; Hamby, pp. 7–9, 16–17, 19; Blum, pp. 231, 262, 247–49; Barber, p. 165.

5 Hopkins, Wallerstein et al., pp. 119–20.

6 Griffith, *passim*, especially pp. 391, 396, 399.

7 Bruhn, pp. 22–24.

8   Fones-Wolf, pp. 26, 37; Irons, pp. 72–89; Sherry (1995), p. 48.

9   Zinn (1980), pp. 417, 420, 422 ff.; Zieger, p. 108 ff.; Sivachyov and Yazkov, pp. 205–09.

10 Kleinfeld, p. 54.

11 Rosenbaum, p. 25.

12 Claessens and Claessens, pp. 210–12; Parenti (1997), p. 58.

13 Parenti (1996), pp. 44–45.

14 Bruhn, pp. 23–25.

15 Kolko (1976), pp. 316–23; O'Connor, pp. 150–58; Chomsky, pp. 47, 106, 111; Galbraith, pp. 231–32; Vidal, pp. 794, 927; Paterson, pp. 203–212; Baran and Sweezy, p. 212.

16 Adams, p. 75.

17 Klare, p.12; Chossudovsky, pp. 99–100; "Military Budget of the United States."

18 See, e.g., Cockburn, p. 736; Greider; Chomsky, pp. 87, 112.

19 Zepezauer and Naiman, pp. 13–15; Adams, p. 117–18.

20 For a critique of Samuelsonian economic concepts such as "public goods," see the study by Linder and Sensat.

21 Vidal, p. 794; Bruhn, *passim*.

CHAPTER 20

1   See the comments on the "gangster theory" of Nazism and fascism in Hoenicke (2010), pp. 88–89, 143, 167, 233–240; also Arato and Gebhardt, p. 34.

2   Pingel, pp. 784–97; Simpson (1993), pp. 13, 85 ff., 269–71; Eisenberg (1996), p. 130 ff.; Kolko (1968), p. 513.

3   Simpson (1993), p 13.

4   Hayes, pp. 361–63, 377–79; Borkin; "Holocaust-Überlebende klagen"; Ponting, pp. 282–83. The "chicken thief" quotation is from Borkin, p. 195.

5   Schmelzer, *passim*.

6   Simpson (1993), *passim*, and especially pp. 290–310.

7   "Big fish" quotation from Steininger, p. 130.

8   Green quotation: Gimbel (1990c), p. 349.

9   Gimbel (1990b), p. 448; Gimbel (1990c); Gimbel (1993), pp. 175–96; monographs by Bower, Hunt, and Jacobsen.

10 Simpson (1993), pp. 150–53, 217 ff.; Berghahn (1993), p. 88; Gimbel (1990b).

11 See, e.g., Borkin, p. 58 ff.; Jonas, p. 222; Junker (1975), p. 104; Kolko (1962),

pp. 721–25; Sampson (1973), pp. 33–38; Simpson (1993), pp. 96–97; Snell, pp. 15–16; Sobel, p. 89; Wilkins and Hill, p. 320.

12 Pendergrast, pp. 218, 226 ff.; "Fanta boooo"; Lindner, p. 118; Reymond, p. 311.

13 Black (2001), pp. 205, 360 ff., 371 ff.; see also Black (2009), pp. 127–60.

14 Hofer and Reginbogin, p. 589; von Hassell and MacRae, pp. 223; Sutton, p. 53–54; Tooze, p. 128; Jeffreys. pp. 196–199; quotation from Black (2009), pp. 107–08.

15 Helms, p. 113; Higham (1983), p. 93 ff.; Greiner, pp. 110–12.

16 Higham (1983), p. 112.

17 Helms, p. 113; Silverstein, pp. 12–13; Greiner, pp. 112–14; Kitman.

18 Billstein et al., p. 25; Neliba; Kugler (1997a), pp. 40–41; Kugler (1997b), p. 69; Helms, p. 113.

19 Snell, pp. 14–15; Kugler (1997a), pp. 53, 67; Kugler (1997b), p. 89; Wilkins and Hill, p. 320; "pioneers of technological development" quotation: Lindner, p. 104.

20 Dobbs (1998a and 1998b).

21 Citation from Helms, p.114; Dobbs (1998a and 1998b).

22 Helms, pp. 14–15; remarks on Transradio in Higham (1983), pp. 104–105.

23 Black , pp. 339, 376, 392–395.

24 Kugler (1997a), p. 65; see also Billstein, pp. 34–36.

25 Silverstein, pp. 15–16; Lindner, p. 121.

26 For the role of the enemy-assets custodian in general, see the study by Lindner.

27 Black (2001), pp. 234–37.

28 Black (2001), pp. 376, 400-02, 405, 415.

29 Kugler (1997a), pp. 52, 61 ff., 67; Kugler (1997b), p. 85.

30 Silverstein, pp. 12, 14; Helms, p. 115; Reich (1990), pp. 121, 123; "Dokumentation uber Zwangsarbeit bei Ford." About wartime profits of "enemy enterprises" in general, see Lindner, pp. 124–27.

31 Billstein, p. 116; Silverstein, pp. 15–16; Greiner, p. 114.

32 Billstein, p. 73; Kugler (1997a), pp. 55, 67; Kugler (1997b), p. 85.

33 Black (2001), pp. 212, 253, 297–99.

34 Black (2001), pp 59–60, 76–77.

35 Message from A. Neugebauer of the city archives of Rüsselsheim to the author, February 4, 2000; Lindner, pp. 126–127.

36 Silverstein.

37 Helms, p. 115 ; Higham (1983), pp. 158–159.

38 Black (2001), pp. 212, 253, 297–99.

39 Quotation from "Hitlers beflissene Hehler."

40 LeBor, p. 206; Trepp (1998), pp. 71–80; Higham (1983), pp. 1–19; Sampson (1973) p. 47; "VS-Banken collaboreerden met nazis"; Clarke.

41 Liebig; "Hitlers beflissene Hehler"; Steinacher, pp. 190–93. Higham (1983), p. 72. Higham (1983), pp. 1–19 devotes an entire chapter to the BIS. On McKittrick, "Hitler's American banker," see Charguéraud's book. See also the documentary *Banking with Hitler*.

CHAPTER 21

1 It is acknowledged here, however, that a capitalist system may occasionally also benefit from relatively high wage levels; for example, dramatic wage increases (possibly combined with other concessions) may serve to defuse a potentially revolutionary situation and thus make it possible for profits — any profits — to continue to be made, thereby allowing the system to continue functioning.

2 Engelmann, pp. 263–64; Recker, *passim*; Kugler (1997b), pp. 71, 86.

3 Lindner, p. 118; Pendergrast, p. 228; Reymond, p. 311; Friedman.

4 Fings, p. 107.

5 "Ford-Konzern wegen Zwangsarbeit verklagt"; Silverstein, p. 14; Billstein, pp. 53 ff., 135 ff.; Lueken; Simpson (1993), pp. 96–97; Kugler (1997a), p. 57; Kugler (1997b), p. 72 ff., quote from p. 76.

6 GM-financed patriotic posters may be found in the National Archives in Washington, DC, Still Pictures Branch.

7 Higham (1983), preface, pp. xv, xxi.

8 Higham (1983), pp. 44–46.

9 Black (2001), pp. 333 ff., 348.

10 Higham (1983), pp. 112–15 (quotation from p. 112); Sampson (1973), p. 40; Bower, pp. 78–79. Pictures of Behn's tomb at Arlington Cemetery and the medal he received from the US government may be viewed on a website devoted to "the heroes and the pathfinders who rest at peace there": www. arlingtoncemetery.com/sbehn.

11 Billstein, pp. 98–100, 118; Helms pp. 115–16; Reich (1990), pp. 124–25, 133; Wilkins and Hill, pp. 344–46.

12 Neugebauer, pp. 170–71; Billstein, pp. 77–79.

13 Black (2001), pp. 406–09.

14 Silverstein, p. 16; Snell, p. 16; Higham (1983), pp. 160, 177; Sampson (1973), p. 47; Reich (1990), p. 123; Link, p. 100; Billstein, pp. 73–75.

15 Eisenberg (1996), p. 142.

16 Cited in Zhilin, p. 10.

17 Higham (1983), p. 212 ff.; Eisenberg (1982), p. 29; Eisenberg (1993), pp. 63–64; Eisenberg (1996), pp. 119–21; Link, pp. 100–06; Berghahn (1993), p. 88; Stone, pp. 21–24; Simpson (1993); Greiner, pp. 262–66; Billstein et al., pp. 96–97; Gaja, pp. 66–67. The quotation is from Eisenberg (1996), p. 144.

18 Minnear, p. 110 ff.; Chomsky, p. 249.

CHAPTER 22

1 Steininger, p. 143; Fisch, pp. 37–38.

2 Loth (1994), pp. 10, 14–15, 19, 22–27; Loth (1995); Eisenberg (1996), p. 303.

3 Eisenberg (1996).

4 Chomsky, p. 40; McCormick, p. 68; Kühnl (1973), p. 129; Hardach, pp. 20–21; Kahler and Link, p. 202.

5 Gatzke, p. 168; Altmann, p. 199.

6 Black (2001), p. 424.

7 Neugebauer, pp. 177–78.

8 Black (2001), pp. 418–19.

9 Reich (1990), p. 116; Eisenberg (1996), pp. 86–87; Chomsky, p. 46.

10 Eisenberg (1996), pp. 12, 233; Leffner (1992), p. 234; McCormick, p. 61; Dieterich, p. 123; Chomsky, p. 47.

11 Leffner (1992), p. 230; Kolko (1968), pp. 515, 572; Eisenberg (1996), p. 317.

12 Henke, pp. 714 ff., 731 ff., 761, 770; Gimbel (1986), p. 437 ff.; Jonscher and Schilling, pp. 267–68; Kolko (1968), p. 572; Weinberg, p. 830; Gardner, p. 241; "Carl Zeiss"; Cohen.

13 Simpson (1988), pp. 30–31; Bower, p. 110; "Das Totengold der Juden."

14 Henke, p. 742 ff.; Gimbel (1986), p. 438 ff.; Jonscher and Schilling, pp. 267–68; Brunzel, pp. 99–100; Bower, pp. 118, 137–40; Cohen.

15 Schäfer, pp. 211–12; Kühnl (1971), p. 122 ff.

16 Horkheimer quotation: Dieterich, p. 70; Mayer, p. 34.

17 Black (2001), p. 420.

18 Eisenberg (1996), pp. 274, 335–36; Kolko (1968), pp. 507–11.

19 Steininger, pp. 117–18; Kolko and Kolko, pp. 125–26; Kühnl (1971), p. 71; Kühnl (1973), pp. 138–39; Altmann, p. 58 ff.; Stuby, pp. 91–101.

20 Reich (1990), p. 135; Altmann, p. 73 ff.; Simpson (1993), pp. 247–48; Eisenberg (1983), *passim*; Eisenberg (1993), pp. 62–63, 73–74; Eisenberg (1996), p. 157; Neugebauer, pp. 179–81, 185–86.

21 Wiesner quotation from Eisenberg (1983), p. 286.

22 Hearden, pp. 89–90; Gaja, p. 17.

23 Eisenberg (1996), pp. 269-76, 334-42; Pfeifer, pp. 40-42; Ruhl, pp. 404, 426-27; Reich (1990), p. 185.

24 Leffner (1991), pp. 231-32, 234; Leffner (1992), p. 8; Chomsky, p. 47.

25 Eisenberg (1983), p. 287 ff.; Eisenberg (1993); Eisenberg (1996), pp. 124-30, 344-45; Steininger, pp. 101-13; Boehling, pp. 281-306; Schäfer, pp. 212-13; Kolko (1968), pp. 507-09; Kühnl (1971), p. 72; Altmann, p. 76 ff.; Simpson (1993), p. 248; Knapp, Link, Schröder, and Schwabe, pp. 164-65; Ruhl, pp. 404-05.

26 Neugebauer, pp. 174-75, 177, 180.

27 Billstein, pp. 119-21; Silverstein, p. 16.

28 Simpson (1993), pp. 185-88; Greiner, pp. 195-97.

29 Quotation of war veteran: Terkel, p. 381.

30 Hoenicke (2010), pp. 334-35.

31 Schäfer, pp. 212-13; Tetens, pp. 236, 241-42.

32 See the study by Zorn.

33 Deschner (1990), *passim*; Lacroix-Riz (1996), pp. 428 ff., 445 ff., 457-60, 463-64, 495-99 ff.; Caretto and Marolo, p. 109 ff.; "Pope Cracks Joke over New Auto."

34 Chomsky, p. 47; Leffner (1992), p. 8; Altmann, p. 198; Livingston, pp. 11-16.

35 Gimbel (1975), p. 278; Eisenberg (1983), p. 303.

36 Hoenicke (2010), p. 345.

37 Kolko (1968), pp. 573-75; Loth (1994), p. 37; Hardach, pp. 21-22; Fisch, p. 74; Paterson, Clifford, and Hagan, p. 449; Williams (1962), pp. 259-60; Backer, pp. 162-63; Overesch (1979), pp. 128-30.

38 On General Clay's suspension of reparations to Soviets: Gimbel (1975); on the issue of reparations and the division of Germany in general, see the study by Kuklick.

39 Eisenberg (1996), p. 322.

40 Hardach, p. 46; Hopkins, Wallerstein, et al., pp. 15-16; Leffner (1992), p. 232 ff.; Paterson, Clifford, and Hagan, pp. 452, 455.

41 Gaddis, p. 260; Williams (1962), pp. 208-09; Ambrose (1997).

42 Eisenberg (1996), pp. 314, 389, 436; Loth (1994), p. 21; Backer, p. 162.

43 Loth (1994), p. 23; Simpson (1988), pp. 55-56.

44 Backer, p. 16.

45 Fisch, pp. 200-01.

46 Loth (1988), p. 70; Loth (1994), p. 15; Backer, p. 162, Linz, p. 21; Millar (1985), pp. 284-85; Ponting, p. 295; Zhilin, p. 6.

47 Gimbel (1990a), p. 296; Gimbel (1993), pp. 182, 186, 192-94.

CHAPTER 23

1 Zinn (1980), pp. 124–46, 514; Loewen, p. 110 ff.; Schäfer, p. 205; Delanty, p. 119; Zezima, p. 61.

2 Zinn (1980), p. 398.

3 Lawrence Wittner quotation: Zinn (1980), p. 416.

4 Millar (1985), p. 289.

5 Parenti (1997), pp. 49, 56; see also Bernal, p. 1176; Gaja, p. 102.

6 Costs and consequences of arms race: Bruhn, *passim*; see also Dowd, pp. 114, 289.

7 Truman as quoted in Matthias, pp. 125–26.

8 Parenti (1997), p. 58.

9 For critical comments on Fukuyama, see Gray, pp. 119–21.

10 "National Debt of the United States."

11 Sampson (1973), p. 46.

12 Zepezauer and Naiman, pp. 69–70.

13 Taxation data: Zepezauer and Naiman, pp. 69–70. More than 30 million poor Americans in 1989: www.census.gov/search-results.html?page=1& stateGeo=none&searchtype=web&q=poverty+statistics+1989. Percentage of officially poor Americans: www.census.gov/hhes/www/poverty/data/census/1960/cphl162.html.

ACKNOWLEDGEMENTS

It is impossible to name here all those who contributed in some way to this book, but some of them deserve special mention. Foremost among them are my parents, grandmother, uncles and aunts, sisters and brothers, and many other relatives, neighbours, friends, and travel companions who experienced the Second World War; through their entertaining stories about that earth-shattering conflict they stimulated the interest of a child who was fortunate to have seen the light of day only after the last bombs had been dropped. The feeling for a more systematic and critical approach to history was primarily inspired by my high school history teacher in the small Flemish town of Eeklo, Carlos De Rammelaere. At the State University of Ghent I was privileged to receive a masterful introduction to contemporary history from Professor Jan Dhondt. And without Professor Michael Kater of York University in Toronto I would know virtually nothing about Hitler's Third Reich and all too little about the Second World War. In the twilight of my protracted student life, finally, a number of political scientists, economists, and other social scientists of the University of Toronto — among them Christian Bay, Stephen Clarkson, Susan Solomon, Michael Trebilcock and Carolyn Tuohy — acquainted me with basic principles of political economy, an academic discipline which in this day and age does not enjoy the popularity it deserves. I also want to mention (in alphabetical order) a handful of authors who have made a deep impression on me: Murray Edelman, Gabriel Kolko, Thomas Kuhn, Reinhard Kühnl, Georg Lukács, Michael Parenti, and Howard Zinn. And I should not forget a number of friends in Europe and North America with whom I have engaged in particularly productive discussions about themes such as fascism, communism, capitalism, and of course the Second World War: Jean-Francois Crombois, John Hill, Mark Lipincott, Hans Oppel, Michael Quinn, Howard Woodhouse. I have also learned an awful lot about the Second World War from many of the Canadian, American, German, Belgian, and British travellers whom I was privileged to accompany as a tour guide on voyages on both sides of the Atlantic. During the research and writing stages, I received valuable help from Bert De Myttenaere, Karola

Fings, Alvin Finkel, Hugo Franssen, Jürgen Harrer, Michiel Horn, Andrea Neugebauer, Anne Willemen, Cy Strom, Jennifer Hutchison, and my son, David, and my daughter, Natalie. Without all these individuals and many others, this book would have looked very different; in fact, it might never have been written at all.

I am of course solely responsible for the inaccuracies and weaknesses of this study, and for the kind of interpretation it offers the reader. It is a historical interpretation, I suppose, that many of my relatives and friends will find somewhat challenging, but I trust that they will read it with an open mind and hope that they will find it a stimulating experience. I will continue to value their friendship even if they do not agree with my views.

Last but certainly not least, I want to say a very heartfelt *"danke"* to my wife Danielle for her interest and her encouragement, and above all for the remarkable patience she displayed while I pursued yet another project that preempted more useful tasks in the house and garden.

— Jacques R. Pauwels

SELECT BIBLIOGRAPHY

For a complete list of sources, visit http://tinyurl.com/mythbiblio

Michael C. C. Adams, *The Best War Ever: America and World War II*, Baltimore and London, 1994.

Les K. Adler and Thomas G. Paterson, "Red Fascism: The Merger of Nazi Germany and Soviet Russia in the American Image of Totalitarianism, 1930's–1950's," *American Historical Review*, Vol. LXXV, No. 4, April 1970, pp. 1047–64.

Gar Alperovitz, *Cold War Essays*, Garden City, NY, 1970.

___, *Atomic Diplomacy: Hiroshima and Potsdam. The Use of the Atomic Bomb and the American Confrontation with Soviet Power*, new edition, Harmondsworth, Middlesex, 1985 (original edition 1965).

___, *The Decision to Use the Atomic Bomb and the Architecture of an American Myth*, New York, 1995.

Stephen E. Ambrose, *Rise to Globalism: American Foreign Policy Since 1938*, 7th, revised edition, New York, 1993.

___, "When the Americans Came Back to Europe," *The International Herald Tribune*, May 28, 1997.

___, *Americans at War*, New York, 1998.

John H. Backer, "From Morgenthau Plan to Marshall Plan," in Robert Wolfe (ed.), *Americans as Proconsuls: United States Military Governments in Germany and Japan, 1944–1952*, Carbondale and Edwardsville, IL, 1984, pp. 155–65.

John Bagguley, "The World War and the Cold War," in David Horowitz (ed.), *Containment and Revolution*, Boston, 1967, pp. 76–124.

Neil Baldwin, *Henry Ford and the Jews: The Mass Production of Hate*, New York, 2001.

William J. Barber, *Designs within Disorder: Franklin D. Roosevelt, the Economists, and the Shaping of American Economic Policy, 1933–1945*, Cambridge, 1996.

Michael Barson, *"Better Dead than Red!": A Nostalgic Look at the Golden Years of Russiaphobia, Red-Baiting, and Other Commie Madness*, New York, 1992.

Edward M. Bennett, *Franklin D. Roosevelt and the Search for Victory: American-Soviet Relations, 1939–1945*, Wilmington, DE, 1990.

Volker Berghahn, "Resisting the Pax Americana? West German Industry and the United States, 1945–55," in Michael Ermarth (ed.), *America and the Shaping of German Society, 1945–1955*, Providence and Oxford, 1993, pp. 85–100.

___, "Writing the History of Business in the Third Reich: Past Achievements and

Future Directions", in Francis R. Nicosia and Jonathan Huener (eds.), *Business and Industry in Nazi Germany*, New York and Oxford, 2004, pp. 129–48.

Barton J. Bernstein (ed.), *Politics and Policies of the Truman Administration*, Chicago, 1970.

Reinhold Billstein, Karola Fings, Anita Kugler, and Nicholas Levis, *Working for the Enemy: Ford, General Motors, and Forced Labor during the Second World War*, New York and Oxford, 2000.

Edwin Black, *IBM and the Holocaust: The Strategic Alliance between Nazi Germany and America's Most Powerful Corporation*, London, 2001.

Edwin Black, *Nazi Nexus: America's Corporate Connections to Hitler's Holocaust*, Washington, DC, 2009.

John Morton Blum, *V Was for Victory: Politics and American Culture During World War II*, New York and London, 1976.

Rebecca Boehling, "US Military Occupation, Grass Roots Democracy, and Local German Government," in Jeffry M. Diefendorf, Axel Frohn, and Hermann-Josef Rupieper (eds.), *American Policy and the Reconstruction of West Germany, 1945–1955*, Cambridge, 1993, pp. 281–306.

Joseph Borkin, *The Crime and Punishment of I.G. Farben*, New York, 1978.

Stuart D. Brandes, *Warhogs: A History of War Profits in America*, Lexington, KY, 1997.

David Brinkley, *Washington Goes to War*, New York and Toronto, 1989.

Russell D. Buhite and Wm. Christopher Hamel, "War or Peace: The Question of an American Preventive War against the Soviet Union, 1945–1955," *Diplomatic History*, Vol. 14, No. 3, Summer 1990, pp. 367–84.

V. R. Cardozier, *The Mobilization of the United States in World War II: How the Government, Military and Industry Prepared for War*, Jefferson, NC, and London, 1995.

Peter N. Carroll and David W. Noble, *The Free and the Unfree: A New History of the United States*, 2nd edition, New York, 1988.

Sean Dennis Cashman, *America, Roosevelt, and World War II*, New York and London, 1989.

Ron Chernow, *The House of Morgan: An American Banking Dynasty and the Rise of Modern Finance*, New York, 1990.

Wayne S. Cole, *Roosevelt and the Isolationists, 1932–45*, Lincoln, NE, 1983.

James V. Compton, "The Swastika and the Eagle," in Arnold A. Offner (ed.), *America and the Origins of World War II, 1933–1941*, New York, 1971, pp. 159–83.

Ed Cray, *Chrome Colossus: General Motors and its Times*, New York, 1980.

Richard G. Davis, "'Operation Thunderclap': The US Army Air Forces and the Bombing of Berlin," *Journal of Strategic Studies*, Vol. 14, No 1, March 1991, pp. 90–111.

Bernard F. Dick, *The Star-Spangled Screen: The American World War II Film*, Lexington, KY, 1985.

Jeffry M. Diefendorf, Axel Frohn, and Hermann-Josef Rupieper (eds.), *American Policy and the Reconstruction of Germany, 1945–1955*, Cambridge, 1993.

John P. Diggins, *Mussolini and Fascism: The View from America*, Princeton, NJ, 1972.

Bill Doares, "The Hidden History of World War II, Part I: Corporate America and the Rise of Hitler," *Workers' World*, New York, May 4, 1995.

Michael Dobbs, "US Automakers Fight Claims of Aiding Nazis," *The International Herald Tribune*, December 3, 1998 (1998a).

___, "Ford and GM Scrutinized for Alleged Nazi Collaboration," *The Washington Post*, December 12, 1998 (1998b).

William E. Dodd, Jr., and Martha Dodd (eds.), *Ambassador Dodd's Diary 1933–1938*, New York, 1941.

Justus D. Doenecke, "Rehearsal for Cold War: United States Anti-Interventionists and the Soviet-Union, 1939–1941," *International Journal of Politics, Culture and Society*, Vol. 7, No. 3, 1994, pp. 375–92.

Justus D. Doenecke and John E. Wilz, *From Isolation to War 1931–1941*, 2nd edition, Arlington Heights, IL, 1991.

Roy Douglas, *The World War 1939–1943: The Cartoonists' Vision*, London and New York, 1990.

Doug Dowd, *Blues for America: A Critique, A Lament, and Some Memories*, New York, 1997.

Richard B. Du Boff, *Accumulation and Power: An Economic History of the United States*, Armonk, NY, and London, 1989.

Murray Edelman, *Constructing the Political Spectacle*, Chicago and London, 1988.

Keith E. Eiler, *Mobilizing America: Robert P. Patterson and the War Effort 1940–1945*, Ithaca, NY, and London, 1997.

Carolyn Woods Eisenberg, "U.S. Policy in Post-war Germany: The Conservative Restoration," *Science and Society*, Vol. XLVI, No. 1, Spring 1982, pp. 24–38.

___, "Working-Class Politics and the Cold War: American Intervention in the German Labor Movement, 1945–49," *Diplomatic History*, Vol.7, No. 4, Fall 1983, pp. 283–306.

___, "The Limits of Democracy: US Policy and the Rights of German Labor, 1945–1949," in Michael Ermarth (ed.), *America and the Shaping of German Society*,

1945–1955, Providence, RI, and Oxford, 1993, pp. 60–81.

___, *Drawing the Line: The American Decision to divide Germany, 1944–1949*, Cambridge, 1996.

Michael Ermarth (ed.), *America and the Shaping of German Society, 1945–1955*, Providence, RI, and Oxford, 1993.

"Fanta boooo," *Ciao!* October 12, 2008, www.ciao.co.uk/Fanta_Orange__ Review_5794341.

David Farber, *Sloan Rules: Alfred P. Sloan and the Triumph of General Motors*, Chicago and London, 2002.

Joe R. Feagin and Kelly Riddell, "The State, Capitalism, and World War II: The US Case," *Armed Forces and Society*, Vol. 17, No. 1, Fall 1990, pp. 53–79.

Peter G. Filene, *American Views of Soviet Russia 1917–1965*, Homewood, IL, 1968.

Philip Sheldon Foner, *History of the Labor Movement in the United States. Volume VIII: Postwar Struggles, 1918–1920*, New York, 1988.

Elizabeth A. Fones-Wolf, *Selling Free Enterprise: The Business Assault on Labor and Liberalism, 1945–60*, Urbana, IL, and Chicago, 1994.

John S. Friedman, "Kodak's Nazi Connections," *The Nation*, March 26, 2001.

Grover Furr, *Khrushchev Lied: The Evidence That Every 'Revelation' of Stalin's (and Beria's) 'Crimes' in Nikita Khrushchev's Infamous 'Secret Speech' to the 20th Party Congress of the Communist Party of the Communist Party of the Soviet Union on February 25, 1956, is Provably False*, Kettering/Ohio, 2010.

Paul Fussell, *Wartime: Understanding and Behavior in the Second World War*, New York and Oxford, 1989.

John Lewis Gaddis, *The United States and the Origins of the Cold War 1941–1947*, New York and London, 1972.

Lloyd C. Gardner, *Architects of Illusion: Men and Ideas in American Foreign Policy 1941–1949*, Chicago, 1970.

John A. Garraty, *Unemployment in History: Economic Thought and Public Policy*, New York, 1978.

Hans W. Gatzke, *Germany and the United States: A "Special Relationship"?*, Cambridge, MA, and London, 1980.

Dieter Georgi, "The Bombings of Dresden," *Harvard Magazine*, Vol. 87, No. 4, March-April 1985, pp. 56–64.

Germany Surrenders 1945, Washington, DC, 1976.

J. Arch Getty, Gabor Rittersporn, and Victor Zemskov, "Victims of the Soviet Penal System in the Pre-War Years: A First Approach on the Basis of Archival Evidence,"

American Historical Review, Vol. 98, October 1993, pp. 1017–49.

John Gimbel, "The American Reparations Stop in Germany: An Essay on the Political Uses of History," *The Historian*, Vol. 37, No. 2, February 1975, pp. 276–96.

___, "U.S. Policy and German Scientists: The Early Cold War," *Political Science Quarterly*, 1986, No. 3, pp. 433–51.

—___, "The American Exploitation of German Technical Know-How after World War II," *Political Science Quarterly*, Vol. 105, No. 2, Summer 1990, pp. 295–309 (1990a).

___, "German Scientists, United States Denazification Policy, and the 'Paperclip' Conspiracy," *The International History Review*, Vol. XII, No. 3, August 1990, pp. 441–65 (1990b).

___, "Project Paperclip: German Scientists, American Policy, and the Cold War," *Diplomatic History*, Vol. 14, No. 3, Summer 1990, pp. 343–65 (1990c).

___, "Science, Technology, and Reparations in Postwar Germany," in Jeffry M. Diefendorf, Axel Frohn, and Hermann-Josef Rupieper (eds.), *American Policy and the Reconstruction of Germany, 1945–1955*, Cambridge, 1993, pp. 175–96.

John Gray, *False Dawn: The Delusions of Global Capitalism*, London, 1998.

A. C. Grayling, *Among the Dead Cities: Was the Allied Bombing of Civilians in WW II a Necessity or a Crime?*, London, 2006.

William Greider, *Fortress America: The American Military and the Consequences of Peace*, New York, 1998.

Robert Griffith, "The Selling of America: The Advertising Council and American Politics, 1942–1960," *Business History Review*, Vol. LVII, Autumn 1983, pp. 388–413.

Peter Grose, *Operation Rollback: America's Secret War Behind the Iron Curtain*, Boston and New York, 2000.

Alfred Grosser, *The Western Alliance: European-American Relations Since 1945*, New York, 1982.

Alonzo L. Hamby, *Beyond the New Deal: Harry S. Truman and American Liberalism*, New York and London, 1973.

Jussi Hanhimaki, "'Containment' in a Borderland: The United States and Finland, 1948–49," *Diplomatic History*, Vol. 18, No. 3, summer 1994, pp. 353–74.

Randall Hansen, *Fire and Fury: the Allied Bombing of Germany, 1942–45*, Toronto, 2008.

Fraser J. Harbutt, *The Iron Curtain: Churchill, America, and the Origins of the Cold War*, New York and Oxford, 1986.

John Lamberton Harper, *American Visions of Europe: Franklin D. Roosevelt, George F. Kennan, and Dean G. Acheson*, Cambridge and New York, 1994.

Peter Hayes, *Industry and Ideology: IG Farben in the Nazi Era*, Cambridge, 1987.

M. J. Heale, *American Anticommunism: Combating the Enemy Within 1830–1970*, Baltimore and London, 1990.

Patrick J. Hearden, *Roosevelt Confronts Hitler: America's Entry into World War II*, Dekalb, IL, 1987.

James Heartfield, *An Unpatriotic History of the Second World War*, Winchester and Washington, 2012.

Charles Higham, *Trading with the Enemy: An Exposé of The Nazi-American Money Plot 1933–1949*, New York, 1983.

Robert L. Hilliard, *Surviving the Americans: The Continued Struggle of the Jews after Liberation*, New York, 1997.

Historical Statistics of the United States: Colonial Times to 1970. Part 2, Washington, 1975.

Christopher Hitchens, "Imagining Hitler," *Vanity Fair*, No. 462, February 1999, pp. 22–27.

Michaela Hoenicke Moore, *Know Your Enemy: The American Debate on Nazism, 1933–1945*, Cambridge, 2010.

David Holloway, "Fear and Competition: The Soviet Response to America's Atomic Monopoly," in Thomas G. Paterson and Robert J. McMahon (eds.), *The Origins of the Cold War*, 3rd edition, Lexington, MA, and Toronto, 1991, pp. 137–47.

David Horowitz (ed.), *The Free World Colossus: A Critique of American Foreign Policy in the Cold War*, London, 1965.

___, *From Yalta to Vietnam: American Foreign Policy in the Cold War*, Harmondsworth, Middlesex, 1967.

Thomas Howell, "The Writers' War Board: U.S. Domestic Propaganda in World War II," *The Historian*, Vol. 59, No. 4, Summer 1997, pp. 795–813.

Linda Hunt, *Secret Agenda: The United States Government, Nazi Scientists, and Project Paperclip, 1945 to 1990*, New York, 1991.

Samuel Hynes, *The Soldiers' Tale: Bearing Witness to Modern War*, New York, 1997.

Akira Iriye, *The Origins of the Second World War in Asia and in the Pacific*, London and New York, 1987.

Peter H. Irons, "American Business and the Origins of McCarthyism: The Cold War Crusade of the American Chamber of Commerce," in Robert Griffith and Athan Theoharis (eds.), *The Specter: Original Essays on the Cold War and the Origins of McCarthyism*, New York, 1974, pp. 72–89.

Noah Isenberg, "Double Enmity," *The Nation*, January 1, 2001.

John W. Jeffries, *Wartime America: The World War II Home Front*, Chicago, 1996.

T. Christopher Jespersen, *American Images of China 1931–1949*, Stanford, CA, 1996.

Manfred Jonas, *The United States and Germany: A Diplomatic History*, Ithaca, NY, and London, 1984.

Miles Kahler and Werner Link, *Europe and America: A Return to History*, New York, 1996.

John Keegan, *The Battle for History: Re-Fighting World War Two*, Toronto, 1995.

Ian Kershaw, *Making Friends with Hitler: Lord Londonderry, the Nazis and the Road to World War II*, New York, 2004.

Helene Keyssar and Vladimir Pozner, *Remembering War: A U.S.-Soviet Dialogue*, New York and Oxford, 1990.

Warren F. Kimball, "FDR and Allied Grand Strategy, 1944-1945: The Juggler's Last Act," in Charles F. Brower (ed.), *World War II in Europe: The Final Year*, New York, 1998, pp. 1538.

Gerald R. Kleinfeld, "The Genesis of American Policy Toward the GDR: Some Working Hypotheses," in Reiner Pommerin (ed.), *The American Impact on Postwar Germany*, Providence, RI, and Oxford, 1995, pp. 53–64.

Gabriel Kolko, "American Business and Germany, 1930–1941," *The Western Political Quarterly*, Vol. XV, No. 4, December 1962, pp. 713–28.

___, *The Politics of War: The World and United States Foreign Policy, 1943–1945*, New York, 1968.

___, *Main Currents in Modern American History*, New York, 1976.

___, *Century of War: Politics, Conflicts, and Society Since 1914*, New York, 1994.

Joyce and Gabriel Kolko, *The Limits of Power: The World and United States Foreign Policy, 1945–1954*, New York, 1972.

Clayton R. Koppes and Gregory D. Black, *Hollywood Goes to War: How Politics, Profits, and Propaganda Shaped World War II Movies*, New York and London, 1987.

Stefan Kühl, *The Nazi Connection: Eugenics, American Racism, and German National Socialism*, New York, 1994.

Judy Kutulas, *The Long War: The Intellectual People's Front and Anti-Stalinism, 1930–1940*, Durham, NC, and London, 1995.

Melvyn P. Leffler, "The American Drive for Security: Marshall Plan, Revival of Germany, and NATO," in Thomas G. Paterson and Robert J. McMahon, *The Origins of the Cold War*, 3rd edition, Lexington, MA, and Toronto, 1991, pp. 229–40.

___, *A Preponderance of Power: National Security, the Truman Administration and the*

Cold War, Stanford, 1992.

Clement Leibovitz and Alvin Finkel, *In Our Time: The Chamberlain-Hitler Collusion*, New York, 1998.

Sidney Lens, *Permanent War: The Militarization of America*, New York, 1987.

Ralph B. Levering, *American Opinion and the Russian Alliance, 1939–1945*, Chapel Hill, NC, 1976.

David Lanier Lewis, *The Public Image of Henry Ford: An American Folk Hero and his Company*, Detroit, 1976.

Eric Lichtblau, *The Nazis Next Door; How America Became A Safe Haven For Hitler's Men*, Boston and New York, 2014.

Marc Linder, in collaboration with Julius Sensat, Jr., *The Anti-Samuelson. Macroeconomics: Basic Problems of the Capitalist Economy*, 2 volumes, New York, 1977.

Richard R. Lingeman, *Don't You Know There's a War on?: The American Home Front, 1941–1945*, New York, 1970.

Susan J. Linz (ed.), *The Impact of World War II on the Soviet Union*, Towota, NJ, 1985.

James W. Loewen, *Lies My Teacher Told Me: Everything Your American History Textbook Got Wrong*, New York, 1995.

Wilfried Loth, *The Division of the World 1941–1955*, London, 1988.

Callum A. MacDonald, "The United States, Appeasement and the Open Door," in Wolfgang J. Mommsen and Lothar Kettenacker (eds.), *The Fascist Challenge and the Policy of Appeasement*, London, 1983, pp. 400–12.

Robert James Maddox, *From War to Cold War: The Education of Harry S. Truman*, Boulder, CO, 1988.

___, *The United States and World War II*, Boulder, CO, 1992.

Thomas R. Maddux, "Watching Stalin Maneuver Between Hitler and the West: American Diplomats and Soviet Diplomacy, 1934–1939," *Diplomatic History*, Vol. 1, No. 2, Spring 1977, pp. 140–54.

___, *Years of Estrangement: American Relations with the Soviet Union, 1933–1941*, Tallahassee, FL, 1980.

Charles S. Maier, "Why the Allies Did It," *Harvard Magazine*, Vol. 87, No. 4, March-April 1985.

Eduard Mark, "October or Thermidor? Interpretations of Stalinism and the Perception of Soviet Foreign Policy in the United States, 1927–1947," *American Historical Review*, Vol. 94 , No. 4, October 1989, pp. 937–62.

Leon Martel, *Lend-Lease, Loans, and the Coming of the Cold War: A Study of the Implementation of Foreign Policy*, Boulder, CO, 1979.

Arthur Marwick, *Class: Image and Reality in Britain, France and the USA since 1930*, New York, 1980.

David Mayers, *The Ambassadors and America's Soviet Policy*, New York and Oxford, 1995.

Laurence W. Mazzeno, "Getting the Word to Willie and Joe," *Military Review*, Vol. LXVII, No. 8, August 1987, pp. 69–82.

Thomas J. McCormick, *America's Half-Century: United States Foreign Policy in the Cold War*, Baltimore and London, 1989.

Alexander McKee, *Dresden 1945: The Devil's Tinderbox*, London, 1982.

Henry Cord Meyer, *Five Images of Germany: Half a Century of American Views on German History*, Washington, 1960.

James V. Milano and Patrick Brogan, *Soldiers, Spies and the Rat Line: America's Undeclared War Against the Soviets*, Washington and London, 1995.

James R. Millar, "Conclusion: Impact and Aftermath of World War II," in Susan J. Linz (ed.), *The Impact of World War II on the Soviet Union*, Towota, NJ, 1985, pp. 283–91.

___, *The Soviet Economic Experiment*, Urbana, IL, 1990.

C. Wright Mills, *The Power Elite*, New York, 1956.

Robert K. Murray, *Red Scare: A Study of National Hysteria, 1919–1920*, New York, 1964.

Williamson Murray and Allan R. Millet (eds.), *Military Innovation in the Interwar Years*, Cambridge, 1996.

Derek Nelson, *The Posters That Won The War*, Osceola, WI, 1991.

"No Canadian Scandal," letter published in *The Globe and Mail*, Toronto, October 4, 1997.

David W. Noble, David A. Horowitz, and Peter N. Carroll, *Twentieth Century Limited: A History of Recent America*, Boston, 1980.

Arnold A. Offner, *American Appeasement: United States Foreign Policy and Germany, 1933–1938*, Cambridge, MA, 1969.

___, "American Appeasement, 1933–1938," in Arnold Offner (ed.), *America and the Origins of World War II, 1933–1941*, Boston, 1971, pp. 54–76.

___, "The United States and National Socialist Germany," in Wolfgang J. Mommsen and Lothar Kettenacker (eds.), *The Fascist Challenge and the Policy of Appeasement*, London, 1983, pp. 413–27.

___, "Harry S Truman as Parochial Nationalist," in Thomas G. Paterson and Robert J. McMahon (eds.), *The Origins of the Cold War*, 3rd edition, Lexington, MA, and Toronto, 1991, pp. 49–60.

David O'Keefe, *One Day in August: The Untold Story behind Canada's Tragedy at Dieppe*, Toronto, 2013.

Mancur Olson, *The Logic of Collective Action: Public Goods and the Theory of Interest Groups*, Cambridge, MA, and London, 1965.

William L. O'Neill, *A Democracy at War: America's Fight at Home and Abroad in World War II*, New York, 1993.

Torsten Oppelland, "Der lange Weg in den Krieg (1900–1918)," in Klaus Larres and Torsten Oppelland (ed.), *Deutschland und die USA im 20. Jahrhundert: Geschichte der politischen Beziehungen*, Darmstadt, 1997, pp. 1–30.

Richard Overy, *Why the Allies Won*, London, 1995.

___, *Russia's War*, London, 1997.

Michael Parenti, *The Anti-Communist Impulse*, New York, 1969.

___, *Power and the Powerless*, New York, 1978.

___, *The Sword and the Dollar: Imperialism, Revolution, and the Arms Race*, New York, 1989.

___, *Against Empire*, San Francisco, 1995 (1995a).

___, *Democracy for the Few*, 6th edition, New York, 1995 (1995b).

___, *Dirty Truths: Reflections on Politics, Media, Ideology, Conspiracy, Ethnic Life and Class Power*, San Francisco, 1996.

___, *Blackshirts and Reds: Rational Fascism and the Overthrow of Communism*, San Francisco, 1997.

___, *History as Mystery*, San Francisco, 1999.

Thomas G. Paterson, "Exaggerations of the Soviet Threat," in Thomas G. Paterson and Robert J. McMahon (eds.), *The Origins of the Cold War*, 3rd edition, Lexington, MA, and Toronto, 1991, pp. 203–12.

Thomas G. Paterson, J. Garry Clifford, and Kenneth J. Hagan, *American Foreign Policy: A History / 1900 to Present*, Lexington, MA, and Toronto, 1991.

Jacques R. Pauwels, "Hitler's Failed Blitzkrieg against the Soviet Union. The 'Battle of Moscow' and Stalingrad: Turning Point of World War II," Global Research, December 6, 2011, *globalresearch.ca/index.php?context=va&aid=28059*.

___, *Big business avec Hitler*, Brussels, 2013.

___, *De Groote Klassenoorlog 1914–1918*, Berchem, 2014.

Mark Pendergrast, *For God, Country, and Coca-Cola: The Unauthorized History of the Great American Soft Drink and the Company That Makes It*, New York, 1993.

Clive Ponting, *Armageddon: The Second World War*, London, 1995.

Walter S. Poole, "From Conciliation to Containment: The Joint Chiefs of Staff and the Coming of the Cold War, 1945–1946," *Military Affairs*, Vol. XLII, No. 1, February 1978, pp. 12–15.

Robert C. Puth, *American Economic History*, 2nd edition, Fort Worth, TX, 1988.

Simon Reich, *The Fruits of Fascism: Postwar Prosperity in Historical Perspective*, Ithaca, NY, and London, 1990.

___, "The Ford Motor Company and the Third Reich," *Dimensions: A Journal of Holocaust Studies*, Vol. 13, No. 2, December 1999, pp. 15–17.

Simon Reich and Lawrence Dowler, *Research Findings About Ford-Werke Under the Nazi Regime*, Dearborn, MI, 2001.

David Reynolds, *Rich Relations: The American Occupation of Britain, 1942–1945*, New York, 1995.

David Reynolds, Warren F. Kimball, and A. O. Chubarian (eds.), *Allies at War: The Soviet, American, and British Experience, 1939–1945*, New York, 1994.

Geoffrey Roberts, *Stalin's Wars from World War to Cold War, 1939–1953*, New Haven, CT, and London, 2006.

George H. Roeder, Jr., *The Censored War: American Visual Experience during World War Two*, New Haven, CT, and London, 1993.

Steven T. Ross, *American War Plans 1941–1945: The Test of Battle*, London and Portland, OR, 1997.

Mario Rossi, "United States Military Authorities and Free France, 1942–1944," *The Journal of Military History*, Vol. 61, No. 1, January 1997, pp. 49–64.

Floyd Rudmin, "Secret War Plans and the Malady of American Militarism," *Counterpunch*, 13:1, February 17–19, 2006, pp. 4–6, www.counterpunch. org/2006/02/17/secret-war-plans-and-the-malady-of-american-militarism.

Keith Sainsbury, *Churchill and Roosevelt at War: The War They Fought and the Peace They Hoped to Make*, New York, 1994.

Anthony Sampson, *The Sovereign State of ITT*, New York, 1973.

___, *The Seven Sisters: The Great Oil Companies and the World They Made*, New York, 1975.

Michael Sayers and Albert E. Kahn, *The Plot against the Peace: A Warning to the Nation!*, New York, 1945.

Ronald Schaffer, "American Military Ethics in World War II: The Bombing of

German Civilians," *The Journal of Military History*, Vol. 67, No. 2, September 1980, pp. 318–34.

David F. Schmitz, "'A Fine Young Revolution': The United States and the Fascist Revolution in Italy, 1919–1925," *Radical History Review*, No. 33, September 1985, pp. 117–38.

___, *Thank God They're on Our Side: The United States and Right-Wing Dictatorships, 1921–1965*, Chapel Hill, NC, and London, 1999.

Michael S. Sherry, *The Rise of American Air Power: The Creation of Armageddon*, New Haven, CT, and London, 1987.

___, *In the Shadow of War: The United States Since the 1930s*, New Haven, CT, and London, 1995.

Michael S. Shull and David E. Wilt, *Doing Their Bit: Wartime American Animated Short Films, 1939–1945*, Jefferson, NC, and London, 1987.

Ken Silverstein, "Ford and the Führer," *The Nation*, January 24, 2000, pp. 11–16.

Christopher Simpson, *Blowback: The First Full Account of America's Recruitment of Nazis, and Its Disastrous Effect on our Domestic and Foreign Policy*, New York, 1988.

___, *The Splendid Blond Beast: Money, Law, and Genocide in the Twentieth Century*, New York, 1993.

Nikolai V. Sivachev and Nikolai N. Yakovlev, *Russia and the United States*, Chicago and London, 1979.

N. Sivachyov and E. Yazkov, *History of the USA Since World War I*, Moscow, 1976.

Robert M. Slusser, "Soviet Policy and the Division of Germany, 1941–1945," in Susan J. Linz (ed.), *The Impact of World War II on the Soviet Union*, Towota, NJ, 1985, pp. 107–25.

Melvin Small, "How We Learned to Love the Russians: American Media and the Soviet Union During World War II," *The Historian*, Vol. 36, May 1974, pp. 455–78.

___, "The 'Lessons' of the Past: Second Thoughts about World War II," in Norman K. Risjord (ed.), *Insights on American History*. Vol. II, San Diego, 1988.

Arthur L. Smith, Jr., *Churchill and the German Army (1945): Some Speculations on the Origins of the Cold War*, Center for the Study of Armament and Disarmament, California State University, Los Angeles, 1974.

___, *Churchill's German Army: Wartime Strategy and Cold War Politics, 1943–1947*, Beverly Hills, CA, 1977.

Bradford Snell, "GM and the Nazis," *Ramparts*, Vol. 12, No. 11, June 1974, pp. 14–16.

Robert Sobel, *ITT: The Management of Opportunity*, New York, 1982.

Richard W. Steele, "'The Greatest Gangster Movie Ever Filmed': Prelude to War," *Prologue: The Journal of the National Archives*, Vol. 11, No. 4, Winter 1979, pp. 221–35.

Alexander Stephan, *"Communazis": FBI Surveillance of German Emigré Writers*, New Haven, CT, and London, 2000.

Robert B. Stinnett, *Day of Deceit: The Truth about FDR and Pearl Harbor*, New York, 2000.

Mark A. Stoler, "The 'Second Front' and American Fear of Soviet Expansion, 1941–1943," *Military Affairs*, Vol. XXXIX, No. 3, October 1975, pp. 136–41.

Anthony C. Sutton, *Wall Street and the Rise of Hitler*, Seal Beach, CA, 1976.

Frederick Taylor, *Dresden: Tuesday, February 13, 1945*, New York, 2005.

Studs Terkel, *"The Good War": An Oral History of World War Two*, New York, 1984.

T. H. Tetens, *The New Germany and the Old Nazis*, London, 1962.

Robert W. Thurston, *Life and Terror in Stalin's Russia 1934–1941*, New Haven, CT, and London, 1996.

Tooze, Adam. *The Wages of Destruction: The Making and Breaking of the Nazi Economy*, London, 2006.

Henry Ashby Turner, Jr., *General Motors and the Nazis: The Struggle for Control of Opel, Europe's Biggest Carmaker*, New Haven, CT, and London, 2005.

William W. Turner, *Hoover's FBI*, New York, 1993.

Harold G. Vatter, *The U.S. Economy in World War II*, New York, 1985.

Milton Viorst, *Hostile Allies: FDR and Charles de Gaulle*, New York and London, 1965.

Agostino von Hassell and Sigrid McRae, *Alliance of Enemies: The Untold Story of the Secret American and German Collaboration to End World War II*, New York, 2006.

Mary-Alice Waters, "1945: When US Troops Said 'No!': A Hidden Chapter in the Fight Against War," *New International: A Magazine of Marxist Politics and Theory*, No. 7, 1991, pp. 279–300.

T. H. Watkins, *The Great Depression: America in the 1930s*, Boston, 1993.

Kenneth E. Weiher, *America's Search for Economic Stability: Monetary and Fiscal Policy Since 1913*, New York, 1992.

Gerhard L. Weinberg, *A World at Arms: A Global History of World War II*, Cambridge, 1994.

Mira Wilkins, *The Maturing of Multinational Enterprise: American Business Abroad from 1914 to 1970*, Cambridge, MA, and London, 1974.

Mira Wilkins and Frank Ernest Hill, *American Business Abroad: Ford on Six Continents*, Detroit, 1964.

William Appleman Williams, *The Tragedy of American Diplomacy*, revised edition, New York, 1962.

___, "American Intervention in Russia: 1917–20," in David Horowitz (ed.), *Containment and Revolution*, Boston, 1967, pp. 26–75.

___, "Empire as a Way of Life," *Radical History Review*, No. 50, Spring 1991, pp. 71–102.

Allan M. Winkler, *The Politics of Propaganda: The Office of War Information 1942–1945*, New Haven and London, 1978.

Neil A. Wynn, "The 'Good War': The Second World War and Postwar American Society," *The Journal of Contemporary History*, Vol. 31, No. 3, July 1996, pp. 463–82.

Wyvetra B. Yeldell, *Publications of the US Army Center of Military History*, Washington, DC, 1997.

Mark Zepezauer and Arthur Naiman, *Take the Rich Off Welfare*, Tucson, AZ, 1996.

Michael Zezima, *Saving Private Power: The Hidden History of the "Good War,"* New York, 2000.

Robert H. Zieger, *American Workers, American Unions*, 2nd edition, Baltimore and London, 1994.

Gerard Colby Zilg, *Du Pont: Behind the Nylon Curtain*, Englewood Cliffs, NJ, 1974.

Howard Zinn, *A People's History of the United States*, s.l., 1980.

___, *Howard Zinn on War*, New York and London, 2001.

INDEX